All-Time
Favorites

Maryland Crab Cakes with
Lemon Rémoulade, page 158

Weight Watchers®
All-Time
Favorites

Over 200 Best-Ever Recipes from
the Weight Watchers Test Kitchens

BICENTENNIAL
1807
WILEY
2007
BICENTENNIAL

WILEY PUBLISHING, INC.

Wiley also publishes its books in a variety of electronic formats. Some content that appears in print may not be available in electronic books. For more information about Wiley products, visit our web site at www.wiley.com.

LIBRARY OF CONGRESS CATALOGING-IN-PUBLICATION DATA:

Weight Watchers all-time favorites : over 200 best-ever recipes from the Weight Watchers test kitchens.

p. cm.

Includes index.

ISBN 978-0-470-43547-2 (cloth)

1. Reducing diets—Recipes. I. Weight Watchers International.

RM222.2.W31135 2007

641.5'635—dc22

2007011315

WEIGHT WATCHERS PUBLISHING GROUP

CREATIVE AND EDITORIAL DIRECTOR: Nancy Gagliardi
FOOD EDITOR: Eileen Runyan
EDITOR: Deborah Mintcheff
PHOTOGRAPHY: Rita Maas
FOOD STYLING: Anne Disrude
PROP STYLING: Lynda White

WILEY PUBLISHING, INC.

PUBLISHER: Natalie Chapman
EXECUTIVE EDITOR: Anne Ficklen
SENIOR EDITORIAL ASSISTANT: Charleen Barila
PRODUCTION MANAGER: Leslie Anglin
ART DIRECTOR: Tai Blanche
COVER DESIGN: Suzanne Sunwoo
INTERIOR DESIGN AND LAYOUT: Richard Oriolo
MANUFACTURING MANAGER: Kevin Watt

Manufactured in China

10 9 8 7 6 5 4 3 2 1

Cover photos: Mini Burgers and Vegetable Salad with Shallot Vinaigrette (page 23), Pan-Seared Scallops with Tomato-Corn Hash (page 9), Broccoli-Tomato Quiche (page 70), Smoky Roast Pork with Peaches and Plums (page 131)

WILEY BICENTENNIAL LOGO: Richard J. Pacifico

Contents

About Weight Watchers

Weight Watchers International, Inc. is the world's leading provider of weight management services, operating globally through a network of Company-owned and franchise operations. Weight Watchers holds over 48,000 weekly meetings, where members receive group support and education about healthful eating patterns, behavior modification, and physical activity. Weight-loss and weight-management results vary by individual. We recommend that you attend Weight Watchers meetings to benefit from the supportive environment you'll find there and follow the comprehensive Weight Watchers program, which includes food plans, an activity plan, and a thinking-skills plan. In addition, Weight Watchers offers a wide range of products, publications and programs for those interested in weight loss and weight control. For the Weight Watchers meeting nearest you, call **800-651-6000**. For information on bringing Weight Watchers to your workplace, call **800-8AT-WORK**. Also, visit us at our Web site, **WeightWatchers.com**, or look for **Weight Watchers Magazine** at your newsstand or in your meeting room.

Introduction

What makes a recipe a favorite? That is, why do you turn to particular recipes over and over again whenever you want to create delicious, memorable meals for family or friends without stepping away from your commitment to embrace a healthy lifestyle?

For more than forty years, the experts at Weight Watchers have created delicious, good-for-you recipes to help you maintain a healthy lifestyle and bring you closer to your weight-loss goals. With our newest book, we are pleased to continue that tradition: The 225 recipes in Weight Watchers *All-Time Favorites* are designed to meet all your mealtime needs. Whether you're looking for a family-friendly weeknight dinner, a perfect-for-company entrée, or a crowd-pleasing holiday menu, these flavorful classics suit every situation and occasion—all while helping you stay on a healthy path.

Inside are 12 chapters bursting with our very best recipes, including quick-and-easy light meals, satisfying one-dish dinners, easy brunches and lunches, no-cook fixes, slow-cooker specials, 15-minute meals, and scrumptious desserts.

What's more, Weight Watchers *All-Time Favorites* transforms many classic, must-make dishes into recipes that work for your busy lifestyle. For family meals, we've included our hands-down favorite recipe for Classic Roast Chicken, the most satisfying Shrimp and Sausage Paella, and the best-ever Barbecue-Sauced Sloppy Joes. For entertaining, enjoy the most delectable Sesame-Lime Grilled Tuna and the most flavorful Beef Tenderloin with Red Wine and Mushrooms. And for dessert, we present the most tempting and delicious Boston Cream Pie, Lemon-Glazed Orange Loaf, and Ruby Port–Poached Plums.

The recipes in *All-Time Favorites*, like those in all Weight Watchers cookbooks, include easy-to-follow, step-by-step instructions; the preparation and cooking time, along with the number of servings, are clearly indicated at the top of each recipe. All 225 recipes are suitable for followers of the **Flex Plan**, and many of them are tailored for followers of the **Core Plan**®. We also provide helpful tips, including make-ahead suggestions, advice on how to substitute ingredients, pointers for cooking and handling food safely, and clever cooking techniques to get you out of the kitchen in record time.

These recipes are favorites in our Weight Watchers kitchens, and they are sure to become favorites in your kitchen too. Whether you are a novice cook or an expert in the kitchen, Weight Watchers *All-Time Favorites* is a book you will turn to again and again.

About Our Recipes

We make every effort to ensure that you will have success with our recipes. For best results and for nutritional accuracy, please keep the following guidelines in mind:

- Recipes in this book have been developed for Weight Watchers members who are following either the **Flex Plan** or the **Core Plan**® on **TurnAround**®. All **Core Plan** recipes are marked with our **Core Plan** recipe icon ☑. We include *POINTS*® values so you can use any of the recipes if you are following the **Flex Plan** on the program. *POINTS* values are assigned based on calories, fat (grams), and fiber (grams) provided for a serving size of a recipe.

- All recipes feature approximate nutritional information; our recipes are analyzed for Calories (Cal), Total Fat (Fat), Saturated Fat (Sat Fat), Trans Fat (Trans Fat), Cholesterol (Chol), Sodium (Sod), Carbohydrates (Carb), Dietary Fiber (Fib), Protein (Prot), and Calcium (Calc).

- Nutritional information for recipes that include meat, poultry, and fish are based on cooked skinless boneless portions (unless otherwise stated), with the fat trimmed. We recommend that you buy lean meat and poultry, then trim it of all visible fat before cooking. When poultry is cooked with the skin on, we suggest removing the skin before eating.

- In our recipes we follow the USDA guidelines for cooking meats and poultry to safe temperatures to prevent foodborne illness, but for beef and lamb (steaks, roasts, and chops) be aware that cooking them to the recommended minimum of 145°F will give you a medium-cooked steak, roast, or chop.
- Before serving, divide foods—including vegetables, sauce, or accompaniments—into portions of equal size according to the designated number of servings per recipe.
- Any substitutions made to the ingredients will alter the "Per serving" nutritional information and may affect the **Core Plan** recipe status or the *POINTS* value.
- We recommend that all fresh fruits, vegetables, and greens in recipes be rinsed before using.

CHAPTER ONE

Starters and Light Meals

Crunchy Vegetable Rolls with Peanut Dipping Sauce

HANDS-ON PREP 25 MIN ■ COOK NONE ■ SERVES 4

2 tablespoons unseasoned rice vinegar

2 teaspoons fresh lime juice

1 tablespoon finely chopped unsalted roasted peanuts

$1/2$ teaspoon sugar

$1/8$ teaspoon salt

1 ounce cellophane noodles (part of 16-ounce package)

1 cup boiling water

4 (8-inch) round rice-paper sheets

1 cucumber, peeled, halved, seeded, and cut into long, thin matchstick strips

1 carrot, shredded

4 scallions (light green parts only), sliced into long, thin strips

$1/4$ cup packed fresh cilantro leaves

$1/4$ cup packed flat-leaf parsley leaves

1   To make the dipping sauce, combine the vinegar, lime juice, peanuts, sugar, and salt in a small bowl; set aside.

2   Combine the noodles with the boiling water in a medium bowl. Soak the noodles for 12 minutes; drain and pat dry with paper towels.

3   Half-fill a large skillet with warm water. Soak 1 rice-paper round in the water just until pliable, 30–45 seconds. Pat with a paper towel to remove the excess water. Place one-fourth of the noodles on the bottom third of the rice paper; top with one-fourth each of the cucumber, carrot, scallions, and cilantro. Tightly roll the rice paper around the filling just enough to cover it. Place one-fourth of the parsley leaves in a single row along the roll, then continue rolling up to form a neat cylinder. Place, seam side down, on a plate and cover with a damp paper towel. Repeat with the remaining rice-paper rounds, noodles, cucumber, carrot, scallions, cilantro, and parsley leaves to make 4 rolls in all.

4   With a serrated knife, slice each roll on the diagonal into 4 pieces. Serve with the dipping sauce.

PER SERVING (1 roll and generous $1/2$ tablespoon sauce): 78 Cal, 1 g Fat, 0 g Sat Fat, 0 g Trans Fat, 4 mg Chol, 87 mg Sod, 15 g Carb, 2 g Fib, 3 g Prot, 37 mg Calc.
POINTS value: 1.

PLAN AHEAD

If you chop and prepare the ingredients in advance, refrigerate them in plastic bags. Then soak the rice-paper wrappers, fill them, and roll them up. It's important to keep the rolls covered as you work, as the wrappers can quickly dry out.

Crunchy Vegetable Rolls with Peanut Dipping Sauce,
Feta and Spinach Triangles, Herbed Mushroom Morsels

Onion-Flavored Cheese Rounds

HANDS-ON PREP 8 MIN ■ COOK 7 MIN ■ SERVES 16

1 cup shredded reduced-fat Monterey
  Jack cheese

2 tablespoons grated Parmesan cheese

1 tablespoon all-purpose flour

2 teaspoons onion powder

1   Preheat the oven to 400°F. Spray 2 baking sheets with nonstick spray.

2   Combine the Monterey Jack, Parmesan, and flour in a small bowl. Drop by table-spoonfuls onto the baking sheets, at least 2 inches apart, making 16 rounds in all. Bake until the cheese is melted and golden with darker brown edges, 5–7 minutes.

3   While the cheese rounds are still slightly warm, sprinkle generously with the onion powder; let cool about 1 minute. With a metal spatula, carefully transfer the cheese rounds to paper towels and let cool completely. Serve at once, or store in an airtight container up to 2 days at room temperature.

PER SERVING (1 round): 25 Cal, 2 g Fat, 1 g Sat Fat, 0 g Trans Fat, 4 mg Chol, 52 mg Sod, 1 g Carb, 0 g Fib, 2 g Prot, 63 mg Calc.

POINTS value: 1.

HOW WE DID IT

For an even coating of onion powder on the cheese rounds, place the powder in a small dish, grasp a good amount of it between your thumb and first two fingers and hold it high (about 14 inches) above the food. Move your hand back and forth over the food as you evenly sprinkle the powder.

Feta and Spinach Triangles

HANDS-ON PREP 35 MIN ■ COOK 25 MIN ■ SERVES 8

1 (10-ounce) box frozen chopped
  spinach, thawed and squeezed dry

1/2 cup crumbled reduced-fat feta cheese

2 tablespoons plain low-fat Greek-style
  yogurt

3 scallions, chopped

2 tablespoons chopped fresh dill

1 egg white

1/4 teaspoon freshly ground pepper

8 (12 x 17-inch) sheets frozen phyllo
  dough, thawed

2 tablespoons olive oil

1 Place an oven rack in the center of the oven and preheat the oven to 375°F. Spray a baking sheet with nonstick spray.

2 Press the spinach between layers of paper towels to remove any excess moisture. Put the feta and yogurt in a medium bowl and mash with a fork until creamy. Add the spinach, scallions, dill, egg white, and pepper, stirring to combine.

3 Set the stack of phyllo sheets to one side of the work surface; cover with damp paper towels and a sheet of plastic wrap to keep them from drying out.

4 Place 1 phyllo sheet on a work surface with a long side facing you. Cover the remaining phyllo with a damp paper towel and plastic wrap to prevent it from drying out. Lightly brush the phyllo sheet with the oil. Top with another sheet and lightly brush with oil. Cut the sheets crosswise into 6 equal strips. Place a scant tablespoon of the spinach mixture at one end of each strip. Fold one corner of the phyllo over the filling, then continue folding, flag style, to form a triangle.

5 Place the phyllo triangles on the baking sheet and repeat with the remaining phyllo sheets and filling to make 24 triangles in all. Brush the triangles with any remaining oil. Bake until golden brown, about 25 minutes. Let cool about 5 minutes before serving.

PER SERVING (3 triangles): 115 Cal, 6 g Fat, 1 g Sat Fat, 0 g Trans Fat, 3 mg Chol, 242 mg Sod, 12 g Carb, 1 g Fib, 5 g Prot, 47 mg Calc.
POINTS value: 3.

FOOD NOTE

Boxes of phyllo dough can be found in the frozen foods section of supermarkets. Phyllo must be completely defrosted overnight in the refrigerator, still in the box, before it can be used. Unroll the defrosted phyllo, keeping in mind that the sheets tear easily, so handle them as gently—and as little—as possible.

Herbed Mushroom Morsels ☑

2 (10-ounce) packages sliced white mushrooms

2 tablespoons basil-infused olive oil

2 teaspoons reduced-sodium soy sauce

1 teaspoon dried oregano

1 teaspoon dried thyme

$1/2$ teaspoon garlic powder

$1/8$ teaspoon freshly ground pepper

1 Preheat the broiler.

2 Spread the mushrooms in a broiler pan or large roasting pan. Whisk together the oil, soy sauce, oregano, thyme, and garlic powder in a small bowl. Drizzle over the mushrooms; toss well. Let stand about 10 minutes to allow the flavors to blend.

3 Broil the mushrooms 5 inches from the heat until golden and crisp, about 2 minutes. Turn the mushrooms and broil until crisp, about 1 minute longer. Sprinkle with the pepper and serve at once.

PER SERVING ($3/4$ cup): 50 Cal, 4 g Fat, 1 g Sat Fat, 0 g Trans Fat, 0 mg Chol, 53 mg Sod, 0 g Carb, 1 g Fib, 2 g Prot, 7 mg Calc.

POINTS value: 1.

GOOD IDEA

You can munch on these treats on their own as an hors d'oeuvre, but they can also be used to add an extra burst of flavor to vegetable soups, cooked brown rice, or to top chicken breast cutlets or fish fillets.

Pita Chips with Black Bean "Caviar"

HANDS-ON PREP 5 MIN ■ COOK NONE ■ SERVES 8

1 (15-ounce) can black beans, rinsed
  and drained

1 tablespoon prepared black olive
  tapenade

1 tablespoon crumbled feta cheese

1 tablespoon extra-virgin olive oil

1 large garlic clove, minced

1/4 teaspoon freshly ground pepper

4 (6-inch) whole-wheat pitas, toasted,
  each cut into 8 wedges

Combine the beans, tapenade, feta, oil, garlic, and pepper in a medium bowl; gently mash with a wooden spoon to break up some of the beans. Transfer to a serving bowl and serve with the pita wedges.

PER SERVING (4 pita wedges and 1/4 cup "caviar"): 108 Cal, 3 g Fat, 0 g Sat Fat, 0 g Trans Fat, 0 mg Chol, 134 mg Sod, 17 g Carb, 3 g Fib, 4 g Prot, 38 mg Calc.
POINTS value: 2.

TRY IT

Black olive tapenade, which is also available made from green olives, is a versatile condiment that can add bold flavor to a variety of foods. Just a spoonful will boost the flavor of grilled fish, oven-roasted or steamed vegetables, turkey burgers, lamb chops, and poached eggs.

Pan-Seared Scallops with Tomato-Corn Hash ☑

HANDS-ON PREP 6 MIN ■ COOK 15 MIN ■ SERVES 4

³/₄ pound jumbo sea scallops

¹/₄ teaspoon salt

¹/₄ teaspoon freshly ground pepper

2 teaspoons extra-virgin olive oil

2 scallions (white and light green parts only), chopped

1 garlic clove, minced

³/₄ cup frozen corn kernels, thawed

1 plum tomato, seeded and chopped

¹/₂ tablespoon balsamic vinegar

2 teaspoons chopped fresh cilantro

1 cup packed torn frisée

1 Sprinkle the scallops with ¹/₈ teaspoon of the salt and ¹/₈ teaspoon of the pepper. Heat 1 teaspoon of the oil in a large nonstick skillet set over medium-high heat. Add the scallops and cook just until browned and opaque in the center, about 3 minutes on each side. Transfer to a plate and keep warm.

2 Heat the remaining 1 teaspoon of oil in the skillet over medium-high heat. Add the scallions and garlic; cook, stirring occasionally, until softened, about 3 minutes. Add the corn and cook, stirring frequently, until lightly browned, about 2 minutes. Add the tomato and cook, stirring occasionally, until softened, 1–2 minutes. Add the vinegar and cook, stirring constantly, until it evaporates, about 30 seconds. Remove the skillet from the heat; stir in the cilantro and the remaining ¹/₈ teaspoon salt and ¹/₈ teaspoon pepper. Divide the scallops, hash, and frisée among 4 plates and serve at once.

PER SERVING (2 scallops and ¹/₄ cup hash): 157 Cal, 6 g Fat, 1 g Sat Fat, 0 g Trans Fat, 28 mg Chol, 312 mg Sod, 13 g Carb, 2 g Fib, 16 g Prot, 31 mg Calc.
POINTS value: 3.

HOW WE DID IT

Scallops pan-sear best when they are thoroughly dry and the skillet is very hot. Blot the scallops with paper towels until there is no trace of moisture on them. The scallops should sizzle when they are placed in the skillet. Keep in mind that just a few additional seconds of cooking time will turn the scallops chewy and dry, so don't overcook them.

Ham and Cheese Soufflé

HANDS-ON PREP 20 MIN ■ COOK 1 HR 20 MIN ■ SERVES 6

3 tablespoons plain dried bread crumbs

3 1/4 cups fat-free milk

3/4 teaspoon salt

1/4 teaspoon freshly ground pepper

1 cup cornmeal

2 egg yolks, lightly beaten

1 tablespoon canola oil

4 scallions, chopped

2 garlic cloves, minced

1 (1/4 pound) slice of lean deli ham, diced

1/4 pound fat-free cheddar cheese, diced

1/2 teaspoon powdered sage

5 egg whites

1 Preheat the oven to 375°F. Spray a 1½-quart soufflé or deep baking dish with non-stick spray; coat with the bread crumbs.

2 Bring the milk, salt, and pepper to a simmer in a large saucepan set over medium-high heat. Gradually add the cornmeal, whisking constantly, until blended. Reduce the heat to medium-low; cook, whisking constantly, until the mixture is thickened and smooth, about 6 minutes. Transfer the cornmeal mixture to a large bowl; let cool about 2 minutes. Stir in the egg yolks and let cool about 20 minutes.

3 Meanwhile, heat the oil in a medium nonstick skillet set over medium-high heat. Add the scallions and garlic; cook, stirring occasionally, until softened, 1–2 minutes. Add the ham and cook until lightly browned, 6–7 minutes. Remove the skillet from the heat; let stand until slightly cooled, about 5 minutes.

4 Stir the ham mixture, cheddar, and sage into the cornmeal mixture; set aside.

5 With an electric mixer on high speed, beat the egg whites in a medium bowl until stiff peaks form. With a rubber spatula, gently fold one-fourth of the beaten egg whites into the cornmeal mixture. Repeat with the remaining beaten whites. Spoon the batter into the soufflé dish and bake until puffed and golden, 55–60 minutes. Serve at once.

PER SERVING (about 1 cup): 251 Cal, 5 g Fat, 2 g Sat Fat, 0 g Trans Fat, 84 mg Chol, 901 mg Sod, 30 g Carb, 2 g Fib, 19 g Prot, 386 mg Calc.
POINTS value: 5.

HOW WE DID IT

The centuries-old secret to a really puffy soufflé is to *never* open the oven door to check on the soufflé's progress. The slightest wisp of cool air during baking will lower the temperature and deflate the delicate expanding egg whites.

Sweet Apple and Cheese Pancakes

HANDS-ON PREP 10 MIN ■ COOK 30 MIN ■ SERVES 6

5 teaspoons unsalted butter

1 apple, peeled, cored, and finely chopped

2 teaspoons sugar

³/₄ cup low-fat buttermilk

1 large egg, lightly beaten

1¹/₃ cups all-purpose flour

1¹/₂ teaspoons baking powder

³/₄ teaspoon baking soda

³/₄ teaspoon salt

¹/₂ teaspoon nutmeg

1 cup fat-free creamy-style cottage cheese

1　Melt 2 teaspoons of the butter in a large nonstick skillet set over medium-high heat. Add the apple and sugar; cook, stirring occasionally, until the apple is lightly browned, about 5 minutes. Transfer to a small bowl and let cool about 5 minutes.

2　Meanwhile, in a microwavable cup, heat the remaining 3 teaspoons of butter on High until melted, about 30 seconds. Whisk together the melted butter, buttermilk, and egg in a large bowl; set aside. Combine the flour, baking powder, baking soda, salt, and nutmeg in another large bowl. Add the flour mixture to the milk mixture, stirring just until blended. Stir in the apple and ¹/₂ cup of the cottage cheese.

3　Wipe the skillet clean. Spray with nonstick spray and set over medium heat. When a drop of water sizzles in the skillet, pour in the batter by ¹/₄ cupfuls. Cook just until bubbles appear along the edges of the pancakes, about 3 minutes. Turn and cook until golden, about 3 minutes longer. Transfer the pancakes to a plate and keep warm. Repeat with the remaining batter to make 12 pancakes in all. Serve at once with the remaining ¹/₂ cup of cottage cheese.

PER SERVING (2 pancakes and 4 teaspoons cottage cheese): 198 Cal, 5 g Fat, 3 g Sat Fat, 0 g Trans Fat, 47 mg Chol, 733 mg Sod, 29 g Carb, 1 g Fib, 9 g Prot, 93 mg Calc.
POINTS value: 4.

FOOD NOTE

When baking powder, baking soda, and buttermilk work in tandem, the result is delectably tender, fluffy pancakes. Stir the milk mixture into the flour mixture just enough to combine the ingredients. Overstirring will result in thin, tough pancakes.

Blueberry Blintzes

HANDS-ON PREP 15 MIN ■ COOK 25 MIN ■ SERVES 8

¹/₃ cup low-fat farmer cheese, at room temperature

¹/₄ cup sugar

¹/₂ teaspoon vanilla extract

1¹/₂ cups whipped low-fat (1%) cottage cheese

2 tablespoons blueberry preserves

1 cup low-fat (1%) milk

1 cup all-purpose flour

2 large eggs

2 egg whites

1 tablespoon unsalted butter, melted

¹/₄ teaspoon salt

2 cups (about 1 pint) fresh or thawed frozen blueberries

1 To make the filling, combine the farmer cheese, sugar, and vanilla in a medium bowl. Add the cottage cheese and blueberry preserves and stir until combined; cover and refrigerate.

2 To make the pancake batter, combine the milk, flour, eggs, egg whites, butter, and salt in a blender or food processor; process until smooth. Pour into a bowl and let stand about 20 minutes.

3 Place the oven rack in the center of the oven and preheat the oven to 350°F. Line a baking sheet with foil and lightly spray with nonstick spray.

4 Spray a small nonstick skillet with nonstick spray and set over medium heat. When a drop of water sizzles in the skillet, pour about 3 tablespoons of the batter into the pan, quickly tilting the pan to coat the bottom evenly with the batter. Cook until lightly browned and dry on the top, about 30 seconds. Turn the pancake and cook until golden, about 5 seconds. Flip onto a plate and place a piece of wax paper on top. Repeat with the remaining batter, lightly spraying the skillet between pancakes, to make 16 pancakes in all, stacking each between sheets of wax paper.

5 To assemble the blintzes, spoon 2 tablespoons of the cheese mixture on the lower third of the paler side of each pancake. Fold the two sides over the filling, then roll up jelly-roll style. Place, seam side down, on the baking sheet and cover loosely with foil. Bake until heated through, about 10 minutes. Transfer the blintzes to a platter and serve with the blueberries.

PER SERVING (2 blintzes and ¹/₄ cup blueberries): 194 Cal, 4 g Fat, 2 g Sat Fat, 0 g Trans Fat, 61 mg Chol, 258 mg Sod, 28 g Carb, 0 g Fib, 12 g Prot, 89 mg Calc.
POINTS value: 4.

TRY IT

Another attractive—though not traditional—way to fill and serve blintzes is to place the filling close to the center of each pancake, then fold it in quarters.

Classic Herbed Omelette ☑

1 large egg

2 egg whites

1 tablespoon water

2 teaspoons chopped flat-leaf parsley

2 teaspoons chopped fresh chives

1 teaspoon chopped fresh tarragon

1 teaspoon chopped fresh thyme

Pinch cayenne

$1/4$ teaspoon salt

$1/8$ teaspoon freshly ground pepper

1 tablespoon fat-free sour cream

1 Whisk together all the ingredients except the sour cream in a medium bowl.

2 Spray a medium nonstick skillet with nonstick spray and set over medium-high heat. When a drop of water sizzles in the skillet, pour in the egg mixture and tilt the pan to coat the bottom evenly with the egg mixture. Cook until the underside starts to set, about 20 seconds. With a spatula, gently lift the edges of the omelette. Continue to cook, lifting the edges occasionally to allow the uncooked egg to run underneath, until the eggs are set but slightly runny on top, 1–2 minutes. Gently fold the omelette in thirds and cook just until set, about 30 seconds longer. Slide onto a plate and top with the sour cream. Serve at once.

PER SERVING (1 omelette with sour cream): 116 Cal, 5 g Fat, 2 g Sat Fat, 0 g Trans Fat, 213 mg Chol, 764 mg Sod, 3 g Carb, 0 g Fib, 14 g Prot, 58 mg Calc.
POINTS value: 3.

EXPRESS LANE

You can use dried herbs in place of the chopped fresh herbs in this dish. If you do, follow the general rule of substituting 1 measure of dried herbs for 3 measures of fresh herbs. To get the most flavor from the dried herbs, crush them between your fingers directly over the omelette before folding it in thirds.

Spicy Corn Pudding

HANDS-ON PREP 10 MIN ■ COOK 40 MIN ■ SERVES 6

1 1/2 tablespoons all-purpose flour

1 cup low-fat (1%) milk

2 cups fresh or frozen corn kernels

1 large water-packed roasted red pepper, drained and finely chopped

2 scallions (white and light green parts only), chopped

1/4 teaspoon hot paprika

1 teaspoon sugar

1/4 teaspoon salt

1 large egg

1 egg white

1/2 cup shredded reduced-fat pepperjack cheese

1 Preheat the oven to 350°F. Spray a 1-quart baking dish with nonstick spray.

2 Put the flour in a medium saucepan and gradually whisk in the milk. Stir in the corn, roasted red pepper, scallions, paprika, sugar, and salt and set over medium heat. Bring to a simmer, stirring constantly; cook, stirring, until slightly thickened, about 2 minutes.

3 Beat the egg and egg white in a small bowl; gradually whisk in about 1/2 cup of the hot milk mixture. Whisk the egg mixture into the saucepan; remove the pan from the heat. Reserve 2 tablespoons of the pepperjack; stir the remaining cheese into the corn mixture. Spoon into the baking dish and sprinkle the reserved cheese on top.

4 Place the baking dish in a large roasting pan. Set the pan on the oven rack; carefully pour enough hot water into the pan to come one-third up the side of the baking dish. Bake until the pudding is just set in the center, about 35 minutes. Carefully remove the pudding from the water bath and serve at once.

PER SERVING (1/6th of pudding): 115 Cal, 3 g Fat, 2 g Sat Fat, 0 g Trans Fat, 42 mg Chol, 190 mg Sod, 16 g Carb, 2 g Fib, 7 g Prot, 130 mg Calc.
POINTS value: 2.

FOOD NOTE

The reason for beating a small amount of the hot milk mixture into the egg mixture first is to warm the egg mixture slowly so it doesn't curdle, which would result in a lumpy—rather than smooth—pudding. The technique, known as tempering, is often used with custards to ensure that they will be silky smooth.

Pasta with Oven-Roasted Tomatoes and Pesto

HANDS-ON PREP 10 MIN ■ COOK 20 MIN ■ SERVES 6

6 plum tomatoes, halved lengthwise

2 tablespoons olive oil

1 teaspoon chopped fresh rosemary

4 fresh thyme sprigs

2 cups packed fresh basil leaves

1 large garlic clove, smashed

2 tablespoons grated Parmesan cheese

1 tablespoon chopped walnuts

1/8 teaspoon freshly ground pepper

2 cups rotelle (fusilli)

1 Preheat the oven to 400°F.

2 Toss together the tomatoes, 1 tablespoon of the oil, and the rosemary in a medium bowl. Place the tomato halves, cut side up, in a shallow medium baking dish and scatter the thyme sprigs on top. Roast the tomatoes until lightly browned but still slightly firm, about 20 minutes. Let cool.

3 To make the pesto, put the basil, garlic, Parmesan, walnuts, the remaining 1 tablespoon of oil, and the pepper in a blender or food processor; pulse until the mixture forms a coarse, bright green paste. Set aside.

4 Meanwhile, cook the rotelle according to the package directions, omitting the salt if desired. Drain, reserving 1 1/2 tablespoons of the cooking water. Transfer the rotelle to a serving bowl. Add the cooking water to the pesto and process 2 seconds. Add the pesto to the pasta and toss well to coat. Discard the thyme sprigs and arrange the roasted tomatoes on top of the pasta. Serve hot or at room temperature.

PER SERVING (2/3 cup pasta and 2 tomato halves): 186 Cal, 7 g Fat, 1 g Sat Fat, 0 g Trans Fat, 1 mg Chol, 47 mg Sod, 26 g Carb, 2 g Fib, 6 g Prot, 60 mg Calc.
POINTS value: 4.

HOW WE DID IT

The tomato-pesto combination is enjoyable with almost any pasta, but rotelle, fusilli, rotini, and other curly pastas offer a double reward. When cooked, the curves of the pasta trap the sauce, making every bite especially juicy and robust.

Fettuccine with Gorgonzola and Toasted Walnuts

HANDS-ON PREP 10 MIN ■ COOK 20 MIN ■ SERVES 6

1/2 (16-ounce) box fettuccine

1/4 cup low-fat (1%) milk

1/2 cup fat-free ricotta cheese

1/4 cup crumbled Gorgonzola cheese

1/4 cup coarsely chopped walnuts, toasted

2 tablespoons chopped flat-leaf parsley

1 (3-inch-long) strip lemon zest, removed with a vegetable peeler and very thinly sliced on the diagonal

1 Cook the fettuccine according to the package directions, omitting the salt if desired. Drain the fettuccine, then transfer to a serving bowl and keep warm.

2 Meanwhile, in a microwavable cup, heat the milk on High until warm, about 30 seconds. Combine the ricotta and Gorgonzola in a medium bowl; stir in the warm milk until almost smooth. Some of the Gorgonzola should remain slightly lumpy. Spoon the cheese mixture over the fettuccine and toss well; sprinkle with the walnuts, parsley, and lemon zest. Serve hot or at room temperature.

PER SERVING (2/3 cup): 208 Cal, 6 g Fat, 1 g Sat Fat, 0 g Trans Fat, 8 mg Chol, 93 mg Sod, 31 g Carb, 2 g Fib, 9 g Prot, 85 mg Calc.
POINTS value: 4.

EXPRESS LANE

This Gorgonzola sauce is equally delicious with fresh fettuccine. Use a 9-ounce package; instead of cooking it as directed in step 1, place the pasta in the boiling water when you begin to make the cheese mixture, following the package directions. Drain the pasta and toss it with the sauce. Fresh pasta takes much less time to cook than dried pasta and will be soft rather than al dente.

Bow Ties with Smoked Salmon, Goat Cheese, and Chives

HANDS-ON PREP 15 MIN ■ COOK 20 MIN ■ SERVES 6

2 cups bow ties (farfalle)

4 teaspoons olive oil

3 scallions (white and light green parts only), chopped

1 small tomato, chopped

4 (1-ounce) slices smoked salmon, coarsely chopped

1 cup packed watercress leaves and tender stems, coarsely chopped

2 ounces fresh (mild) goat cheese, crumbled

1/8 teaspoon salt

1/8 teaspoon freshly ground pepper

1/4 cup chopped fresh chives

1 Cook the bow ties according to the package directions, omitting the salt if desired. Drain and transfer to a large bowl.

2 Heat the oil in a large nonstick skillet set over medium heat. Add the scallions and cook, stirring constantly, until fragrant, about 30 seconds. Add the tomato and cook until heated through, about 1 minute. Remove the skillet from the heat. Let the tomato mixture cool 1 minute, then add to the pasta and toss well. Add the smoked salmon, watercress, goat cheese, salt, and pepper; toss thoroughly. Sprinkle with the chives. Serve hot or at room temperature.

PER SERVING (1 cup): 158 Cal, 7 g Fat, 3 g Sat Fat, 0 g Trans Fat, 12 mg Chol, 481 mg Sod, 16 g Carb, 2 g Fib, 9 g Prot, 48 mg Calc.
POINTS value: 3.

PLAY IT SAFE

Instead of lifting a heavy pot of hot water and risking injury from the steam when draining the pasta, you could use a "spider" to remove the pasta from the pot. A spider is a woven-wire spoon with a long bamboo handle, available in several sizes at kitchen-supply stores and Asian housewares shops.

Lima Bean–Tomato Succotash ☑

1 (10-ounce) box frozen lima beans, thawed

1 tablespoon olive oil

1/2 small red onion, finely chopped

1 zucchini, quartered lengthwise and cut into 1/4-inch pieces

2 small tomatoes, chopped

2 cups fresh or thawed frozen corn kernels

1 teaspoon chopped fresh thyme or 1/2 teaspoon dried

1/2 teaspoon salt

1/8 teaspoon cayenne

1 Cook the lima beans according to the package directions; drain and set aside.

2 Meanwhile, heat the oil in a large nonstick skillet set over medium-high heat. Add the red onion and cook, stirring, until softened, about 4 minutes. Add the zucchini and tomatoes; cook, stirring occasionally until softened, about 3 minutes.

3 Add the lima beans, corn, thyme, salt, and cayenne to the skillet; cook, stirring occasionally, until heated through, about 3 minutes.

PER SERVING (1 1/4 cups): 147 Cal, 4 g Fat, 2 g Sat Fat, 0 g Trans Fat, 8 mg Chol, 301 mg Sod, 28 g Carb, 5 g Fib, 5 g Prot, 48 mg Calc.
POINTS value: 2.

PLAN AHEAD

This recipe makes a terrific summer salad. Prepare as directed and let the succotash cool to room temperature or cover and refrigerate up to 2 days. Stir in 1/4 cup slivered fresh basil leaves and 1 tablespoon balsamic vinegar just before serving.

CHAPTER TWO

Fresh Salads

Mini Burgers and Vegetable Salad with Shallot Vinaigrette ✓

HANDS-ON PREP 10 MIN ■ COOK 25 MIN ■ SERVES 4

1 (10-ounce) box frozen asparagus spears

1 (9-ounce) box frozen artichoke hearts

2 tablespoons vegetable broth

2 tablespoons chopped shallots

1 tablespoon chopped fresh oregano

1 tablespoon white-wine or Champagne vinegar

4 teaspoons olive oil

2 teaspoons Dijon mustard

1 garlic clove, minced

¾ teaspoon salt

¼ teaspoon freshly ground pepper

½ pound ground lean beef (7% or less fat)

1 Cook the asparagus and artichoke hearts according to the package directions. Drain well; set aside in a serving bowl.

2 Put the broth, shallots, oregano, vinegar, oil, mustard, garlic, ¼ teaspoon of the salt, and the pepper in a blender or food processor; process until smooth. Drizzle the dressing evenly over the vegetables; toss well to coat. Cover tightly with plastic wrap and refrigerate up to 8 hours.

3 Mix the ground beef with the remaining ½ teaspoon of salt. Divide the meat into 4 equal portions and shape each into a mini burger. Spray a medium nonstick skillet with nonstick spray and set over medium-high heat. Add the burgers and cook, turning once, until an instant-read thermometer inserted into the side of a burger registers 160°F, about 8 minutes. Transfer the burgers to a plate and let cool about 5 minutes. Serve with the vegetable salad.

PER SERVING (1 cup salad and 1 mini burger): 165 Cal, 8 g Fat, 2 g Sat Fat, 0 g Trans Fat, 31 mg Chol, 592 mg Sod, 10 g Carb, 4 g Fib, 16 g Prot, 45 mg Calc.
POINTS value: 3.

EXPRESS LANE

You can hasten the cooking time of the frozen vegetables by microwaving them instead of boiling them on the stovetop. To quickly cool the vegetables (and maintain their bright green color), plunge them into a bowl of ice water as soon as they're done cooking.

Roast Beef and Baby Greens Salad

HANDS-ON PREP 10 MIN ■ COOK NONE ■ SERVES 4

$^1/_2$ cup plain fat-free yogurt

4 teaspoons canola oil

1 tablespoon balsamic vinegar

$^1/_2$ teaspoon sugar

1 garlic clove, minced

$^1/_2$ teaspoon salt

$^1/_8$ teaspoon freshly ground pepper

1 (10-ounce) bag mixed baby salad greens

1 Belgian endive, root end trimmed and leaves thinly sliced

$^1/_2$ pound thinly sliced deli roast beef, cut into strips

1 tablespoon chopped fresh chives

1 To make the dressing, put the yogurt, oil, vinegar, sugar, garlic, salt, and pepper in a food processor or blender; process until smooth. Transfer to a bowl; cover and refrigerate until ready to serve.

2 Combine the salad greens and endive in a serving bowl. Briefly whisk the dressing and drizzle evenly over the salad. Top with the roast beef and toss well. Sprinkle with the chives and serve at once.

PER SERVING (2 cups): 158 Cal, 7 g Fat, 1 g Sat Fat, 0 g Trans Fat, 28 mg Chol, 929 mg Sod, 11 g Carb, 6 g Fib, 16 g Prot, 150 mg Calc.
POINTS value: 3.

TRY IT

If you're lucky enough to live near a farmers' market or other gourmet produce source, replace the mixed baby salad greens with some of the more exotic varieties, such as tatsoi, mizuna, radish sprouts, snow pea shoots, and/or baby mustard greens.

Pork Chop Salad with Pear-Roquefort Dressing

HANDS-ON PREP 15 MIN ■ COOK 10 MIN ■ SERVES 6

1 pound lean boneless center-cut pork chops, lightly pounded

3/4 teaspoon salt

1/2 teaspoon freshly ground pepper

2 tablespoons red-wine vinegar

1 tablespoon olive oil

2 teaspoons honey

1 teaspoon Dijon mustard

4 cups mixed salad greens

3 celery stalks, thinly sliced on the diagonal

1 ripe Bosc pear, halved, cored, and chopped

6 tablespoons coarsely chopped toasted walnuts

3 tablespoons crumbled Roquefort cheese

1   Sprinkle the pork chops on both sides with 1/2 teaspoon of the salt and the pepper. Spray a nonstick ridged grill pan with nonstick spray and set over medium-high heat. Add the pork chops and cook until browned and cooked through, 3–4 minutes on each side. Transfer to a cutting board; let rest about 5 minutes. Cut the pork on the diagonal into 1/4-inch-thick slices.

2   Whisk together the vinegar, oil, honey, mustard, and the remaining 1/4 teaspoon salt in a large bowl until blended. Add the pork, salad greens, celery, and pear; toss to coat. Divide the salad evenly among 6 plates; top with the walnuts and sprinkle with the Roquefort. Serve at once.

PER SERVING (1 1/3 cups salad, 1 tablespoon walnuts, and 1/2 tablespoon cheese): 220 Cal, 11 g Fat, 2 g Sat Fat, 0 g Trans Fat, 49 mg Chol, 446 mg Sod, 12 g Carb, 3 g Fib, 20 g Prot, 79 mg Calc.
POINTS value: 5.

GOOD IDEA

For easier eating, it's always a good idea to peel the strings from the outside of the celery stalks. It can be done in just seconds with a vegetable peeler and will save diners the embarrassment of having to remove the strings as they chew.

Ham and Chickpea Salad ☑

HANDS-ON PREP 10 MIN ■ COOK NONE ■ SERVES 4

1 (15-ounce) can chickpeas, rinsed and drained

1/4 pound sliced lean ham, cut into strips

1 red bell pepper, seeded and chopped

1 yellow bell pepper, seeded and chopped

1 small red onion, chopped

2 tablespoons apple-cider vinegar

2 teaspoons olive oil

1/4 teaspoon dried thyme

1/4 teaspoon salt

1/4 teaspoon freshly ground pepper

Combine all the ingredients in a large bowl. Serve at once or refrigerate, covered, up to overnight.

PER SERVING (1 cup): 153 Cal, 4 g Fat, 1 g Sat Fat, 0 g Trans Fat, 14 mg Chol, 642 mg Sod, 21 g Carb, 4 g Fib, 9 g Prot, 33 mg Calc.
POINTS value: 3.

PLAN AHEAD

Prepare the chickpea salad without the ham and refrigerate, covered, up to 3 days. The flavors will meld and deepen while the chickpeas marinate. Just before serving, sprinkle the ham strips over the salad.

Sautéed Cauliflower, Broccoli, and Bacon Salad ☑

4 cups fresh cauliflower florets	$^1/_2$ teaspoon ground allspice
4 cups fresh broccoli florets	$^1/_2$ teaspoon salt
1 tablespoon olive oil	$^1/_8$ teaspoon cayenne
4 (1-ounce) slices Canadian bacon, coarsely chopped	1$^1/_2$ tablespoons sherry vinegar
	1 teaspoon grated orange zest

1 Bring a large pot of lightly salted water to a boil. Add the cauliflower and return to a boil; cook 3 minutes. Add the broccoli and cook until the vegetables are crisp-tender, about 2 minutes. Drain in a colander, then rinse under cold running water and drain again.

2 Heat the oil in a large nonstick skillet set over medium-high heat. Add the bacon and vegetables; cook, stirring frequently, until heated through, about 1 minute. Stir in the allspice, salt, and cayenne. Cook, stirring constantly, 1–2 minutes.

3 Remove the skillet from the heat; stir in the vinegar and orange zest. Spoon the salad into a serving bowl and let cool about 10 minutes before serving.

PER SERVING (1$^1/_2$ cups): 113 Cal, 6 g Fat, 1 g Sat Fat, 0 g Trans Fat, 10 mg Chol, 887 mg Sod, 9 g Carb, 6 g Fib, 9 g Prot, 59 mg Calc.
POINTS value: 2.

TRY IT

Oven-roasting the vegetables for this dish will deepen their flavors. Preheat the oven to 425°F. Combine all of the ingredients in a large bowl. Divide the mixture between 2 large rimmed baking sheets. Roast, stirring once halfway through the roasting time, until the vegetables are tender and slightly caramelized around the edges, about 25 minutes.

Coleslaw-Chicken Salad with Peppery Dressing

HANDS-ON PREP 15 MIN ■ COOK NONE ■ SERVES 4

6 tablespoons fat-free mayonnaise

1 tablespoon Dijon mustard

1 tablespoon apple-cider vinegar

1/2 teaspoon caraway seeds, lightly crushed

1 teaspoon whole peppercorns, lightly crushed

2 teaspoons sugar

1 (1-pound) bag coleslaw mix

3/4 pound cooked chicken breast, shredded (about 2 cups)

1 tomato, chopped

4 slices bacon, crisp-cooked, drained, and crumbled

1 To make the dressing, whisk together the mayonnaise, mustard, vinegar, caraway seeds, peppercorns, and sugar in a small bowl until blended; set aside.

2 Combine the coleslaw mix, chicken, and tomato in a large bowl. Drizzle with the dressing and toss well to coat. Divide the mixture evenly among 4 plates and sprinkle with the bacon. Serve at once.

PER SERVING (1 1/2 cups slaw and 1 slice crumbled bacon): **214 Cal, 7 g Fat, 2 g Sat Fat, 0 g Trans Fat, 63 mg Chol, 448 mg Sod, 14 g Carb, 3 g Fib, 25 g Prot, 77 mg Calc.**
POINTS value: 4.

GOOD IDEA

Serving the chicken salad with warm squares of corn bread turns this dish into a Southern-style meal (a 2-inch square of corn bread will increase the per-serving *POINTS* value by *3*).

Penne-Chicken Salad with Creamy Ranch Dressing

HANDS-ON PREP 20 MIN ■ COOK 20 MIN ■ SERVES 6

1/2 cup fat-free mayonnaise

1/4 cup reduced-fat buttermilk

3 scallions, chopped

1 tablespoon fresh lemon juice

1 teaspoon Dijon mustard

1/4 teaspoon salt

1/2 (16-ounce) box penne

4 (1/4-pound) skinless boneless chicken breast halves, lightly pounded

1 bunch arugula, tough stems trimmed, leaves coarsely chopped

1 cup diced celery

1 cup grape or cherry tomatoes, halved

1 To make the dressing, combine the mayonnaise, buttermilk, scallions, lemon juice, mustard, and salt in a medium bowl; set aside.

2 Cook the penne according to the package directions, omitting the salt if desired; drain. Rinse under cold running water; drain again. Transfer to a large bowl; set aside.

3 Spray a large nonstick skillet with nonstick spray and set over medium-high heat. Add the chicken and cook until browned and cooked through, about 4 minutes on each side. Transfer the chicken to a cutting board; let rest 5 minutes. Cut the chicken on the diagonal into thin slices.

4 Add the chicken to the pasta. Add the arugula, celery, and tomatoes; toss well. Drizzle with the dressing and toss well to coat. Serve at once.

PER SERVING (1 1/2 cups): 270 Cal, 4 g Fat, 1 g Sat Fat, 0 g Trans Fat, 46 mg Chol, 490 mg Sod, 36 g Carb, 2 g Fib, 23 g Prot, 64 mg Calc.
POINTS value: 5.

GOOD IDEA

Drizzle this delicious ranch dressing over a crisp salad of mixed greens, tomato wedges, and cucumber, or use it as a dip for crunchy vegetables, such as red peppers, celery, and carrots.

Chicken Salad with Grapes and Walnuts

HANDS-ON PREP 10 MIN ■ COOK NONE ■ SERVES 4

$^1/_2$ cup plain fat-free yogurt

2 tablespoons reduced-fat mayonnaise

1 tablespoon honey

1 teaspoon apple-cider vinegar

$^1/_2$ teaspoon Dijon mustard

$^1/_8$ teaspoon nutmeg

$^1/_4$ teaspoon salt

$^1/_8$ teaspoon freshly ground pepper

2 cups chopped cooked chicken breast

1 $^1/_2$ cups seedless green grapes, halved

$^1/_4$ cup chopped walnuts

Combine the yogurt, mayonnaise, honey, vinegar, mustard, nutmeg, salt, and pepper in a large bowl. Add the chicken, grapes, and walnuts; toss to coat evenly. Cover and refrigerate at least 1 hour or up to 8 hours.

PER SERVING ($^3/_4$ cup): 277 Cal, 11 g Fat, 2 g Sat Fat, 0 g Trans Fat, 66 mg Chol, 303 mg Sod, 16 g Carb, 1 g Fib, 29 g Prot, 95 mg Calc.
POINTS value: 6.

PLAY IT SAFE

The chicken in this salad can easily become a health threat if left out in warm weather. To prevent the risk of illness, don't let the salad sit out of the refrigerator longer than 2 hours and only for 1 hour if the temperature is 80°F or higher. When transporting cooked chicken or chicken salad, stow it in an insulated carrying case or ice chest and keep the temperature below 40°F.

Cajun Shrimp and Arugula Salad ☑

HANDS-ON PREP 10 MIN ■ COOK 5 MIN ■ SERVES 4

1/2 cup fat-free mayonnaise

2 scallions, finely chopped

2 teaspoons fresh lemon juice

2 teaspoons Cajun seasoning

1 pound large shrimp, peeled and deveined

2 teaspoons olive oil

2 (5-ounce) bags baby arugula

1 To make the sauce, combine the mayonnaise, scallions, lemon juice, and 1/2 teaspoon of the Cajun seasoning in a small bowl; set aside.

2 Combine the shrimp and the remaining 1 1/2 teaspoons Cajun seasoning in a medium bowl; set aside.

3 Heat the oil in a large nonstick skillet set over medium-high heat. Add the shrimp and cook just until lightly browned on the outside and opaque in the center, 1 1/2–2 minutes on each side. Divide the arugula evenly among 4 plates; place the shrimp on top, dividing it evenly. Serve at once with the sauce.

PER SERVING (1 salad and 2 tablespoons sauce): 149 Cal, 5 g Fat, 1 g Sat Fat, 0 g Trans Fat, 171 mg Chol, 492 mg Sod, 7 g Carb, 2 g Fib, 20 g Prot, 154 mg Calc.
POINTS value: 3.

PLAN AHEAD

It's a good idea to add a 16-ounce bag of frozen peeled and deveined shrimp to your shopping cart. Place the shrimp in the refrigerator in the morning, and they'll be defrosted by evening. Toss them with the Cajun seasoning, then cover and refrigerate until ready to cook—this salad almost puts itself together.

Frisée Salad with Truffled Poached Eggs

HANDS-ON PREP 10 MIN ■ COOK 10 MIN ■ SERVES 4

1/4 cup finely chopped onion

2 tablespoons Champagne vinegar

1 tablespoon Dijon mustard

1/4 teaspoon salt

1/8 teaspoon freshly ground pepper

1 tablespoon distilled white vinegar

4 large eggs

8 cups frisée lettuce, torn into bite-size pieces

1 teaspoon truffle butter, softened

1 To make the dressing, whisk together the onion, vinegar, mustard, salt, and pepper in a large bowl until blended; set aside.

2 Line a large plate with a triple layer of paper towels. Bring 2 inches of water just to a boil in a large skillet; stir in the vinegar. Reduce the heat to a very gentle simmer. One at a time, break the eggs into a cup and slip them into the skillet, being careful not to break the yolks. Cook until the whites are set and the yolks begin to thicken but not harden, 2–3 minutes. With a slotted spoon, transfer the eggs, one at a time, to the paper towels to drain.

3 Add the frisée to the dressing in the bowl and toss to coat. Divide the frisée evenly among 4 plates and top each with a poached egg. Place 1/4 teaspoon of the truffle butter on top of each egg and serve at once.

PER SERVING (1 salad): 101 Cal, 7 g Fat, 2 g Sat Fat, 0 g Trans Fat, 215 mg Chol, 319 mg Sod, 4 g Carb, 2 g Fib, 8 g Prot, 64 mg Calc.
POINTS value: 2.

FOOD NOTE

Truffle butter is a relatively inexpensive and delicious way to add decadent truffle flavor to food. It is a combination of unsalted butter and finely chopped white or black truffles; both varieties are very tasty. Truffle butter is packed in little plastic containers and is available in specialty food stores.

Diner-Style Greek Salad

HANDS-ON PREP 15 MIN ■ COOK NONE ■ SERVES 4

1/4 cup vegetable broth

1 tablespoon olive oil

1 tablespoon red-wine vinegar

1 teaspoon dried oregano

1 garlic clove, minced

1/4 teaspoon salt

1/8 teaspoon freshly ground pepper

6 cups baby romaine lettuce leaves

1/2 cucumber, thinly sliced

1/2 red bell pepper, seeded and cut into strips

1 tomato, cut into 8 wedges

1/2 cup crumbled reduced-fat feta cheese

1/4 cup coarsely chopped fresh dill

10 pitted kalamata olives, sliced

1 To make the dressing, whisk together the broth, oil, vinegar, oregano, garlic, salt, and pepper in a small bowl. Let stand until the flavors blend, about 5 minutes.

2 Meanwhile, make separate piles of the lettuce, cucumber, bell pepper, tomato, feta, dill, and olives in a serving bowl. Serve the dressing alongside.

PER SERVING (2 1/2 cups): 112 Cal, 8 g Fat, 2 g Sat Fat, 0 g Trans Fat, 5 mg Chol, 558 mg Sod, 8 g Carb, 3 g Fib, 5 g Prot, 74 mg Calc.
POINTS value: 2.

EXPRESS LANE

Many supermarket salad bars and specialty food stores have "olive bars" with as many as a dozen or more varieties to choose from. Making a Greek salad is twice as easy when you buy pre-sliced, pitted olives. Kalamatas are the olives of choice for this salad, but niçoise and picholine olives are also tasty.

Spicy Tabbouleh-Pomegranate Salad ☑

HANDS-ON PREP 15 MIN ■ COOK 5 MIN ■ SERVES 4

1 cup water	1 tablespoon olive oil
1 cup bulgur	2 teaspoons cumin
2 tomatoes, chopped	$1/4$ teaspoon cayenne
$1/2$ cup fresh pomegranate seeds	1 garlic clove, minced
$1/2$ cup chopped fresh parsley	$1/2$ teaspoon salt
$1/4$ cup fresh lemon juice	$1/4$ teaspoon freshly ground pepper

1 Bring the water to a boil in a small saucepan. Stir in the bulgur and remove the pan from the heat. Cover and let stand until the water is absorbed, about 15 minutes.

2 Fluff the bulgur with a fork; transfer to a medium bowl and let cool. Stir in the tomatoes, pomegranate seeds, parsley, lemon juice, oil, cumin, cayenne, garlic, salt, and pepper. Serve at once or cover and refrigerate up to 3 days.

PER SERVING (1 cup): 191 Cal, 5 g Fat, 1 g Sat Fat, 0 g Trans Fat, 0 mg Chol, 311 mg Sod, 36 g Carb, 8 g Fib, 6 g Prot, 39 mg Calc.

POINTS value: 3.

TRY IT

Fresh pomegranate seeds add an authentic Moroccan touch to this salad. The seeds are often available, packed in clear plastic containers, in specialty food stores and in some supermarkets. Pomegranates are high in antioxidants, making them a healthful addition to the salad.

I ♡ Tomatoes Salad ☑

HANDS-ON PREP 10 MIN ■ COOK NONE ■ SERVES 4

2 red tomatoes, each cut into 6 wedges

2 yellow tomatoes, each cut into 6 wedges

4 cups grape or cherry tomatoes, halved

1/2 red onion, cut into paper-thin slices

1/4 cup thinly sliced fresh basil leaves

1/4 cup chopped flat-leaf parsley

1 tablespoon balsamic vinegar

1 tablespoon basil-flavored olive oil

1/2 teaspoon salt

1/8 teaspoon freshly ground pepper

Toss together all of the ingredients in a serving bowl. Serve at once or let stand at room temperature up to 30 minutes.

PER SERVING (1 1/2 cups): **105 Cal, 4 g Fat, 1 g Sat Fat, 0 g Trans Fat, 0 mg Chol, 404 mg Sod, 15 g Carb, 3 g Fib, 3 g Prot, 32 mg Calc.**

POINTS value: 2.

FOOD NOTE

This surefire refresher is made even better when prepared with a variety of heirloom tomatoes when in season. The mild flavor of basil-infused oil gives the fresh basil and parsley a little flavor boost. To slice the basil leaves easily, stack a few at a time, roll up lengthwise, and slice crosswise into the thinnest strips possible.

Pickled Beet Salad with Raspberry Vinaigrette

HANDS-ON PREP 2 MIN ■ COOK NONE ■ SERVES 4

2 tablespoons vegetable broth

3 tablespoons apple-cider vinegar

1 tablespoon raspberry vinegar

2 teaspoons sugar

2 teaspoons olive oil

$1/4$ teaspoon salt

$1/4$ teaspoon freshly ground pepper

2 (15-ounce) cans sliced beets, drained

1 red onion, chopped

2 tablespoons grated lemon zest

Combine the broth, cider vinegar, raspberry vinegar, sugar, oil, salt, and pepper in a large bowl. Add the beets and red onion; toss to coat. Cover tightly and refrigerate at least 30 minutes or up to 1 day to allow the flavors to blend. Sprinkle the beets with the lemon zest and serve at once.

PER SERVING ($3/4$ cup): 117 Cal, 3 g Fat, 0 g Sat Fat, 0 g Trans Fat, 0 mg Chol, 278 mg Sod, 23 g Carb, 3 g Fib, 3 g Prot, 35 mg Calc.

POINTS value: 2.

FOOD NOTE

It's fun to experiment with different-flavored vinegars, such as the apple-cider and raspberry versions in this salad. Try other combinations, including Champagne, balsamic, tarragon, red-wine, white-wine, or sherry.

Fruit Salad with Creamy Mint Dressing

HANDS-ON PREP 8 MIN ■ COOK NONE ■ SERVES 4

2 cups strawberries, hulled and sliced

1 mango, peeled, pitted, and cubed (about 2 cups)

1 banana, sliced

1 cup blueberries

3 tablespoons orange juice

1/2 cup vanilla low-fat yogurt

2 tablespoons chopped fresh mint

Fresh mint sprigs

1 Toss together the strawberries, mango, banana, blueberries, and 1 tablespoon of the orange juice in a serving bowl.

2 Put the yogurt, chopped mint, and the remaining 2 tablespoons of orange juice in a food processor and puree until smooth. Pour the yogurt dressing over the fruit mixture and gently toss to coat. Refrigerate, covered, until thoroughly chilled, at least 1 hour or up to 8 hours. Garnish with the mint sprigs and serve at once.

PER SERVING (3/4 cup): 135 Cal, 1 g Fat, 0 g Sat Fat, 0 g Trans Fat, 2 mg Chol, 25 mg Sod, 32 g Carb, 5 g Fib, 3 g Prot, 79 mg Calc.

POINTS value: 2.

MAKE IT CORE

Replace the orange juice with a fresh orange, cut into segments and substitute plain fat-free yogurt for the vanilla yogurt.

Robust Soups

Chunky Vegetable-Beef Soup

HANDS-ON PREP 20 MIN ■ COOK 1 HOUR 10 MIN ■ SERVES 6

1 pound beef top round steak, cut into
   1-inch chunks

1 large onion, chopped

3 carrots, chopped

3 garlic cloves, minced

1 slice thick-cut bacon, chopped

3 (14 $\frac{1}{2}$-ounce) cans reduced-sodium
   beef broth

1 (14 $\frac{1}{2}$-ounce) can diced tomatoes

$\frac{1}{2}$ cup long-grain white rice

3 cups small broccoli florets

$\frac{1}{4}$ teaspoon freshly ground pepper

1 Spray a large nonstick pot or Dutch oven with nonstick spray and set over medium-high heat. Add the beef and cook, stirring frequently, until browned on all sides, about 10 minutes. Transfer the beef to a medium bowl; set aside. Add the onion, carrots, garlic, and bacon to the pot. Reduce the heat to medium. Cook, stirring frequently, until the bacon is lightly browned and the vegetables are softened, about 10 minutes.

2 Add enough water to the broth to equal 6 cups. Return the beef to the pot. Add the broth and tomatoes; bring to a boil. Reduce the heat and simmer, covered, until the beef is just tender, about 30 minutes. Stir in the rice and bring to a boil. Reduce the heat and simmer, covered, until the rice is tender and the beef is fork-tender, about 15 minutes longer. Add the broccoli and pepper; return to a boil. Reduce the heat and simmer, covered, until the broccoli is tender, about 6 minutes.

PER SERVING (scant 2 cups): 225 Cal, 3 g Fat, 1 g Sat Fat, 0 g Trans Fat, 41 mg Chol, 563 mg Sod, 25 g Carb, 4 g Fib, 23 g Prot, 53 mg Calc.
POINTS value: 4.

GOOD IDEA

Serving this hearty soup with toasted thinly sliced Italian or French bread adds tempting crunch (3 thin slices of bread toasts will increase the per-serving **POINTS** value by **3**).

Smoky Black Bean Soup ☑

HANDS-ON PREP 20 MIN ▪ COOK 20 MIN ▪ SERVES 4

1 teaspoon canola oil

1 large onion, chopped

2 garlic cloves, minced

1 (14½-ounce) can reduced-sodium chicken broth

2 cups fresh or frozen corn kernels

1 (15-ounce) can black beans, rinsed and drained

1 cup prepared mild salsa

1 teaspoon chipotle chile powder

1 teaspoon ground cumin

1 cup chopped cooked boneless pork loin

3 tablespoons chopped fresh cilantro

1 teaspoon fresh lime juice

4 tablespoons fat-free sour cream

2 tablespoons chopped scallions

1 Heat the oil in a large nonstick saucepan set over medium heat. Add the onion and garlic; cook, stirring occasionally, until golden, about 8 minutes.

2 Add enough water to the broth to equal 2 cups. Add the broth, corn, beans, salsa, chipotle chile powder, and cumin to the saucepan; bring to a boil. Reduce the heat and simmer, covered, until the flavors are blended, about 5 minutes. Stir in the pork, cilantro, and lime juice; simmer until heated through, about 3 minutes. Ladle the soup into 4 bowls and top with the sour cream and scallions.

PER SERVING (1¾ cups soup, 1 tablespoon sour cream, and 1/2 tablespoon scallion): **283 Cal, 5 g Fat, 1 g Sat Fat, 0 g Trans Fat, 28 mg Chol, 934 mg Sod, 41 g Carb, 9 g Fib, 21 g Prot, 67 mg Calc.**

POINTS value: 5.

HOW WE DID IT

For really fresh cumin flavor, toast and grind whole cumin seeds. Here's how: Toast 2 tablespoons cumin seeds in a small nonstick skillet set over medium heat, tossing frequently, until fragrant, 3 to 4 minutes. Transfer to a plate to cool, then grind the seeds in a spice or coffee grinder. The cumin will keep in a sealed jar up to 3 months.

Garlicky Chicken and Escarole Soup ☑

HANDS-ON PREP 10 MIN ■ COOK 35 MIN ■ SERVES 6

2 teaspoons extra-virgin olive oil

1 onion, chopped

4 garlic cloves, minced

1 tablespoon chopped fresh thyme

3/4 pound Yukon Gold potatoes, scrubbed and diced

4 cups chopped fresh escarole

1 (32-ounce) carton reduced-sodium chicken broth

1 (14 1/2-ounce) can diced tomatoes

1 pound skinless boneless chicken breast halves, cut into chunks

1 1/2 cups frozen peas

1 Heat the oil in a large nonstick saucepan set over medium heat. Add the onion, garlic, and thyme; cook, stirring frequently, until softened, about 2 minutes. Add the potatoes and escarole; cook until the escarole starts to wilt, 4–5 minutes. Stir in the broth and tomatoes; bring to a boil. Reduce the heat and simmer, covered, about 15 minutes.

2 Stir in the chicken and peas; simmer, covered, until the potatoes are tender and the chicken is cooked through, about 10 minutes.

PER SERVING (1 1/3 cups): 215 Cal, 4 g Fat, 1 g Sat Fat, 0 g Trans Fat, 42 mg Chol, 569 mg Sod, 24 g Carb, 6 g Fib, 22 g Prot, 56 mg Calc.
POINTS value: 4.

GOOD IDEA

Other potatoes would work equally well here—red potatoes, long white potatoes, and fingerlings are all good choices.

Curried Chicken and Vegetable Soup ☑

HANDS-ON PREP 25 MIN ▪ COOK 35 MIN ▪ SERVES 6

2 teaspoons canola oil

1 leek, cleaned and thinly sliced (white and light green parts only)

3 garlic cloves, minced

1 tablespoon curry powder

3 (14½-ounce) cans reduced-sodium chicken broth

2 large red potatoes, scrubbed and diced

2 carrots, diced

2 cups small cauliflower florets

¾ pound skinless boneless chicken thighs, cut into ½-inch chunks

¼ cup chopped fresh cilantro

1 teaspoon garam masala

¼ teaspoon salt

¼ cup plain fat-free Greek-style yogurt

1 Heat the oil in a large nonstick pot or Dutch oven set over medium heat. Add the leek and garlic; cook, stirring occasionally, until golden, 7–10 minutes. Add the curry powder and cook, stirring constantly, until fragrant, about 1 minute. Stir in the broth, potatoes, carrots, and cauliflower; bring to a boil. Reduce the heat and simmer until tender, about 15 minutes.

2 Stir in the chicken, cilantro, garam masala, and salt; return the soup to a boil. Reduce the heat and simmer, covered, until the chicken is cooked through, about 10 minutes. Serve the yogurt alongside.

PER SERVING (about 1⅓ cups soup and 2 teaspoons yogurt): 206 Cal, 7 g Fat, 2 g Sat Fat, 0 g Trans Fat, 35 mg Chol, 557 mg Sod, 16 g Carb, 3 g Fib, 19 g Prot, 59 mg Calc.
POINTS value: 4.

TRY IT

Garam masala is a mixture of spices that is essential to Indian cooking. In fact, *masala* means "seasonings" in Arabic. Some of the seasonings often included in garam masala are cinnamon, bay leaves, fennel, cardamom, black pepper, coriander, cloves, mace, and nutmeg. Look for it in specialty food stores and in the spice section of large supermarkets.

Turkey and Sweet Potato Soup

HANDS-ON PREP 25 MIN ■ COOK 50 MIN ■ SERVES 6

1 tablespoon olive oil

1 large Vidalia onion, chopped

3 garlic cloves, minced

2 tablespoons minced peeled
  fresh ginger

1 small jalapeño pepper, seeded and
  chopped (wear gloves to prevent
  irritation)

1 teaspoon ground cardamom

3 (14½-ounce) cans low-sodium
  chicken broth

3 large sweet potatoes (about
  2 pounds), peeled and cut into
  1-inch chunks

1½ cups chopped cooked turkey breast

1 tablespoon packed light brown sugar

2 teaspoons fresh lime juice

¼ cup fat-free half-and-half

2 tablespoons chopped fresh cilantro

1 Heat the oil in a nonstick Dutch oven or large pot set over medium-high heat. Add the onion and cook, stirring frequently, until softened, about 8 minutes. Add the garlic, ginger, jalapeño, and cardamom; cook, stirring constantly, until fragrant, about 2 minutes.

2 Add enough water to the broth to equal 6 cups. Add the sweet potatoes and 3 cups of the broth to the Dutch oven; bring to a boil. Reduce the heat and simmer, covered, until the potatoes are tender, about 20 minutes. Remove the Dutch oven from the heat and let the mixture cool 5 minutes.

3 Transfer the mixture, in batches if necessary, to a blender and puree. Return to the Dutch oven. Stir in the remaining 3 cups of broth, the turkey, brown sugar, and lime juice; bring to a boil. Reduce the heat and simmer until heated through, about 3 minutes. Remove the Dutch oven from the heat; stir in the half-and-half. Ladle the soup into 6 bowls. Sprinkle with the cilantro and serve at once.

PER SERVING (1¾ cups): **262 Cal, 5 g Fat, 1 g Sat Fat, 0 g Trans Fat, 34 mg Chol, 162 mg Sod, 38 g Carb, 3 g Fib, 17 g Prot, 73 mg Calc.**
POINTS value: **5.**

PLAY IT SAFE

When transferring hot soup from a pot to a blender, we recommend first letting the mixture cool for at least 5 minutes. Do not fill the blender more than halfway with the hot liquid. We also like to remove the center part of the lid to allow the steam to escape and, instead, hold a folded clean kitchen towel on the lid while the machine is running.

Asian-Style Shrimp and Vegetable Soup

HANDS-ON PREP 20 MIN ■ COOK 20 MIN ■ SERVES 8

2 (32-ounce) cartons reduced-sodium chicken broth

1 pound small fresh or frozen shrimp, peeled and deveined

3/4 pound snow peas, trimmed and cut into 1-inch pieces

1/2 pound Napa cabbage, shredded (about 4 cups)

1 tablespoon reduced-sodium soy sauce

1 tablespoon Asian (dark) sesame oil

1 bunch scallions, trimmed and sliced

1 (8-ounce) can bamboo shoots, drained and thinly sliced

1/4 (16-ounce) box capellini

1 teaspoon rice or white-wine vinegar

Freshly ground pepper

1 Bring the broth to a boil in a large saucepan set over medium-high heat. Add the shrimp, snow peas, cabbage, soy sauce, and sesame oil; return to a boil. Reduce the heat and simmer just until the cabbage wilts slightly, the snow peas are crisp-tender, and the shrimp are opaque in the center, about 5 minutes.

2 Stir in the scallions, bamboo shoots, capellini, vinegar, and pepper. Cook until the capellini is barely tender and the soup is heated through, about 5 minutes. Serve at once.

PER SERVING (1¾ cups): 112 Cal, 2 g Fat, 0 g Sat Fat, 0 g Trans Fat, 1 mg Chol, 683 mg Sod, 17 g Carb, 3 g Fib, 7 g Prot, 50 mg Calc.
POINTS value: 2.

TRY IT

Napa cabbage, also known as Chinese cabbage, has firmly packed pale green oblong-shaped leaves. It belongs to the same family as green cabbage but has a sweeter, milder flavor. It can be found in the produce section of most supermarkets and in Asian markets.

Manhattan Clam Chowder ☑

HANDS-ON PREP 20 MIN ■ COOK 25 MIN ■ SERVES 6

4 teaspoons olive oil

1½ cups chopped fennel bulb

1 onion, chopped

1 carrot, chopped

1 celery stalk, chopped

1 (32-ounce) carton reduced-sodium chicken broth

1 cup canned no-salt added stewed tomatoes, coarsely chopped, juice reserved

1 (8-ounce) bottle clam juice

1 large Yukon Gold potato, scrubbed and chopped

1½ teaspoons chopped fresh thyme or ½ teaspoon dried

1½ teaspoons chopped fresh oregano or ½ teaspoon dried

¼ teaspoon crushed red pepper

1 (6½-ounce) can minced clams

½ teaspoon grated lemon zest

1 teaspoon fresh lemon juice

1 Heat the oil in a large nonstick saucepan set over medium-high heat. Add the fennel, onion, carrot, and celery; cook, stirring occasionally, until softened, about 5 minutes.

2 Add the broth, tomatoes and their juice, clam juice, potato, thyme, oregano, and crushed red pepper to the saucepan; bring to a boil. Reduce the heat and simmer until the potatoes and vegetables are tender, about 15 minutes. Stir in the clams with their juice, and the lemon zest and juice. Simmer until heated through (do not let boil).

PER SERVING (1 cup): 133 Cal, 4 g Fat, 1 g Sat Fat, 0 g Trans Fat, 10 mg Chol, 415 mg Sod, 18 g Carb, 3 g Fib, 7 g Prot, 54 mg Calc.
POINTS value: 2.

GOOD IDEA

Be sure to stir in the clams at the last minute, and cook them over low heat just until heated through. Boiling the clams, even for a few minutes, will toughen them.

Italian Bean Soup

HANDS-ON PREP 25 MIN ■ COOK 1 HR 40 MIN ■ SERVES 8

3/4 cup dried cannellini (white kidney) beans, picked over, rinsed, and drained

2 (32-ounce) cartons reduced-sodium chicken broth

1/4 teaspoon salt

1/4 teaspoon freshly ground pepper

4 teaspoons olive oil

2 onions, chopped

2 carrots, chopped

2 celery stalks, chopped

2 garlic cloves, minced

1 (28-ounce) can Italian-style peeled tomatoes, drained and chopped, 1 cup juice reserved

3 zucchini, chopped

1 (9-ounce) box frozen cut green beans

3 ounces ditalini or other small pasta (about 2/3 cup)

1/2 cup chopped fresh basil

1/4 cup grated Parmesan cheese

1 Soak the beans according to the package directions. Drain.

2 Combine the beans, broth, salt, and pepper in a large pot; bring just to a boil. Reduce the heat and simmer, covered, until the beans are barely tender, about 1 hour.

3 Heat the oil in a large nonstick skillet set over medium-high heat. Add the onions, carrots, celery, and garlic; cook, stirring frequently, until softened, about 5 minutes.

4 Stir the vegetable mixture into the bean mixture; add the tomatoes with their juice, the zucchini, and green beans. Simmer, stirring occasionally, until the vegetables are tender, about 10 minutes. Stir in the ditalini and cook until barely tender, about 10 minutes. Stir in the basil. Serve sprinkled with the Parmesan.

PER SERVING (1 1/2 cups soup and 1/2 tablespoon Parmesan): 196 Cal, 1 g Fat, 0 g Sat Fat, 0 g Trans Fat, 2 mg Chol, 877 mg Sod, 35 g Carb, 8 g Fib, 13 g Prot, 142 mg Calc.
POINTS value: 3.

MAKE IT CORE

If you're following the **Core Plan,** use whole-wheat pasta and substitute fat-free mozzarella for the Parmesan.

Watercress–Egg Drop Soup ☑

HANDS-ON PREP 10 MIN ■ COOK 15 MIN ■ SERVES 4

1 (32-ounce) carton reduced-sodium chicken broth

1 tablespoon minced peeled fresh ginger

1 tablespoon reduced-sodium soy sauce

3 large eggs, lightly beaten

1 bunch watercress, tough stems removed

2 scallions, thinly sliced

1 Combine the broth, ginger, and soy sauce in a large saucepan; bring to a boil. Reduce the heat and simmer until the flavors are blended, about 10 minutes.

2 Slowly add the eggs, whisking constantly, until strands form, about 1 minute. Remove the saucepan from the heat. Add the watercress and scallions, stirring just until the watercress wilts. Serve at once.

PER SERVING (1¼ cups): 82 Cal, 4 g Fat, 1 g Sat Fat, 0 g Trans Fat, 159 mg Chol, 840 mg Sod, 4 g Carb, 1 g Fib, 8 g Prot, 32 mg Calc.
POINTS value: 2.

ZAP IT

This tasty soup can be reheated quickly by microwaving on High until heated through, about 1 minute 30 seconds for a 1¼-cup portion, stirring once.

Mushroom-Rice Soup

HANDS-ON PREP 20 MIN ■ COOK 1 HR ■ SERVES 8

4 teaspoons olive oil

2 onions, chopped

3 carrots, chopped

3 celery stalks, chopped

$1/2$ cup dry white wine or water

5 ($14^1/2$-ounce) cans reduced-sodium chicken broth

$1/3$ cup brown rice

2 (10-ounce) packages sliced white mushrooms

3 tablespoons chopped fresh thyme

Freshly ground pepper

1 Heat the oil in a large nonstick skillet set over medium-high heat. Add the onions, carrots, and celery; cook, stirring frequently, until softened, about 5 minutes. Add the wine; simmer until the liquid is reduced by one-fourth. Add the broth and bring to a boil.

2 Stir in the rice. Simmer, covered, stirring occasionally, until the rice is almost tender, about 30 minutes.

3 Stir in the mushrooms and thyme and season to taste with pepper; bring just to a boil. Reduce the heat and simmer, covered, stirring occasionally, until the mushrooms are tender, about 10 minutes longer.

PER SERVING ($1^1/2$ cups): 117 Cal, 3 g Fat, 0 g Sat Fat, 0 g Trans Fat, 0 mg Chol, 737 mg Sod, 18 g Carb, 3 g Fib, 7 g Prot, 33 mg Calc.
POINTS value: 2.

EXPRESS LANE

To shorten the cooking time, use quick-cooking brown rice and simmer for just 10 minutes in step 1.

Creamiest Asparagus Soup

HANDS-ON PREP 10 MIN ■ COOK 40 MIN ■ SERVES 6

2 teaspoons olive oil

3 scallions, sliced

1 large all-purpose potato, peeled and cut into 1-inch chunks

1 tablespoon chopped fresh thyme

1 (32-ounce) carton reduced-sodium chicken broth

1 pound asparagus, trimmed and cut into 1-inch pieces

1 tablespoon grated lemon zest

1 cup fat-free half-and-half

1/4 teaspoon salt

1/4 teaspoon freshly ground pepper

1/4 teaspoon nutmeg

6 tablespoons fat-free sour cream

1 Heat the oil in a large nonstick saucepan set over medium heat. Add the scallions and cook, stirring occasionally, until softened, about 3 minutes. Add the potato and thyme; cook, stirring frequently, about 1 minute. Stir in the broth, asparagus, and lemon zest; bring to a boil. Reduce the heat and simmer until the vegetables are tender, about 20 minutes. Stir in the half-and-half, salt, pepper, and nutmeg; cook until heated through, about 5 minutes.

2 Remove the saucepan from the heat; let the mixture cool about 5 minutes. Transfer, in batches if necessary, to a blender and puree. Return the soup to the saucepan; cook over low heat until heated through, about 3 minutes. Ladle the soup into 6 bowls and swirl 1 tablespoon of sour cream into each serving.

PER SERVING (1 cup): 118 Cal, 2 g Fat, 0 g Sat Fat, 0 g Trans Fat, 0 mg Chol, 559 mg Sod, 19 g Carb, 2 g Fib, 6 g Prot, 96 mg Calc.
POINTS value: 2.

TRY IT

Turn this hot soup into a delicious chilled one. Follow the directions in step 2 for pureeing the soup, then refrigerate until well chilled. Top each serving with the sour cream and sprinkle with a little chopped fresh thyme, scallions, or chives.

Silky Butternut Squash Soup ☑

2 teaspoons olive oil

1 onion, chopped

1 (2-pound) butternut squash, peeled, halved, seeded, and cut into 1-inch chunks

1 (32-ounce) carton reduced-sodium chicken broth

1¼ cups water

2 tablespoons chopped fresh thyme

¼ cup fat-free sour cream

4 teaspoons chopped fresh chives

1 Heat the oil in a large nonstick saucepan set over medium-high heat. Add the onion and cook, stirring, until softened, about 5 minutes. Add the squash, broth, water, and thyme; bring to a boil. Reduce the heat and simmer until the squash is very soft, about 20 minutes. Remove the saucepan from the heat and let cool about 30 minutes.

2 Pour the squash mixture through a sieve set over a medium bowl; reserve the liquid. Transfer the squash mixture, in batches if necessary, to a blender or food processor and puree. With the machine running, add 1–1½ cups of the reserved cooking liquid, ½ cup at a time, until the soup has the consistency of cream.

3 Return the soup to the saucepan and set over medium heat. Cook, stirring, just until heated through, about 5 minutes. Remove the saucepan from the heat and stir in the sour cream. Ladle the soup into 4 bowls; top each serving with 1 teaspoon of the chives.

PER SERVING (1 cup): 184 Cal, 4 g Fat, 1 g Sat Fat, 0 g Trans Fat, 0 mg Chol, 489 mg Sod, 33 g Carb, 7 g Fib, 8 g Prot, 136 mg Calc.
POINTS value: 3.

EXPRESS LANE

To cut the prep time in half, use packaged precut butternut squash. Most supermarkets carry packaged precut vegetables in the refrigerated section of the produce department. You will need approximately 1½ pounds of squash chunks.

Leek and Sweet Potato Soup ☑

HANDS-ON PREP 25 MIN ■ COOK 35 MIN ■ SERVES 8

2 (32-ounce) cartons reduced-sodium chicken broth

2 1/2 pounds sweet potatoes, peeled and chopped

3 leeks, cleaned and thinly sliced (white and light green parts only)

1/4 teaspoon salt

1/8 teaspoon freshly ground white pepper

2 tablespoons minced fresh chives or parsley

1 Combine the broth, sweet potatoes, leeks, salt, and pepper in a large pot and bring to a boil. Reduce the heat and simmer, covered, until the vegetables are very soft, about 30 minutes. Remove the saucepan from the heat; uncover and let the mixture cool about 5 minutes.

2 Transfer the sweet potato mixture, in batches if necessary, to a blender or food processor and puree. Return the sweet potato mixture to the saucepan and set over medium heat. Cook, stirring, until heated through, about 5 minutes. Serve at once, sprinkled with the chives, or refrigerate and serve chilled.

PER SERVING (1 1/2 cups): 151 Cal, 0 g Fat, 0 g Sat Fat, 0 g Trans Fat, 0 mg Chol, 692 mg Sod, 33 g Carb, 3 g Fib, 5 g Prot, 44 mg Calc.
POINTS value: 2.

HOW WE DID IT

Here's the best way to clean leeks: Trim the roots, leaving the root end intact to hold the layers together. Slice the leeks lengthwise, fan open the layers, and swish in a large bowl of cool water. Let the leeks rest in the water for a few minutes to give the grit time to fall to the bottom of the bowl. Lift out the leeks and shake dry before using.

Chilled Minted Zucchini Soup ☑

HANDS-ON PREP 10 MIN ■ COOK 15 MIN ■ SERVES 4

3 (14 1/2-ounce) cans reduced-sodium chicken broth

3 zucchini, coarsely chopped

1 onion, chopped

1 garlic clove, minced

2 tablespoons fresh lemon juice

3 tablespoons chopped mint

4 tablespoons fat-free sour cream

1 Add enough water to the broth to equal 6 cups. Combine the broth, zucchini, onion, and garlic in a large saucepan; bring to a boil. Reduce the heat and simmer, covered, until the zucchini is very tender, about 15 minutes. Remove the saucepan from the heat. Uncover and let cool about 5 minutes.

2 Strain the zucchini mixture through a strainer set over a medium bowl; reserve the liquid. Transfer the zucchini mixture to a blender or food processor. Add the lemon juice and mint; puree. With the machine running, add the reserved liquid, 1/4 cup at a time, until the soup has the consistency of cream. Let cool to room temperature, then cover tightly and refrigerate until well chilled, at least 3 hours or up to 1 day. Ladle the soup into 4 bowls and top each serving with a dollop of sour cream.

PER SERVING (1 1/2 cups soup and 1 tablespoon sour cream): **70 Cal, 0 g Fat, 0 g Sat Fat, 0 g Trans Fat, 0 mg Chol, 841 mg Sod, 12 g Carb, 3 g Fib, 7 g Prot, 60 mg Calc.**
POINTS value: 1.

TRY IT

Be as creative as you like with this delicious soup. Use broccoli, frozen peas, or any leafy green vegetable, or a combination of all three in place of the zucchini.

Gazpacho with Garlic Croutons

HANDS-ON PREP 30 MIN ■ COOK NONE ■ SERVES 4

4 large plum tomatoes, peeled and coarsely chopped

1 medium cucumber, peeled, halved, seeded, and coarsely chopped

1 red bell pepper, seeded and coarsely chopped

4 scallions, thickly sliced

3 garlic cloves (2 minced and 1 crushed)

1 jalapeño pepper, seeded and minced (wear gloves to prevent irritation)

2 cups reduced-sodium tomato juice

1/4 cup chopped fresh cilantro

3 tablespoons chopped fresh basil

2 tablespoons red-wine vinegar

1 tablespoon fresh lime juice

1/4 teaspoon salt

1 tablespoon extra-virgin olive oil

2 slices firm-textured white or whole-wheat bread, cut into 1-inch pieces

4 lime slices, for garnish (optional)

1 To make the soup, put the tomatoes, cucumber, bell pepper, scallions, the minced garlic, and jalapeño in a food processor; pulse until chopped. Transfer to a large bowl. Stir in the tomato juice, cilantro, basil, vinegar, lime juice, and salt. Cover and refrigerate until well chilled, at least 3 hours or up to 2 days.

2 To make the croutons, heat the oil in a medium nonstick skillet set over medium-high heat. Add the crushed garlic and cook, stirring, until fragrant, about 30 seconds; discard the garlic. Add the bread pieces and cook, stirring frequently, until just beginning to brown. Remove the skillet from the heat. Ladle the chilled soup into 4 glasses or bowls. Top with the warm croutons and garnish with the lime slices (if using). Serve at once.

PER SERVING (1 1/4 cups soup and 1/4 cup croutons): 128 Cal, 4 g Fat, 1 g Sat Fat, 0 g Trans Fat, 0 mg Chol, 463 mg Sod, 20 g Carb, 3 g Fib, 4 g Prot, 64 mg Calc.
POINTS value: 2.

HOW WE DID IT

To peel the tomatoes, immerse them in boiling water for 1 minute. With a slotted spoon, transfer the tomatoes to a bowl of ice water to cool them down. As soon as the tomatoes are cool enough to handle, slip off the skins.

CHAPTER FOUR

Easy Brunches
and Lunches

Bacon, Egg, and Cheese Casserole

HANDS-ON PREP 10 MIN ■ COOK 30 MIN ■ SERVES 6

6 slices turkey bacon, cut crosswise into
  ¼-inch-wide strips

1 (12-ounce) bag frozen hash-brown
  potatoes

1 onion, chopped

3 large eggs

3 egg whites

¾ cup part-skim ricotta cheese

⅔ cup shredded reduced-fat Swiss
  cheese

3 tablespoons grated Parmesan cheese

3 tablespoons all-purpose flour

½ teaspoon baking powder

¼ teaspoon salt

¼ teaspoon freshly ground pepper

Pinch cayenne

1 Preheat the oven to 375°F. Spray three 2-cup oval baking dishes, casseroles, or ramekins with nonstick spray.

2 Spray a nonstick skillet with nonstick spray and set over medium-high heat. Add the bacon and cook, stirring, until crisp, about 4 minutes. Add the potatoes and onion; cook, stirring, until the potatoes are tender and golden, about 6 minutes. Remove the skillet from the heat; let cool slightly.

3 Meanwhile, beat the eggs and egg whites in a large bowl. Add the ricotta, ⅓ cup of the Swiss cheese, the Parmesan, flour, baking powder, salt, pepper, and cayenne, stirring until blended. Stir in the potato mixture and pour evenly into the baking dishes. Sprinkle evenly with the remaining ⅓ cup of Swiss cheese. Bake until the casseroles are slightly puffed and golden and the cheese is melted, 20–25 minutes.

PER SERVING (½ of a casserole): 220 Cal, 9 g Fat, 4 g Sat Fat, 0 g Trans Fat, 134 mg Chol, 445 mg Sod, 17 g Carb, 1 g Fib, 18 g Prot, 271 mg Calc.
POINTS value: 5.

ZAP IT

If you find yourself with leftovers, you can refrigerate them up to 2 days; reheat individual portions in the microwave on High until heated through, about 3 minutes. You can also bake the casserole in a 7 x 11-inch baking dish. Increase the baking time by 10 minutes.

Cheese and Chive Omelette ☑

HANDS-ON PREP 5 MIN ■ COOK 10 MIN ■ SERVES 2

4 egg whites

1 large egg

1 tablespoon chopped fresh chives

1 tablespoon water

$1/4$ teaspoon salt

$1/4$ teaspoon freshly ground pepper

$1/2$ teaspoon olive oil

$1/2$ cup shredded fat-free cheddar cheese

1 Beat the egg whites, egg, chives, water, salt, and pepper in a medium bowl until frothy.

2 Heat $1/4$ teaspoon of the oil in a small nonstick skillet set over medium-high heat. Add half of the egg mixture and cook, lifting the edges frequently with a spatula to allow the uncooked egg to run underneath, until the eggs are just set, about 2 minutes. Sprinkle $1/4$ cup of the cheddar over half of the egg mixture. Loosen the edges of the omelette and fold over the unfilled portion of eggs to enclose the filling. Reduce the heat to low and cook until the eggs are set and the cheese begins to melt, about 1 minute longer.

3 Slide the omelette onto a plate; keep warm. Repeat with the remaining oil, egg mixture, and cheese to make another omelette.

PER SERVING (1 omelette): 122 Cal, 4 g Fat, 1 g Sat Fat, 0 g Trans Fat, 111 mg Chol, 702 mg Sod, 2 g Carb, 0 g Fib, 19 g Prot, 269 mg Calc.

POINTS value: 3.

TRY IT

There are an endless number of ways to fill an omelette, and it only takes a couple of tasty ingredients to create something wonderful. You might like to substitute fat-free mozzarella cheese for the cheddar and some torn fresh basil leaves for the chives, and add $1/4$ cup of diced roasted red peppers (not oil-packed).

Green Chile and Cheddar Strata

HANDS-ON PREP 10 MIN ■ COOK 45 MIN ■ SERVES 6

5 slices whole-wheat bread, quartered

1 (4-ounce) can mild green chiles, drained and chopped

1/2 cup shredded reduced-fat cheddar cheese

3 scallions, thinly sliced

1/2 cup chopped fresh cilantro

2 cups low-fat (1%) milk

2 large eggs

3 egg whites

1/2 teaspoon hot pepper sauce

1/4 teaspoon salt

1/4 teaspoon freshly ground pepper

1 Spray a 2-quart baking dish with nonstick spray. Arrange the bread pieces in the baking dish, overlapping them slightly; scatter the green chiles, cheddar, scallions, and cilantro on top.

2 Whisk together the milk, eggs, egg whites, pepper sauce, salt, and pepper in a medium bowl until blended. Pour evenly over the bread; let stand, covered, for at least 1 hour or refrigerate up to overnight.

3 Meanwhile, preheat the oven to 350°F.

4 Bake the strata until puffed and golden and a knife inserted into the center comes out clean, 40–45 minutes. Let stand 10 minutes; serve hot or warm.

PER SERVING (1/6 of strata): 199 Cal, 9 g Fat, 5 g Sat Fat, 0 g Trans Fat, 89 mg Chol, 451 mg Sod, 18 g Carb, 2 g Fib, 13 g Prot, 261 mg Calc.
POINTS value: 4.

PLAN AHEAD

One of the best things about a strata—a savory casserole consisting of bread, cheese, and/or vegetables, meat, or fish with a custard mixture to bind it all together—is that once assembled, it can be refrigerated several hours or up to overnight and baked the next day.

Mini Artichoke Frittatas

HANDS-ON PREP 10 MIN ■ COOK 25 MIN ■ SERVES 6

6 slices turkey bacon, sliced crosswise into 1/4-inch-wide strips

1 cup low-fat (1%) milk

3 large eggs

3 egg whites

1/4 cup grated Parmesan cheese

1/4 teaspoon salt

1/4 teaspoon pepper

1 (8 1/2-ounce) can quartered artichoke hearts, drained and coarsely chopped

1 Preheat the oven to 350°F. Spray a 12-cup muffin pan with nonstick spray.

2 Spray a nonstick skillet with nonstick spray and set over medium-high heat. Add the bacon and cook, stirring, until crisp, about 4 minutes. Remove the skillet from the heat; set aside.

3 Whisk together the milk, eggs, egg whites, Parmesan, salt, and pepper in a large bowl until blended. Stir in the artichoke hearts and bacon. Spoon the mixture into the muffin cups, dividing it evenly. Bake until a knife inserted into the center comes out clean, about 20 minutes. To remove the frittatas, run a narrow metal spatula around the edge of each muffin cup, invert the pan, and flip them out.

PER SERVING (2 mini frittatas): 108 Cal, 4 g Fat, 2 g Sat Fat, 0 g Trans Fat, 121 mg Chol, 441 mg Sod, 4 g Carb, 0 g Fib, 11 g Prot, 110 mg Calc.
POINTS value: 2.

FOOD NOTE

A frittata is an Italian-style omelette. Unlike a French-style omelette, where the filling is folded inside the eggs, in a frittata the filling ingredients are mixed with the eggs. It is usually cooked in a skillet and broiled until the top is nice and browned. For a nice variation, our artichoke frittata can be cooked up in a skillet and cut into wedges for serving.

Santa Fe–Style Baked Eggs

HANDS-ON PREP 10 MIN ■ COOK 25 MIN ■ SERVES 4

4 (6-inch) corn tortillas

1 (14 1/2-ounce) can Mexican-style
stewed tomatoes

1 (15 1/2-ounce) can black beans, rinsed
and drained

1/2 cup jarred roasted red peppers, diced

3 tablespoons chopped fresh parsley

3/4 teaspoon chipotle pepper sauce

4 large eggs

1/4 cup shredded reduced-fat Monterey
Jack cheese

1 Preheat the oven to 425°F.

2 Lightly spray both sides of the tortillas with nonstick spray. Invert 4 custard cups on a baking sheet; drape a tortilla over each cup, lightly pressing the tortilla to the cup to help shape it. Bake until the tortillas are crisp and light golden around the edges, about 10 minutes. Transfer the tortillas, right side up, to a rack and let cool.

3 Combine the tomatoes, beans, roasted red peppers, 2 tablespoons of the parsley, and the pepper sauce in an ovenproof skillet; bring to a boil over medium heat. Reduce the heat and simmer until the flavors are blended, about 4 minutes. One at a time, break the eggs and slip on top of the sauce, spacing them evenly. Bake until the eggs are almost set, 6–8 minutes. Sprinkle the Monterey Jack and the remaining 1 tablespoon of parsley on top of the eggs; bake until the cheese is melted, about 1 minute. Place the tortilla cups on plates and spoon the eggs and sauce into the cups, dividing evenly. Serve at once.

PER SERVING (1 filled tortilla cup): 289 Cal, 8 g Fat, 3 g Sat Fat, 0 g Trans Fat, 216 mg Chol, 840 mg Sod, 40 g Carb, 8 g Fib, 17 g Prot, 200 mg Calc.
POINTS value: 6.

ZAP IT

If you prefer soft tortillas, stack the tortillas and wrap them in a sheet of wax paper. Microwave on High just until heated through, about 1 minute. To serve, place the tortillas on plates and spoon the eggs and sauce on top.

Golden Cornmeal Pancakes

HANDS-ON PREP 10 MIN ■ COOK 15 MIN ■ SERVES 6

1 cup all-purpose flour

1/2 cup cornmeal

2 tablespoons sugar

1 teaspoon baking powder

1/4 teaspoon baking soda

1/8 teaspoon salt

1 1/4 cups low-fat buttermilk

1 large egg, lightly beaten

3 teaspoons butter

6 tablespoons unsweetened applesauce

6 (1/2-ounce) slices reduced-fat cheddar cheese

1 Whisk together the flour, cornmeal, sugar, baking powder, baking soda, and salt in a large bowl. Beat the buttermilk and egg in a small bowl. Add the buttermilk mixture to the flour mixture, stirring just until the flour mixture is moistened.

2 Melt 1 teaspoon of the butter in a large nonstick skillet set over medium heat. Pour 1/4 cupfuls of the batter into the skillet. Cook until bubbles appear and the edges of the pancakes look dry, about 2 minutes. Turn and cook until golden, about 2 minutes longer. Repeat with the remaining butter and batter to make 12 pancakes in all. Serve with the applesauce and cheddar.

PER SERVING (2 pancakes, 1 tablespoon applesauce, and 1 slice cheddar): 233 Cal, 7 g Fat, 4 g Sat Fat, 0 g Trans Fat, 53 mg Chol, 350 mg Sod, 33 g Carb, 2 g Fib, 9 g Prot, 181 mg Calc. POINTS value: 5.

PLAN AHEAD

Prepare the flour mixture and store in a zip-close plastic bag up to 2 weeks. The next time the mood strikes, combine the flour mixture with the buttermilk mixture and cook the pancakes. The cornmeal adds both an earthy flavor and great texture that is very appealing. For true country appeal, use stone-ground cornmeal, available in large supermarkets and specialty food stores.

Easy Mushroom-Ham Crêpes

HANDS-ON PREP 10 MIN ■ COOK 30 MIN ■ SERVES 6

3/4 cup low-fat (1%) milk

3/4 cup reduced-sodium chicken broth

3 tablespoons all-purpose flour

5 tablespoons dry marsala wine

1/4 teaspoon freshly ground pepper

1/8 teaspoon nutmeg

1/8 teaspoon cayenne

1/2 cup grated Parmesan cheese

2 teaspoons chopped fresh thyme or
   1/2 teaspoon dried

1 (8-ounce) package sliced white
   mushrooms

3 garlic cloves, minced

1/4 teaspoon salt

6 (7-inch) ready-to-use crêpes (from a
   5-ounce package)

6 thin slices lean deli ham (about
   6 ounces)

1 Whisk together the milk, broth, flour, 3 tablespoons of the marsala, the pepper, nutmeg, and cayenne in a medium saucepan until smooth; set over medium heat. Cook, whisking constantly, until bubbly and thickened, 6–7 minutes. Remove the saucepan from heat and stir in the Parmesan and 1 teaspoon of the thyme; keep warm.

2 Spray a large nonstick skillet with nonstick spray and set over medium-high heat. Add the mushrooms, garlic, and salt; cook, stirring, until softened, about 6 minutes. Stir in the remaining 2 tablespoons of marsala and cook until the liquid is evaporated, 2–3 minutes. Remove the skillet from the heat and stir in the remaining 1 teaspoon of thyme. Let cool slightly.

3 Meanwhile, preheat the oven to 425°F. Spray a 7 x 11-inch baking dish with nonstick spray.

4 Place the crêpes on a work surface. Lay 1 slice of the ham across the center of each crêpe. Spread with 1 tablespoon of the sauce and top with 2 tablespoons of the mushroom mixture. Roll the crêpes up, jelly-roll style, and transfer to the baking dish, seam side down. Top with the remaining sauce. Bake until the sauce is bubbly and lightly browned, about 15 minutes.

PER SERVING (1 filled crêpe): 134 Cal, 4 g Fat, 2 g Sat Fat, 0 g Trans Fat, 19 mg Chol, 696 mg Sod, 13 g Carb, 1 g Fib, 11 g Prot, 136 mg Calc.
POINTS value: 3.

FOOD NOTE

Marsala is an Italian wine that is fortified with brandy and is sometimes flavored with herbs and spices. Its slightly sweet taste nicely balances out the other flavors in this dish. You can substitute sherry or any good dry white wine for the marsala, if you like.

Broccoli-Tomato Quiche

HANDS-ON PREP 15 MIN ■ COOK 50 MIN ■ SERVES 8

2 teaspoons olive oil

1 onion, chopped

1 garlic clove, minced

1 (10-ounce) box frozen chopped broccoli, thawed

1 (9-inch) refrigerated piecrust

3/4 cup fat-free evaporated milk

2 large eggs

1 egg white

1/4 cup fat-free sour cream

1/2 teaspoon salt

1/8 teaspoon freshly ground pepper

1/2 cup shredded reduced-fat Swiss cheese

2 plum tomatoes, thinly sliced

1 tablespoon grated Parmesan cheese

2 teaspoons chopped fresh thyme

1 Heat the oil in a large nonstick skillet set over medium-high heat. Add the onion and garlic; cook, stirring, until softened, about 5 minutes. Add the broccoli and cook, stirring, 2 minutes. Remove the skillet from the heat; set aside.

2 Preheat the oven to 375°F.

3 Roll out the piecrust on a lightly floured surface to an 11-inch round; ease into a 9-inch pie plate, pressing the dough against the side of the plate. Trim the dough, leaving a 1-inch overhang. Crimp the edge to form a decorative rim; set aside.

4 Lightly beat the evaporated milk, eggs, egg white, sour cream, salt, and pepper in a medium bowl until blended. Sprinkle the Swiss cheese over the bottom of the crust. Top evenly with the broccoli mixture, then pour in the egg mixture. Arrange the tomato slices on top in a decorative pattern; sprinkle with the Parmesan and thyme. Bake until a knife inserted into the center comes out clean, 35–40 minutes. Let stand about 10 minutes to serve hot or serve at room temperature.

PER SERVING (1/8 of quiche): 215 Cal, 11 g Fat, 4 g Sat Fat, 0 g Trans Fat, 65 mg Chol, 334 mg Sod, 21 g Carb, 1 g Fib, 9 g Prot, 178 mg Calc.
POINTS value: 5.

TRY IT

Other green vegetables would also be tasty in this quiche, including frozen sliced zucchini, chopped spinach, or kale. Just be sure to remove any excess water once the vegetable has thawed.

Scrambled Egg and Bacon Melt ☑

HANDS-ON PREP 5 MIN ■ COOK 10 MIN ■ SERVES 4

2 large eggs

2 egg whites

1/4 cup shredded fat-free cheddar cheese

1/4 teaspoon salt

1/8 teaspoon freshly ground pepper

4 slices Canadian bacon

1 tablespoon canola oil

1/2 green bell pepper, seeded and chopped

1 Whisk together the eggs, egg whites, cheddar, salt, and pepper in a medium bowl; set aside.

2 Cook the Canadian bacon in a medium nonstick skillet set over medium-high heat until lightly browned, about 2 minutes on each side. Transfer to a plate; keep warm.

3 Heat the oil in the same skillet set over medium heat. Add the bell pepper and cook, stirring, until softened, about 4 minutes. Add to the egg mixture. Spray the skillet with nonstick spray. Add the egg mixture and cook, stirring, until the eggs are set and the cheese is melted, about 2 minutes.

4 Place 1 slice of bacon and one-fourth of the egg mixture on each of 4 plates and serve at once.

PER SERVING (1 plate): 135 Cal, 8 g Fat, 2 g Sat Fat, 0 g Trans Fat, 121 mg Chol, 632 mg Sod, 2 g Carb, 0 g Fib, 13 g Prot, 80 mg Calc.
POINTS value: 3.

GOOD IDEA

Vary this quick and delicious breakfast dish by using thinly sliced lean turkey instead of the Canadian bacon and fat-free Swiss or mozzarella cheese instead of the cheddar cheese.

Grilled Swiss with Avocado and Tomato

HANDS-ON PREP 10 MIN ■ COOK 4 MIN ■ SERVES 4

2 tablespoons low-fat mayonnaise

8 slices multigrain bread

4 (1/2-ounce) slices low-fat Swiss or cheddar cheese

1/2 small avocado, pitted, peeled, and thinly sliced

2 carrots, shredded

2 cups alfalfa sprouts

1 tomato, cut into 8 slices

1 Spread 1 1/2 teaspoons of the mayonnaise on each of 4 of the bread slices; layer with 1 slice of Swiss cheese, one-fourth of the avocado, one-fourth of the carrots, 1/2 cup of the alfalfa sprouts, and 2 tomato slices. Cover with the remaining 4 slices of bread.

2 Set a large nonstick skillet over medium heat. Lightly spray both sides of each sandwich with nonstick spray; place in the skillet. Cook, covered, turning once, until the cheese is melted and the bread well toasted, about 4 minutes. Cut each sandwich in half and serve at once.

PER SERVING (1 sandwich): 228 Cal, 6 g Fat, 1 g Sat Fat, 0 g Trans Fat, 5 mg Chol, 386 mg Sod, 34 g Carb, 6 g Fib, 11 g Prot, 202 mg Calc.
POINTS value: 4.

GOOD IDEA

Take this sandwich to another level by adding crisp cooked turkey bacon (3 slices will increase the per-serving POINTS value by 2).

Almond Butter and Jam–Stuffed French Toast

HANDS-ON PREP 15 MIN ■ COOK 10 MIN ■ SERVES 4

8 slices whole-grain bread

8 teaspoons almond butter

8 teaspoons raspberry jam

3/4 cup fat-free egg substitute

1 teaspoon vanilla extract

1/2 teaspoon cinnamon

2 teaspoons canola oil

1 Spread each of 4 slices of the bread with 2 teaspoons of the almond butter. Spread each of the remaining 4 slices of bread with 2 teaspoons of the jam. Put the slices of bread together to make 4 almond butter and jam sandwiches; set aside.

2 Beat the egg substitute, vanilla, and cinnamon in a large shallow bowl. Dip 1 sandwich in the egg mixture until evenly soaked, about 30 seconds on each side. Transfer to a flat plate. Repeat with the remaining sandwiches.

3 Heat 1 teaspoon of the oil in a large nonstick skillet set over medium-high heat. Add 2 of the sandwiches and cook until browned, about 2 minutes on each side. Repeat with the remaining oil and sandwiches. Cut each sandwich in half and serve at once.

PER SERVING (1 sandwich): 255 Cal, 10 g Fat, 2 g Sat Fat, 0 g Trans Fat, 0 mg Chol, 397 mg Sod, 31 g Carb, 4 g Fib, 12 g Prot, 66 mg Calc.

POINTS value: 5.

FOOD NOTE

Almond butter contains more calcium than peanut butter. Look for it in large supermarkets and in natural-foods stores.

Berry and Cream Cheese
Open-Face Sandwiches

HANDS-ON PREP 10 MIN ■ COOK 2 MIN ■ SERVES 4

4 large strawberries, hulled and sliced

$1/2$ cup raspberries

$1 1/2$ tablespoons sugar

$1/2$ teaspoon grated orange zest

2 teaspoons fresh orange juice

4 tablespoons light cream cheese (Neufchâtel)

2 teaspoons honey

$1/4$ teaspoon vanilla extract

4 slices cinnamon-raisin bread

1 Combine the strawberries, raspberries, sugar, and orange zest and juice in a small bowl. Let stand, stirring occasionally, until the sugar is dissolved, about 5 minutes.

2 Meanwhile, combine the cream cheese, honey, and vanilla in another small bowl.

3 Toast the bread; let cool about 30 seconds. Spread 1 tablespoon of the cream cheese mixture on each slice of bread. Cut each slice in quarters and top each quarter with about 2 teaspoons of the strawberry mixture. Serve at once.

PER SERVING (4 quarters of sandwich): 147 Cal, 4 g Fat, 1 g Sat Fat, 0 g Trans Fat, 6 mg Chol, 162 mg Sod, 25 g Carb, 2 g Fib, 4 g Prot, 41 mg Calc.
POINTS value: 3.

GOOD IDEA

Kids will love these tasty little treats. For fun, use cookie cutters to cut the bread into stars, triangles, or hearts.

Greek-Style Pizza with Feta and Artichokes

HANDS-ON PREP 10 MIN ■ COOK 5 MIN ■ SERVES 6

1 (10-ounce) bag baby spinach

1/2 cup marinated artichoke hearts, rinsed, drained, and chopped

1 (10-ounce) prebaked thin pizza crust

1/2 cup part-skim ricotta cheese

1 teaspoon dried oregano

1/8 teaspoon crushed red pepper

6 cherry tomatoes, halved

1/2 cup crumbled feta cheese

1 Preheat the broiler.

2 Cook the spinach according to the package directions. Transfer to a colander and rinse under cold running water until cool. Squeeze the excess water from the spinach, then coarsely chop. Put in a small bowl and add the artichokes, stirring until well mixed.

3 Place the pizza crust on a pizza pan or baking sheet. Broil 4–5 inches from the heat until golden, 30–60 seconds on each side.

4 Spread the ricotta evenly over the crust; sprinkle with the oregano and crushed red pepper. Top with the spinach mixture, cherry tomatoes, and feta. Broil until the feta is softened, about 1 minute. Cut into 6 wedges and serve at once.

PER SERVING (1 wedge): 220 Cal, 8 g Fat, 4 g Sat Fat, 0 g Trans Fat, 18 mg Chol, 531 mg Sod, 31 g Carb, 6 g Fib, 12 g Prot, 226 mg Calc.
POINTS value: 4.

TRY IT

Instead of plain feta, try feta cheese flavored with sun-dried tomatoes and basil or Mediterranean herbs. For convenience, buy microwavable bags of triple-washed baby spinach.

Spicy Chicken Tostadas

HANDS-ON PREP 10 MIN ▪ COOK 4 MIN ▪ SERVES 4

4 (6-inch) corn tortillas

1 cup cubed cooked smoked chicken or turkey breast

6 tablespoons tomatillo salsa

$1/3$ cup chopped red bell pepper

1 tablespoon fat-free mayonnaise

$1/2$ cup shredded light Mexican four-cheese blend

1 Preheat the broiler. Place the tortillas on a baking sheet. Broil 4 inches from the heat until golden, 1–2 minutes on each side.

2 Combine the chicken, salsa, bell pepper, and mayonnaise in a small bowl; stir until combined. Top each tortilla with a generous $1/4$ cup of the chicken mixture, spreading it almost to the edge; sprinkle with 2 tablespoons of the cheese. Broil the tostadas until the cheese melts, 1–2 minutes.

PER SERVING (1 tostada): 149 Cal, 5 g Fat, 2 g Sat Fat, 0 g Trans Fat, 29 mg Chol, 699 mg Sod, 17 g Carb, 2 g Fib, 12 g Prot, 172 mg Calc.
POINTS value: 3.

FOOD NOTE

The tomatillo, also called a Mexican green tomato, is a fruit that belongs to the same nightshade family as other tomatoes. Tomatillos resemble very small tomatoes but are covered with a parchment-paper–like skin. They are widely used in Mexican and Southwestern cooking. The tomatillo salsa in this recipe adds a tempting smoky, citrusy flavor.

Turkey-Cheddar Tacos

HANDS-ON PREP 10 MIN ■ COOK 8 MIN ■ SERVES 4

1 cup shredded cooked turkey breast

2 tablespoons drained pickled jalapeño pepper slices, finely chopped

4 teaspoons fat-free mayonnaise

2 tablespoons chopped fresh cilantro

1 teaspoon grated lime zest

1 teaspoon lime juice

4 (6-inch) fat-free flour tortillas

1 cup shredded green leaf lettuce

1 cup yellow or red cherry tomatoes, quartered

1/2 cup shredded reduced-fat cheddar cheese

1 Combine the turkey, pickled jalapeño, mayonnaise, cilantro, and lime zest and juice in a medium bowl.

2 Spray a large nonstick skillet with nonstick spray and set over medium-high heat. Add the tortillas, one at a time, and cook until crispy and dark brown in spots, about 1 minute on each side.

3 Top each tortilla with 1/4 cup of the turkey mixture, spreading it almost to the edge; top with 1/4 cup of the lettuce, about 1/4 cup of the tomatoes, and 2 tablespoons of the cheddar.

PER SERVING (1 taco): 173 Cal, 4 g Fat, 2 g Sat Fat, 0 g Trans Fat, 40 mg Chol, 413 mg Sod, 18 g Carb, 3 g Fib, 16 g Prot, 116 mg Calc.
POINTS value: 3.

GOOD IDEA

Tacos are fun to eat and can be prepared with various ingredients. We love our tacos with good-for-you green leaf lettuce, but if crisp lettuce is more to your liking, use iceberg instead. When picking out a head of iceberg, choose one that is soft when pressed, which will ensure fewer pale green leaves. As for the cheese, cheddar is traditional, but Monterey Jack, pepperjack, or a combination of the two is also delicious.

CHAPTER FIVE

Best-Ever Poultry

Grilled Whole Chicken with Garlic and Herbs ☑

HANDS-ON PREP 15 MIN ■ COOK 2 HR 10 MIN ■ SERVES 6

6 garlic cloves, thinly sliced

1 tablespoon olive oil

1 tablespoon grated lemon zest

1 tablespoon chopped fresh sage +
3 sage leaves

1 teaspoon salt

¹/₄ teaspoon freshly ground pepper

1 (3¹/₂–4-pound) chicken, giblets
discarded

1 medium onion, halved

1 lemon, cut into quarters

1 Spray the grill rack with nonstick spray; preheat the grill to medium or prepare a medium fire using the indirect method (see How We Did It below).

2 Combine the garlic, oil, lemon zest, chopped sage, salt, and pepper in a small bowl. With your fingers, loosen the skin on the chicken breasts, legs, and thighs. Rub the garlic mixture into the meat under the skin. Place the onion, lemon, and sage leaves inside the cavity of the chicken. Tie the legs together with kitchen string.

3 Place the chicken, breast side up, on the cooler part of the grill rack; cover the grill. Grill the chicken, without turning, until an instant-read thermometer inserted into a thigh registers 180°F, about 2 hours 10 minutes. Transfer the chicken to a cutting board and let stand about 10 minutes before carving. Remove the skin before eating.

PER SERVING (¹/₆ of chicken): 198 Cal, 9 g Fat, 2 g Sat Fat, 0 g Trans Fat, 81 mg Chol, 473 mg Sod, 1 g Carb, 0 g Fib, 27 g Prot, 20 mg Calc.
POINTS value: 5.

HOW WE DID IT

To set up a grill for indirect cooking, preheat only one side of a gas grill or mound the charcoal on one side of a charcoal grill. With indirect grilling, larger items, such as a whole chicken, can be grilled for a long time without getting charred while acquiring a delicious smoky taste.

Classic Roast Chicken ☑

HANDS-ON PREP 15 MIN ■ COOK 2 HR ■ SERVES 8

1 (4 1/2-pound) chicken, giblets discarded
3/4 teaspoon salt
1/2 teaspoon freshly ground pepper

1 lemon, halved
5 garlic cloves, peeled
5 fresh rosemary or thyme sprigs

1 Preheat the oven to 350°F.

2 Rub the chicken inside and out with the salt and pepper. Squeeze the lemon over the outside of the chicken. Place the lemon halves, garlic, and rosemary sprigs inside the cavity of the chicken. Tie the legs together with kitchen string.

3 Place the chicken, breast side up, on a rack in a large roasting pan. Roast until an instant-read thermometer inserted into a thigh registers 180°F, 2–2 1/4 hours. Transfer the chicken to a carving board and let stand about 10 minutes. Remove the lemon, garlic, and rosemary sprigs from the cavity and discard. Carve the chicken. Remove the skin before eating.

PER SERVING (1/8 of chicken): 161 Cal, 6 g Fat, 2 g Sat Fat, 0 Trans Fat, 74 mg Chol, 287 mg Sod, 0 g Carb, 0 g Fib, 26 g Prot, 19 mg Calc.
POINTS value: 4.

PLAY IT SAFE

If you use a frozen chicken, be sure to defrost it in the refrigerator, not on the counter. This will ensure that the chicken defrosts evenly, resulting in a tasty and moist chicken. Also, if thawed at room temperature, poultry becomes a perfect environment for the growth of salmonella bacteria.

Easy Chicken Cacciatore

HANDS-ON PREP 15 MIN ■ COOK 35 MIN ■ SERVES 8

1 (2 1/2 –3-pound) chicken, skinned and
   cut into 8 pieces

1/2 teaspoon salt

1/4 teaspoon freshly ground pepper

3 teaspoons olive oil

1 onion, chopped

3 garlic cloves, minced

2 red bell peppers, seeded and chopped

1/4 pound fresh cremini mushrooms,
   sliced

1/2 cup chopped fennel or celery

1/2 teaspoon dried oregano

Pinch cayenne

2 cups prepared marinara sauce

1   Sprinkle the chicken with the salt and ground pepper. Heat 2 teaspoons of the oil in a large nonstick skillet set over medium-high heat. Add the chicken and cook until browned, 3–4 minutes on each side. Transfer the chicken to a plate; set aside.

2   Heat the remaining 1 teaspoon of oil in the same skillet. Add the onion and garlic; cook, stirring occasionally, until softened, about 3 minutes. Add the bell peppers, mushrooms, fennel, oregano, and cayenne; cook, stirring occasionally, until softened, 5–6 minutes. Return the chicken to the skillet; add the marinara sauce and spoon it over the chicken; bring to a boil. Reduce the heat and simmer, covered, until the chicken is cooked through and the vegetables are tender, about 20 minutes.

PER SERVING (1 piece chicken and scant 1/2 cup vegetables with sauce): 203 Cal, 8 g Fat, 2 g Sat Fat, 0 g Trans Fat, 48 mg Chol, 510 mg Sod, 16 g Carb, 2 g Fib, 18 g Prot, 33 mg Calc. *POINTS* value: 4.

PLAN AHEAD

This hearty dish tastes even better if prepared a day or two ahead and refrigerated in an airtight container. When ready to serve, transfer the cacciatore to a large nonstick skillet and gently simmer, covered, until heated through, about 15 minutes, being sure to stir occasionally to prevent the sauce from burning.

Pineapple and Honey–Glazed Chicken

HANDS-ON PREP 15 MIN ◼ COOK 50 MIN ◼ SERVES 8

$1/2$ cup canned crushed pineapple in juice

2 tablespoons reduced-sodium soy sauce

2 tablespoons honey

2 tablespoons fresh lime juice

1 tablespoon grated peeled fresh ginger

1 shallot, minced

1 small jalapeño pepper, preferably red, seeded and minced (wear gloves to prevent irritation)

1 (4-pound) chicken, skinned and cut into 8 pieces

$1/2$ teaspoon cornstarch

2 teaspoons water

1 tablespoon chopped fresh parsley

1 Combine the pineapple, soy sauce, honey, lime juice, ginger, shallot, and jalapeño in a large zip-close plastic bag; add the chicken. Squeeze out the air and seal the bag; turn to coat the chicken. Refrigerate, turning the bag occasionally, at least 4 hours or up to overnight.

2 Meanwhile, preheat the oven to 375°F. Place a rack in a large roasting pan.

3 Remove the chicken pieces from the marinade and place on the rack; reserve the marinade. Bake the chicken until browned and an instant-read thermometer inserted into a thigh registers 180°F, about 45 minutes. Baste with the reserved marinade twice during the first 25 minutes of cooking. Discard the marinade.

4 Stir together the cornstarch and water in a small bowl until smooth. Transfer the chicken to a platter; keep warm. Remove the rack from the roasting pan. With a spoon, skim off any fat from the pan juices; pour the pan juices into a small saucepan and set over medium heat. Cook until the juices are reduced by half, about 2 minutes. Add the cornstarch mixture and cook, stirring constantly, until the mixture bubbles and thickens, about 10 seconds; stir in the parsley. Serve the chicken with the sauce.

PER SERVING (1 piece chicken and 2 tablespoons sauce): 199 Cal, 6 g Fat, 2 g Sat Fat, 0 g Trans Fat, 78 mg Chol, 210 mg Sod, 8 g Carb, 0 g Fib, 26 g Prot, 18 mg Calc.
POINTS value: 4.

GOOD IDEA

Serve this Asian-inspired dish with a side of fragrant jasmine rice ($1/2$ cup cooked rice for each serving will increase the *POINTS* value by *2*).

Baked Mediterranean-Style Chicken ☑

HANDS-ON PREP 15 MIN ■ COOK 40 MIN ■ SERVES 6

3 (³/₄-pound) bone-in chicken breast halves, skinned and cut crosswise in half

3 garlic cloves, minced

1 tablespoon chopped fresh rosemary

1 tablespoon chopped fresh thyme

1 tablespoon grated orange zest

2 teaspoons olive oil

¹/₂ teaspoon crushed red pepper

¹/₂ teaspoon salt

Pinch dried lavender buds (optional)

1 tablespoon balsamic vinegar

1   Preheat the oven to 400°F.

2   Toss together the chicken, garlic, rosemary, thyme, orange zest, oil, crushed red pepper, salt, and lavender (if using) in a large zip-close plastic bag until the chicken is coated.

3   Place the chicken pieces on a rimmed baking sheet. Bake 30 minutes. Increase the oven temperature to 450°F. Sprinkle the vinegar over the chicken. Continue baking until the chicken is browned and an instant-read thermometer inserted into a breast registers 170°F, about 10 minutes longer. Transfer the chicken to a platter and let stand about 5 minutes.

4   Meanwhile, skim off any fat from the pan juices. Serve the pan juices with the chicken.

PER SERVING (1 piece chicken and 2 teaspoons pan juices): 168 Cal, 5 g Fat, 1 g Sat Fat, 0 g Trans Fat, 74 mg Chol, 265 mg Sod, 1 g Carb, 0 g Fib, 27 g Prot, 18 mg Calc. *POINTS* value: 4.

GOOD IDEA

If you like, toss some pimiento-stuffed olives onto the baking sheet when you sprinkle the chicken with the vinegar in step 3. (Decrease the salt to ¹/₄ teaspoon to keep the sodium in check.) Five pimiento-stuffed olives with each serving will increase the **POINTS** value by *1.*

Grilled Chicken with Fresh Corn Salsa ☑

HANDS-ON PREP 15 MIN ■ COOK 30 MIN ■ SERVES 4

3 ears of corn, husks and silk removed

1 pint grape tomatoes, quartered

1 small onion, chopped

1 jalapeño pepper, seeded and finely chopped (wear gloves to prevent irritation)

2 tablespoons fresh lime juice

1 tablespoon chopped fresh cilantro

1/4 teaspoon salt

2 (3/4-pound) bone-in chicken breast halves, skinned and cut crosswise in half

1 tablespoon olive oil

2 teaspoons chili powder

1 Spray the grill rack with nonstick spray; preheat the grill to medium or prepare a medium fire.

2 To make the salsa, place the corn on the grill rack. Grill, turning every 2 minutes, until tender and well marked, about 6 minutes. Transfer the corn to a cutting board and let cool about 5 minutes. With a sharp knife, cut the kernels from the cobs; transfer the kernels to a large bowl. Add the tomatoes, onion, jalapeño, lime juice, cilantro, and salt; mix well and set aside.

3 Meanwhile, rub the chicken with the oil and sprinkle with the chili powder; place on the grill rack. Grill, turning once, until an instant-read thermometer inserted into a breast registers 170°F, 20–24 minutes. Serve the chicken with the salsa.

PER SERVING (1 piece chicken and 1 cup salsa): 221 Cal, 7 g Fat, 1 g Sat Fat, 0 g Trans Fat, 42 mg Chol, 474 mg Sod, 24 g Carb, 3 g Fib, 19 g Prot, 17 mg Calc.
POINTS value: 4.

GOOD IDEA

Here's a clever way to use some of the corn husks for serving. Place a grilled chicken breast in a husk and top with the salsa. To keep to the **Core Plan**, serve the chicken with unsweetened ice tea.

Soy-Ginger Chicken Breasts

HANDS-ON PREP 15 MIN ■ COOK 25 MIN ■ SERVES 4

3 teaspoons Asian (dark) sesame oil

2 (³/₄-pound) bone-in chicken breast halves, skinned and cut crosswise in half

5 scallions, finely chopped

1 tablespoon + 2 teaspoons grated peeled fresh ginger

1 cup reduced-sodium chicken broth

3 tablespoons reduced-sodium soy sauce

3 tablespoons red-wine vinegar

2 tablespoons chopped fresh cilantro

5 teaspoons honey

1 Heat 2 teaspoons of the sesame oil in a large nonstick skillet set over medium-high heat. Add the chicken and cook until browned, 3–4 minutes on each side. Transfer the chicken to a plate; set aside.

2 Add 4 of the scallions and 1 tablespoon of the ginger to the skillet; cook, stirring constantly, until fragrant, about 1 minute. Add the broth and 2 tablespoons of the soy sauce; bring to a boil. Reduce the heat and simmer, covered, 4 minutes. Add the chicken and return to a gentle simmer; cook, covered, until cooked through, about 12 minutes. Remove the skillet from the heat; set aside 10 minutes. With a slotted spoon, transfer the chicken to a platter; discard the pan liquid.

3 Combine the remaining 1 teaspoon of sesame oil, scallion, 2 teaspoons of ginger, 1 tablespoon of soy sauce, and the vinegar, cilantro, and honey in a small bowl. Serve with the chicken.

PER SERVING (1 piece chicken and 1¹/₂ tablespoons sauce): 205 Cal, 6 g Fat, 1 g Sat Fat, 0 g Trans Fat, 74 mg Chol, 299 mg Sod, 10 g Carb, 0 g Fib, 28 g Prot, 22 mg Calc.
POINTS value: 5.

FOOD NOTE

When shopping for fresh ginger, look for pieces with smooth, shiny skin. When wrinkled or cracked, the ginger is past its prime. If you have extra ginger, store it just as you would potatoes, at cool room temperature.

Baked Chicken Provençal ☑

HANDS-ON PREP 15 MIN ■ COOK 1 HR ■ SERVES 6

3 (³/₄-pound) bone-in chicken breast halves, skinned and cut crosswise in half

1 (14¹/₂-ounce) can no-salt-added diced tomatoes

1 cup reduced-sodium chicken broth

2 fennel bulbs, trimmed and thinly sliced (about 4 cups)

10 pitted green olives, rinsed and chopped

1 onion, chopped

1 (3-inch) strip orange zest, removed with a vegetable peeler

1 bay leaf, preferably Turkish

1 teaspoon chopped fresh rosemary or ¹/₂ teaspoon dried

1 teaspoon chopped fresh thyme or ¹/₂ teaspoon dried

¹/₄ teaspoon salt

¹/₄ teaspoon freshly ground pepper

Large pinch saffron threads

3 tablespoons cornmeal

1 Preheat the oven to 350°F.

2 Spray a Dutch oven or large flameproof casserole dish with olive oil nonstick spray and set over medium-high heat. Add the chicken and cook until browned, about 2 minutes on each side. Add the tomatoes and broth; bring to a boil, scraping up any browned bits from the bottom of the dish. Add all the remaining ingredients except the cornmeal, stirring to make sure the chicken is partially submerged.

3 Bake, covered, 45 minutes. Uncover and slowly whisk the cornmeal into the liquid. Bake, uncovered, until an instant-read thermometer inserted into a breast registers 170°F and the sauce is slightly thickened, about 10 minutes longer. Remove the bay leaf before serving.

PER SERVING (1 piece chicken and ³/₄ cup vegetables with sauce): 217 Cal, 5 g Fat, 1 g Sat Fat, 0 g Trans Fat, 74 mg Chol, 429 mg Sod, 12 g Carb, 4 g Fib, 30 g Prot, 79 mg Calc.
POINTS value: 4.

TRY IT

Saffron, the yellow-orange stigmas of a small crocus, is prized for its aroma and exotic flavor. Just before adding the saffron threads, crush them between your fingers. Saffron can be stored at least 6 months at room temperature and up to 2 years in the freezer.

Chicken Tandoori ☑

HANDS-ON PREP 15 MIN ■ COOK 10 MIN ■ SERVES 8

³/₄ cup plain fat-free yogurt

1 small red onion, finely chopped

2 tablespoons grated peeled fresh ginger

2 tablespoons white-wine vinegar

1 tablespoon Dijon mustard

1 garlic clove, minced

2 teaspoons paprika

1 teaspoon ground cumin

¹/₂ teaspoon ground coriander

¹/₂ teaspoon cinnamon

¹/₈ teaspoon cayenne

8 (¹/₄-pound) chicken cutlets

1 Combine all the ingredients except the chicken in a large zip-close plastic bag. Add the cutlets. Squeeze out the air and seal the bag; turn to coat the cutlets. Refrigerate, turning the bag occasionally, at least 2 hours or up to overnight.

2 Preheat the broiler and spray the broiler pan with nonstick spray.

3 Remove the cutlets from the marinade; discard the marinade. Place the cutlets in the broiler pan and broil 5 inches from the heat, turning once, until cooked through, about 8 minutes.

PER SERVING (1 cutlet): 156 Cal, 3 g Fat, 1 g Sat Fat, 0 Trans Fat, 67 mg Chol, 83 mg Sod, 2 g Carb, 0 g Fib, 27 g Prot, 43 mg Calc.
POINTS value: 3.

EXPRESS LANE

Tandoori spice blends are available in Indian and specialty food stores. Use about 4 teaspoons of the blend and omit the paprika, cumin, coriander, cinnamon, and cayenne in the recipe.

Skillet Chicken with Lemon and Capers

4 (1/4-pound) chicken cutlets

1/2 teaspoon salt

1/4 teaspoon freshly ground pepper

1 tablespoon + 1 teaspoon unsalted butter

1/2 cup reduced-sodium chicken broth

1/4 cup fresh lemon juice

1/2 lemon, thinly sliced

1 tablespoon drained capers

1 tablespoon chopped flat-leaf parsley

1 Sprinkle the cutlets with 1/4 teaspoon of the salt and 1/8 teaspoon of the pepper.

2 Melt 1 tablespoon of the butter in a large nonstick skillet set over medium-high heat. Add the cutlets and cook until lightly browned, about 2 minutes on each side. Add the broth, lemon juice and slices, capers, and parsley; bring to a simmer. Reduce the heat and simmer, turning the chicken once to coat with the sauce, until cooked through, about 2 minutes.

3 Remove the skillet from the heat and swirl in the remaining 1 teaspoon of butter; add the remaining 1/4 teaspoon of salt and 1/8 teaspoon of pepper. Transfer the chicken and sauce to a platter.

PER SERVING (1 cutlet and generous 1 tablespoon sauce): 182 Cal, 8 g Fat, 3 g Sat Fat, 0 g Trans Fat, 79 mg Chol, 477 mg Sod, 1 g Carb, 0 g Fib, 26 g Prot, 19 mg Calc.
POINTS value: 4.

MAKE IT CORE

To fit this recipe into the **Core Plan,** substitute 1 tablespoon plus 1 teaspoon of extra-virgin olive oil for the butter.

Thai Chicken Satay

HANDS-ON PREP 25 MIN ■ COOK 10 MIN ■ SERVES 8

2¹/₂ tablespoons Asian fish sauce

¹/₂ small onion, finely chopped

1 tablespoon minced peeled fresh ginger

2 teaspoons grated lime zest

2 teaspoons + 1 tablespoon fresh lime juice

1¹/₂ pounds skinless, boneless chicken breast halves, cut into 2-inch-long thin strips (about 40)

6 tablespoons light coconut milk

3 tablespoons reduced-fat creamy peanut butter

4 teaspoons honey

¹/₈ teaspoon crushed red pepper

1 Combine 1¹/₂ tablespoons of the fish sauce, the onion, ginger, 1 teaspoon of the lime zest, and 2 teaspoons of the lime juice in a large zip-close plastic bag; add the chicken. Squeeze out the air and seal the bag; turn to coat the chicken. Refrigerate, turning the bag occasionally, at least 1 hour or up to 6 hours.

2 Meanwhile, soak 40 (6–8-inch) wooden skewers in water for at least 30 minutes.

3 To make the peanut sauce, whisk together the coconut milk, peanut butter, honey, the remaining 1 tablespoon of fish sauce, 1 tablespoon of lime juice, 1 teaspoon of lime zest, and the crushed red pepper in a serving bowl until smooth.

4 Spray the broiler rack with nonstick spray and preheat the broiler.

5 Thread the chicken strips onto the skewers. Wrap the ends of the skewers in foil to prevent charring. Place the skewers on the broiler rack; broil 4 inches from the heat, turning once, until cooked through, 6–8 minutes. Serve with the peanut sauce.

PER SERVING (5 chicken skewers and about 2 tablespoons sauce): 162 Cal, 6 g Fat, 2 g Sat Fat, 0 Trans Fat, 47 mg Chol, 200 mg Sod, 7 g Carb, 0 g Fib, 21 g Prot, 18 mg Calc.
POINTS value: 4.

GOOD IDEA

Double the peanut sauce and refrigerate the extra portion in an airtight container up to 4 days. Serve it at another meal alongside grilled steak, broiled pork chops, or steamed green beans or zucchini.

Tex-Mex Chicken Wraps

HANDS-ON PREP 20 MIN ■ COOK 10 MIN ■ SERVES 4

4 (¹/₄-pound) skinless boneless chicken breast halves

1 teaspoon canola oil

2 teaspoons Mexican or taco seasoning

¹/₄ teaspoon salt

¹/₃ cup fat-free mayonnaise

2 tablespoons chopped fresh cilantro

1 tablespoon fresh lime juice

2 teaspoons chopped chipotle en adobo

4 (8-inch) fat-free flour tortillas

4 green leaf lettuce leaves

1 plum tomato, seeded and chopped

1 small onion, chopped

1 Toss together the chicken and oil in a small bowl. Sprinkle with the Mexican seasoning and salt; toss to coat.

2 Spray a nonstick ridged grill pan with nonstick spray and set over medium-high heat. Add the chicken and grill until cooked through, 5–6 minutes on each side. Transfer the chicken to a cutting board; let stand about 5 minutes. Cut the chicken on the diagonal into ¹/₄-inch-thick slices.

3 Combine the mayonnaise, cilantro, lime juice, and chipotle en adobo in a small bowl.

4 Spread each tortilla with 1¹/₂ tablespoons of the mayonnaise mixture. Layer 1 lettuce leaf, 1 chicken breast half, one-fourth of the tomato, and one-fourth of the onion on each tortilla. Fold the bottom edge of each tortilla over the filling, then fold in the sides and roll up, jelly-roll style, to form a neat package.

PER SERVING (1 wrap): 256 Cal, 5 g Fat, 1 g Sat Fat, 0 g Trans Fat, 65 mg Chol, 767 mg Sod, 25 g Carb, 5 g Fib, 28 g Prot, 108 mg Calc.
POINTS value: 5.

GOOD IDEA

If you like, enfold the bottom half of each wrap in foil. The foil will prevent the wraps from opening so you won't lose a drop of the tasty filling.

Chicken with Green Sauce

HANDS-ON PREP 20 MIN ■ COOK 30 MIN ■ SERVES 4

2 teaspoons olive oil

1 onion, chopped

1 green bell pepper, seeded and chopped

1 carrot, chopped

1 celery stalk, chopped

4 (1/4-pound) skinless boneless chicken breast halves

3 cups reduced-sodium chicken broth

1/2 cup dry white wine

2 tablespoons chopped flat-leaf parsley

1 teaspoon herbes de Provence

1 garlic clove

1/4 teaspoon freshly ground pepper

SAUCE

1/2 cup packed flat-leaf parsley leaves

1/2 cup packed fresh cilantro leaves

5 small green olives, pitted and chopped

1 tablespoon fresh lemon juice

1/2 tablespoon plain dried bread crumbs

1 teaspoon capers, drained

1 teaspoon extra-virgin olive oil

1 garlic clove

1/4 teaspoon freshly ground pepper

Pinch cayenne

1 Heat the oil in a large nonstick skillet set over medium-high heat. Add the onion, bell pepper, carrot, and celery; cook, stirring, until softened, about 5 minutes. Add the chicken, broth, wine, parsley, herbes de Provence, garlic, and ground pepper. Bring to a boil; reduce the heat and simmer, covered, until the chicken is cooked through, 12–15 minutes.

2 Meanwhile, to make the sauce, combine all the ingredients in a food processor and pulse until the mixture forms a coarse pestolike sauce.

3 With a slotted spoon, transfer the chicken and vegetables to a warm platter. Reserve the cooking liquid for another use. Serve the chicken and vegetables with the sauce.

PER SERVING (1 chicken breast, 1/4 cup vegetables, and 2 tablespoons sauce): 213 Cal, 8 g Fat, 2 g Sat Fat, 0 Trans Fat, 62 mg Chol, 302 mg Sod, 9 g Carb, 2 g Fib, 27 g Prot, 62 mg Calc.
POINTS value: 5.

FOOD NOTE

Don't discard the cooking liquid in step 3; it can be reused in any dish calling for chicken broth, including risottos, soups, and stews. Refrigerate in an airtight container up to 2 days or freeze up to 2 months.

Hunan Chicken Stir-Fry

HANDS-ON PREP 15 MIN ■ COOK 10 MIN ■ SERVES 4

1 cup orange juice

3 tablespoons reduced-sodium soy sauce

2 tablespoons cornstarch

2 tablespoons honey

¼ teaspoon crushed red pepper or more to taste

4 teaspoons Asian (dark) sesame oil

1 pound chicken cutlets, cut into 1-inch pieces

1 green bell pepper, seeded and diced

2 cups small broccoli florets

1 tablespoon grated peeled fresh ginger

1 teaspoon toasted sesame seeds (optional)

1   Stir together the orange juice, soy sauce, cornstarch, honey, and crushed red pepper in a small bowl until smooth.

2   Heat 2 teaspoons of the sesame oil in a large nonstick skillet or wok set over medium-high heat until a drop of water sizzles in it. Add the chicken and stir-fry until browned and cooked through, about 4 minutes. Transfer the chicken to a plate; set aside.

3   Heat the remaining 2 teaspoons of sesame oil in the same skillet. Add the bell pepper, broccoli, and ginger; stir-fry until crisp-tender, about 1 minute. Return the chicken to the skillet along with the orange juice mixture; cook, stirring constantly, until the sauce bubbles and thickens, about 1 minute. Transfer to a platter; sprinkle with the sesame seeds if using.

PER SERVING (1 cup without sesame seeds): 265 Cal, 6 g Fat, 1 g Sat Fat, 0 g Trans Fat, 75 mg Chol, 452 mg Sod, 24 g Carb, 2 g Fib, 28 g Prot, 35 mg Calc.
POINTS value: 5.

GOOD IDEA

Hot cooked rice is the perfect complement to this spicy dish (½ cup cooked white or brown rice per serving will increase the **POINTS** value by **2**).

Smoky Buffalo Chicken Fingers

HANDS-ON PREP 10 MIN ■ COOK 10 MIN ■ SERVES 8

$^1/_2$ cup Louisiana-style hot sauce

1 teaspoon hot pepper sauce

3 tablespoons unsalted butter

$^1/_4$ teaspoon hickory liquid smoke

2 pounds chicken tenders

4 carrots, cut into matchstick strips

4 celery stalks, cut into matchstick strips

$^1/_2$ cup fat-free blue cheese dressing

1 Spray the grill rack with nonstick spray; preheat the grill to medium or prepare a medium fire.

2 Bring the hot sauce and hot pepper sauce to a simmer in a small saucepan set over medium heat; cook 1 minute. Remove the saucepan from the heat and swirl in 1$^1/_2$ tablespoons of the butter.

3 Put the remaining 1$^1/_2$ tablespoons of butter in a microwavable dish and heat on High until melted, about 10 seconds. Stir in the liquid smoke. Toss together the chicken and butter mixture in a large bowl. Place the chicken on the grill rack. Grill until cooked through, 4–5 minutes on each side. Transfer the chicken to another large bowl and toss with the hot sauce mixture. Serve with the carrots, celery, and blue cheese dressing.

PER SERVING (about 2 chicken tenders, a few vegetable sticks, and 1 tablespoon dressing): 224 Cal, 8 g Fat, 4 g Sat Fat, 0 g Trans Fat, 80 mg Chol, 456 mg Sod, 12 g Carb, 1 g Fib, 26 g Prot, 29 mg Calc.

POINTS value: 5.

MAKE IT CORE

To fit this recipe into the **Core Plan**, substitute canola oil for the butter and fat-free Italian dressing for the blue cheese dressing.

Spanish Chicken and Rice

HANDS-ON PREP 15 MIN ■ COOK 35 MIN ■ SERVES 4

4 (5-ounce) skinless bone-in chicken thighs

³/₄ teaspoon salt

¹/₄ teaspoon freshly ground pepper

2 teaspoons olive oil

2 red bell peppers, seeded and chopped

1 onion, chopped

3 garlic cloves, minced

1 cup long-grain white rice

¹/₂ teaspoon saffron threads, lightly crushed with your fingers

1 (3-inch) strip lemon zest, removed with a vegetable peeler

¹/₄ teaspoon dried oregano

1 (14¹/₂-ounce) can Italian diced tomatoes

1 cup reduced-sodium chicken broth

1 cup frozen peas

12 small pimiento-stuffed green olives

¹/₄ cup chopped fresh cilantro

1   Sprinkle the chicken with ¹/₄ teaspoon of the salt and ¹/₈ teaspoon of the ground pepper. Heat 1 teaspoon of the oil in a large nonstick skillet set over medium-high heat. Add the chicken and cook until browned, 3–4 minutes on each side. Transfer chicken to a plate; set aside.

2   Heat the remaining 1 teaspoon of oil in the same skillet. Add the bell peppers, onion, and garlic; cook, stirring, until softened, about 7 minutes. Stir in the rice, saffron, and lemon zest; cook, stirring constantly, about 1 minute. Add the oregano, tomatoes, broth, and chicken; bring to a boil, stirring occasionally.

3   Reduce the heat and simmer, covered, until the liquid is absorbed and the chicken is cooked through, about 20 minutes. Stir in the peas and olives and the remaining ¹/₂ teaspoon of salt and ¹/₈ teaspoon of ground pepper. Cook, stirring occasionally, until heated through, about 1 minute. Remove the skillet from the heat and let stand, covered, 5 minutes. Spoon the chicken and rice mixture onto a platter and sprinkle with the cilantro.

PER SERVING (1 chicken thigh and 1¹/₃ cups rice mixture): 450 Cal, 12 g Fat, 3 g Sat Fat, 0 g Trans Fat, 57 mg Chol, 1,042 mg Sod, 56 g Carb, 5 g Fib, 28 g Prot, 100 mg Calc.
POINTS value: 9.

Lemon Chicken with Artichokes

HANDS-ON PREP 10 MIN ■ COOK 30 MIN ■ SERVES 6

6 ounces ditalini or orzo (about 1 1/3 cups)

2 ounces reduced-fat feta cheese

8 pitted gaeta olives, sliced

6 (1/2-pound) whole chicken legs, skinned

3/4 teaspoon salt

1/4 teaspoon freshly ground pepper

1 (20-ounce) can artichoke hearts, drained and quartered

3 garlic cloves, minced

1/2 teaspoon dried marjoram

1 cup reduced-sodium chicken broth

2 tablespoons fresh lemon juice

1 Cook the ditalini according to the package directions, omitting the salt if desired. Drain and transfer to a large bowl. Stir in the feta and olives; keep warm.

2 Meanwhile, sprinkle the chicken with the salt and pepper. Spray a large nonstick skillet with nonstick spray and set over medium-high heat. Add the chicken and cook until browned, 3–4 minutes on each side. Transfer the chicken to a plate; set aside.

3 Add the artichoke hearts, garlic, and marjoram to the same skillet; cook, stirring, until fragrant, about 1 minute. Return the chicken to the skillet along with the broth and lemon juice; bring to a boil. Reduce the heat and simmer, covered, until the chicken is cooked through, about 20 minutes.

4 Transfer the chicken to a plate. Pour 1 cup of the artichoke sauce over the pasta and toss well. Divide the pasta evenly among 6 plates and place 1 chicken leg on each plate. Serve with the remaining sauce.

PER SERVING (1 chicken leg, 1/2 cup pasta mixture, and scant 1/4 cup sauce): 365 Cal, 10 g Fat, 4 g Sat Fat, 0 g Trans Fat, 91 mg Chol, 864 mg Sod, 32 g Carb, 5 g Fib, 36 g Prot, 127 mg Calc. *POINTS* value: 7.

GOOD IDEA

For extra lemon flavor, grate the zest from the lemon before you juice it, then stir the zest into the pasta just before serving in step **4**.

Grilled Margarita Chicken

HANDS-ON PREP 10 MIN ■ COOK 15 MIN ■ SERVES 4

1/2 cup orange juice

3 tablespoons tequila

1/2 jalapeño pepper, seeded and minced
(wear gloves to prevent irritation)

2 garlic cloves, minced

2 teaspoons grated lime zest

2 tablespoons fresh lime juice

1 tablespoon canola oil

1 teaspoon chili powder

4 (1/4-pound) skinless boneless
chicken thighs

1/2 teaspoon salt

1/4 teaspoon freshly ground pepper

1 Combine the orange juice, tequila, jalapeño, garlic, lime zest and juice, oil, and chili powder in a large zip-close plastic bag; add the chicken. Squeeze out the air and seal the bag; turn to coat the chicken. Refrigerate, turning the bag occasionally, at least 8 hours or up to overnight.

2 Spray the grill rack with nonstick spray; preheat the grill to medium or prepare a medium fire.

3 Remove the chicken from the marinade and shake off the excess marinade. Discard the marinade. Sprinkle the chicken with the salt and pepper; place on the grill rack. Grill until cooked through, 6–7 minutes on each side.

PER SERVING (1 chicken thigh): 202 Cal, 10 g Fat, 3 g Sat Fat, 0 g Trans Fat, 71 mg Chol, 359 mg Sod, 1 g Carb, 0 g Fib, 24 g Prot, 29 mg Calc.
POINTS value: 5.

GOOD IDEA

Serve these slightly tangy thighs with grilled corn tortillas. Toast the tortillas on the grill rack for about 1 minute on each side. A 6-inch corn tortilla with each serving will increase the **POINTS** value by **2**.

Creole Chicken and Okra ☑

HANDS-ON PREP 15 MIN ■ COOK 15 MIN ■ SERVES 4

2 teaspoons canola oil

1 pound skinless boneless chicken thighs, cut into 1-inch pieces

1/4 teaspoon salt

1/8 teaspoon freshly ground pepper

1 green bell pepper, seeded and chopped

1 onion, chopped

1 celery stalk with leaves, chopped

2 garlic cloves, minced

1 cup frozen sliced okra

1 (14 1/2 -ounce) can diced tomatoes with jalapeños

1/2 teaspoon dried thyme

1/4 teaspoon cayenne

1/4 cup chopped scallions (dark green part only)

1 Heat 1 teaspoon of the oil in a large nonstick skillet set over medium-high heat. Add the chicken and sprinkle with the salt and ground pepper. Cook, stirring frequently, until browned and cooked through, 4–5 minutes. Transfer the chicken to a plate; set aside.

2 Heat the remaining 1 teaspoon of oil in the same skillet. Add the bell pepper, onion, celery, and garlic; cook, stirring frequently, until crisp-tender, about 2 minutes. Add the okra and cook, stirring occasionally, until tender, about 4 minutes. Return the chicken to the skillet along with the tomatoes, thyme, and cayenne; bring to a boil. Reduce the heat and simmer until the liquid is slightly thickened, about 4 minutes longer. Just before serving, sprinkle with the scallions.

PER SERVING (1 cup): 222 Cal, 6 g Fat, 2 g Sat Fat, 0 g Trans Fat, 94 mg Chol, 508 mg Sod, 15 g Carb, 4 g Fib, 27 g Prot, 111 mg Calc.
POINTS value: 4.

FOOD NOTE

Creole dishes often contain the "holy trinity" of chopped green bell pepper, onion, and celery, as well as generous amounts of tomato. The most famous Creole dish is gumbo, a thick stew-like dish that may contain, okra, tomato, the "holy trinity," and meat, chicken, shellfish, and/or some spicy tasso ham.

Grilled Asian-Style Drumsticks

HANDS-ON PREP 5 MIN ■ COOK 20 MIN ■ SERVES 4

1/3 cup miso

1/4 cup mirin

1/4 cup orange juice

1 tablespoon grated peeled fresh ginger

1 teaspoon Asian (dark) sesame oil

4 (6-ounce) chicken drumsticks, skinned

1 teaspoon finely chopped fresh parsley

1/2 teaspoon black sesame seeds (optional)

1 Combine the miso, mirin, orange juice, ginger, and sesame oil in a large zip-close plastic bag; add the chicken. Squeeze out the air and seal the bag; turn to coat the chicken. Refrigerate, turning the bag occasionally, at least 30 minutes or up to overnight.

2 Meanwhile, spray the grill rack with nonstick spray; preheat the grill to medium or prepare a medium fire.

3 Remove the chicken from the marinade and wipe off the excess marinade. Discard the marinade. Place the chicken on the grill rack and cover the grill. Grill, turning once, until an instant-read thermometer inserted into a leg registers 180°F, about 20 minutes. Transfer the chicken to a platter. Sprinkle with the parsley and sesame seeds, if using.

PER SERVING (1 chicken drumstick without sesame seeds): 172 Cal, 8 g Fat, 2 g Sat Fat, 0 g Trans Fat, 57 mg Chol, 261 mg Sod, 3 g Carb, 0 g Fib, 20 g Prot, 26 mg Calc.
POINTS value: 4.

TRY IT

Miso (MEE-soh), a paste made from fermented soybeans, and *mirin* (MEER-in), a sweet Japanese rice wine, can be found in Asian markets, natural-foods stores, and the gourmet section of large supermarkets.

Madras Curry Drumsticks ☑

HANDS-ON PREP 15 MIN ■ COOK 20 MIN ■ SERVES 4

1/2 cup plain fat-free yogurt

2 tablespoons fresh lemon juice

1 tablespoon curry powder, preferably Madras

1 tablespoon grated peeled fresh ginger

2 garlic cloves, minced

1 teaspoon ground cumin

1/4 teaspoon hot pepper sauce

8 (1/4-pound) chicken drumsticks, skinned

3/4 teaspoon salt

1 Combine the yogurt, lemon juice, curry powder, ginger, garlic, cumin, and pepper sauce in a large zip-close plastic bag; add the chicken. Squeeze out the air and seal the bag; turn to coat the chicken. Refrigerate, turning the bag occasionally, at least 30 minutes or up to overnight.

2 Meanwhile, spray the grill rack with nonstick spray; preheat the grill to medium or prepare a medium fire.

3 Remove the chicken from the marinade and sprinkle with the salt. Discard the marinade. Place the chicken on the grill rack. Grill, turning occasionally, until an instant-read thermometer inserted into a drumstick registers 180°F, about 18 minutes.

PER SERVING (2 chicken drumsticks): 158 Cal, 4 g Fat, 1 g Sat Fat, 0 g Trans Fat, 99 mg Chol, 525 mg Sod, 2 g Carb, 0 g Fib, 26 g Prot, 61 mg Calc.
POINTS value: 3.

GOOD IDEA

Cool and crisp cucumber slices and flatbread are perfect accompaniments to our delectably spiced curry drumsticks (1/3 cup thinly sliced cucumber and 3/4 ounce of flatbread will increase the per-serving **POINTS** value by 1).

Best-Ever Chicken Meatloaf

HANDS-ON PREP 20 MIN ■ COOK 1 HR 15 MIN ■ SERVES 6

1 onion, chopped

2 celery stalks, chopped

2 Gala apples, cored and finely chopped

1 1/2 pounds ground skinless chicken breast

2 egg whites, lightly beaten

1 cup fresh whole-wheat bread crumbs

2 tablespoons chopped fresh dill

1 teaspoon grated lemon zest

1/2 teaspoon salt

1/4 teaspoon ground nutmeg

1/4 teaspoon freshly ground pepper

2 teaspoons Dijon mustard

1 Spray a medium nonstick skillet with nonstick spray and set over medium heat. Add the onion and celery; cook, stirring frequently, until slightly softened, about 2 minutes. Add the apples and cook, stirring occasionally, until softened, about 8 minutes. Transfer to a large bowl and let cool about 15 minutes.

2 Meanwhile, preheat the oven to 350°F. Spray a 5 x 9-inch loaf pan with nonstick spray.

3 Add the chicken, egg whites, bread crumbs, dill, lemon zest, salt, nutmeg, and pepper to the onion mixture; mix well. Spoon into the pan and pack down. Spread the mustard over the top of the meatloaf. Bake until an instant-read thermometer inserted into the middle of the meatloaf registers 165°F, about 1 hour 15 minutes. Let stand about 5 minutes, then unmold and cut into 6 slices.

PER SERVING (1/6 of meatloaf): 203 Cal, 4 g Fat, 1 g Sat Fat, 0 g Trans Fat, 68 mg Chol, 351 mg Sod, 13 g Carb, 2 g Fib, 27 g Prot, 33 mg Calc.
POINTS value: 4.

HOW WE DID IT

Chopped apple is our secret to keeping the meatloaf moist even though it's prepared with lean ground chicken breast. The apple also adds a pleasant hint of sweetness.

Tex-Mex–Spiced Turkey Breast ☑

HANDS-ON PREP 10 MIN ■ COOK 2 HRS ■ SERVES 10 + LEFTOVERS

1 1/2 tablespoons chipotle chile powder

1 teaspoon ground cumin

1 teaspoon garlic powder

1 teaspoon onion powder

1 tablespoon canola oil

2 teaspoons fresh lime juice

1 (5-pound) bone-in turkey breast

1/4 cup reduced-sodium chicken broth (optional)

1 Place an oven rack in the lower third of the oven and preheat the oven to 350°F. Spray a large roasting pan with canola nonstick spray.

2 Combine the chipotle chili powder, cumin, garlic powder, and onion powder in a small bowl; stir in the oil and lime juice until the mixture forms a thick paste. If needed, moisten the paste with a little bit of water.

3 With your fingers, separate the skin from the meat beginning at the tip of the breast halves. Spread the spice mixture evenly over the meat; pat the skin back in place.

4 Place the turkey breast in the roasting pan. Roast, basting with the pan juices every 20 minutes, until an instant-read thermometer inserted into the thickest part of the breast registers 170°F, about 2 hours. If the pan juices dry out before the turkey is cooked through, use the broth to baste the bird occasionally. Transfer the turkey breast to a cutting board and let stand about 10 minutes before carving. Remove the skin before eating.

PER SERVING (2 slices): 191 Cal, 3 g Fat, 1 g Sat Fat, 0 g Trans Fat, 107 mg Chol, 93 mg Sod, 1 g Carb, 0 g Fib, 38 g Prot, 24 mg Calc.
POINTS value: 4.

PLAN AHEAD

You'll have about 1 cup of leftover turkey from the roast, which can be refrigerated in an airtight container up to 3 days. Chop the turkey and stir it into vegetable soup or whole-wheat pasta for a hearty meal later in the week.

Turkey Parmesan

HANDS-ON PREP 15 MIN ■ COOK 10 MIN ■ SERVES 4

2 egg whites

$^1/_3$ cup plain dried bread crumbs

$^1/_3$ cup grated Parmesan cheese

$^3/_4$ teaspoon dried oregano

$^1/_2$ teaspoon salt

$^1/_4$ teaspoon freshly ground pepper

3 tablespoons all-purpose flour

4 ($^1/_4$-pound) turkey cutlets

1 tablespoon extra-virgin olive oil

1 $^2/_3$ cups fat-free prepared marinara sauce

$^1/_2$ cup shredded part-skim mozzarella cheese

1 Lightly beat the egg whites in a shallow bowl. Combine the bread crumbs, Parmesan, oregano, salt, and pepper on a sheet of wax paper. Spread the flour on another sheet of wax paper.

2 Working with 1 cutlet at a time, lightly coat with the flour, shaking off the excess. Dip the cutlets in the egg whites, then lightly coat with the bread crumb mixture. Place on a plate. Discard any remaining flour, egg whites, and bread crumb mixture.

3 Heat the oil in a large nonstick skillet set over medium-high heat. Add the cutlets and cook until browned and cooked through, about 3 minutes on each side. Reduce the heat and pour the marinara sauce over the cutlets. Top each cutlet with 2 tablespoons of the mozzarella. Simmer, covered, until the sauce is hot and the cheese is melted, about 4 minutes.

PER SERVING (1 cutlet and about $^1/_3$ cup sauce): 318 Cal, 9 g Fat, 4 g Sat Fat, 0 g Trans Fat, 88 mg Chol, 666 mg Sod, 20 g Carb, 1 g Fib, 37 g Prot, 232 mg Calc.
POINTS value: 7.

HOW WE DID IT

This recipe works best if the cutlets are a scant $^1/_4$ inch thick. If they are thicker, place each one between 2 sheets of wax paper or plastic wrap. With a meat mallet or the bottom of a heavy saucepan, pound the cutlets using an outward motion, starting at the center of each cutlet.

Ham and Cheese–Stuffed Turkey Cutlets

HANDS-ON PREP 20 MIN ■ COOK 30 MIN ■ SERVES 4

4 (1/4-pound) turkey cutlets

4 (1/2-ounce) slices lean deli ham

4 thin slices part-skim mozzarella cheese

I large egg

4 tablespoons all-purpose flour

1/2 teaspoon salt

1/4 teaspoon freshly ground pepper

Pinch cayenne

1/2 cup cornflake crumbs

1/2 cup reduced-fat (2%) milk

1/2 cup reduced-sodium chicken broth

I tablespoon dry sherry

1/8 teaspoon ground nutmeg

2 tablespoons grated Parmesan cheese

1 Preheat the oven to 400°F. Spray a baking sheet with nonstick spray.

2 Lay the cutlets on a work surface. Top each with 1 slice of ham and 1 slice of mozzarella. Roll the cutlets up and secure each one with a toothpick; set aside.

3 Lightly beat the egg in a shallow bowl. Combine 2 tablespoons of the flour, 1/4 teaspoon of the salt, 1/8 teaspoon of the pepper, and the cayenne on a sheet of wax paper. Put the cornflake crumbs on another sheet of wax paper.

4 Working with 1 cutlet roll at a time, lightly coat with the flour mixture, shaking off the excess. Dip the cutlets in the egg, then lightly coat with the cornflake crumbs. Place on the baking sheet. Discard any remaining flour mixture, egg, and crumbs. Lightly spray the turkey rolls with nonstick spray. Bake until an instant-read thermometer inserted into the thickest part of each roll registers 160°F, 30–35 minutes.

5 Meanwhile, to make the sauce, whisk together the milk, broth, sherry, nutmeg, and the remaining 2 tablespoons of flour, 1/4 teaspoon of salt, and 1/8 teaspoon of pepper in a medium saucepan until smooth. Cook over medium heat, whisking constantly, until bubbly and thickened, about 6 minutes. Remove the saucepan from the heat and stir in the Parmesan. Place the turkey rolls on a platter and spoon the sauce over.

PER SERVING (I turkey roll and 1/4 cup sauce): 294 Cal, 9 g Fat, 4 g Sat Fat, 0 Trans Fat, 0 mg Chol, 744 mg Sod, 14 g Carb, 0 g Fib, 38 g Prot, 280 mg Calc.
POINTS value: 7.

HOW WE DID IT

Using sheets of wax paper for the flour mixture and for the cornflake crumbs really cuts down on the cleanup. Foil and parchment paper also work well.

Saucy Turkey Meatballs

HANDS-ON PREP 15 MIN ■ COOK 20 MIN ■ SERVES 4

3/4 pound ground skinless turkey breast

3 tablespoons plain dried bread crumbs

1 egg white, lightly beaten

2 tablespoons chopped flat-leaf parsley

1 tablespoon Dijon mustard

4 teaspoons olive oil

1 zucchini, chopped

1 onion, finely chopped

1 red bell pepper, seeded and finely chopped

1 (28-ounce) can diced tomatoes

1 (10-ounce) package frozen peas and carrots, thawed

1/4 teaspoon salt

1/4 teaspoon freshly ground pepper

1 Combine the turkey, bread crumbs, egg white, parsley, and mustard in a large bowl. Form into 20 meatballs.

2 Heat the oil in a large nonstick skillet set over medium heat. Add the meatballs and cook, turning frequently, until browned on all sides, about 6 minutes. With a slotted spoon, transfer the meatballs to a plate; keep warm.

3 Heat the same skillet over medium-high heat. Add the zucchini, onion, and bell pepper; cook, stirring occasionally, until softened, about 5 minutes. Stir in the tomatoes, peas and carrots, salt, and ground pepper; bring to a simmer. Add the meatballs to the sauce; simmer, partially covered, frequently spooning the sauce over the meatballs, until cooked through and tender, about 10 minutes.

PER SERVING (5 meatballs and 1/2 cup sauce): 257 Cal, 8 g Fat, 2 g Sat Fat, 0 Trans Fat, 50 mg Chol, 631 mg Sod, 22 g Carb, 6 g Fib, 26 g Prot, 129 mg Calc.
POINTS value: 5.

GOOD IDEA

These herb-laced meatballs and tomato sauce are great spooned over mashed potatoes or egg noodles (1/2 cup cooked potatoes or noodles will increase the per-serving **POINTS** value by **2**).

Barbecue-Sauced Sloppy Joes

HANDS-ON PREP 10 MIN ■ COOK 10 MIN ■ SERVES 6

2 teaspoons canola oil

1 onion, chopped

1 green bell pepper, seeded and chopped

2 garlic cloves, minced

1 1/2 teaspoons chili powder

3/4 teaspoon ground cumin

1/2 teaspoon dried oregano

1/2 teaspoon mustard powder

1 pound ground skinless turkey breast

1 cup prepared barbecue sauce

6 multigrain hamburger rolls

6 lettuce leaves

6 thick tomato slices

1 Heat the oil in a large nonstick skillet set over medium heat. Add the onion, bell pepper, and garlic; cook, stirring occasionally, until softened, about 5 minutes. Stir in the chili powder, cumin, oregano, and mustard powder. Add the turkey and cook, breaking it apart with a wooden spoon, until no longer pink, 3–4 minutes. Stir in the barbecue sauce and cook until slightly thickened, about 2 minutes.

2 Spoon 1/2 cup of the turkey mixture onto the bottom half of each roll. Top each with 1 lettuce leaf, 1 tomato slice, and the top of the roll.

PER SERVING (1 sandwich): 273 Cal, 6 g Fat, 2 g Sat Fat, 0 g Trans Fat, 49 mg Chol, 603 mg Sod, 30 g Carb, 3 g Fib, 24 g Prot, 79 mg Calc.
POINTS value: 5.

FOOD NOTE

If you like your sloppy joes on the fiery side, add 1 seeded and finely chopped jalapeño pepper to the vegetable mixture in step 1, then sprinkle 2 tablespoons chopped fresh cilantro into the turkey mixture just before serving.

Turkey Sausage with Peppers and Polenta

HANDS-ON PREP 10 MIN ▪ COOK 25 MIN ▪ SERVES 4

4 (3-ounce) hot Italian-style turkey sausages

3 teaspoons extra-virgin olive oil

1 teaspoon red-wine vinegar

1 large onion, cut into 1 1/4-inch-thick rounds

1 red bell pepper, seeded and cut lengthwise into 8 strips

1 yellow bell pepper, seeded and cut lengthwise into 8 strips

1/4 teaspoon salt

1/8 teaspoon freshly ground pepper

1 (8-ounce) tube refrigerated fat-free plain polenta, cut into 8 rounds

4 teaspoons grated Parmesan cheese

1 Spray the grill rack with nonstick spray; preheat the grill to medium or prepare a medium fire.

2 Place the sausages on the grill rack. Grill, turning occasionally, until browned and cooked through, 12–15 minutes. Transfer to a platter and keep warm.

3 Meanwhile, whisk together 2 teaspoons of the oil and the vinegar in a small bowl. Brush the onion and bell peppers with the oil mixture and sprinkle with the salt and ground pepper. Place the onion and bell peppers on the grill rack. Grill until softened, 6–7 minutes on each side. Transfer to the platter; keep warm.

4 Brush both sides of the polenta slices with the remaining 1 teaspoon of oil. Place the polenta slices on the grill rack. Grill until crispy and golden, about 3 minutes. Carefully turn the polenta slices and sprinkle with the Parmesan; grill until crispy and golden, about 3 minutes longer. Add the polenta to the platter and serve at once.

PER SERVING (1 sausage, 2 slices polenta, and 1/2 cup vegetables): 260 Cal, 14 g Fat, 4 g Sat Fat, 0 g Trans Fat, 51 mg Chol, 797 mg Sod, 16 g Carb, 2 g Fib, 17 g Prot, 55 mg Calc.
POINTS value: 6.

FOOD NOTE

Look for tubes of refrigerated prepared polenta in the produce section of your supermarket. Besides being grilled, it can also be cooked until crispy in a skillet set over medium-high heat.

Citrus-Glazed Duck Breasts

HANDS-ON PREP 10 MIN ■ COOK 30 MIN ■ SERVES 8

1¼ cups tangerine or tangerine-orange juice

½ cup balsamic vinegar

8 (4–5-ounce) skinless boneless duck breast halves

1 small onion, finely chopped

½ cup reduced-sodium chicken broth

1 tablespoon grated tangerine zest

½ teaspoon salt

¼ teaspoon freshly ground pepper

2 (6-ounce) bags baby spinach, washed and dried

2 tablespoons chopped fresh parsley

1 Combine 1 cup of the tangerine juice and ¼ cup of the vinegar in a large zip-close plastic bag; add the duck. Squeeze out the air and seal the bag; turn to coat the duck. Refrigerate, turning the bag occasionally, at least 2 hours or up to overnight. Remove the duck from the marinade; discard the marinade.

2 Spray the grill rack with nonstick spray; preheat the grill to medium or prepare a medium fire.

3 Meanwhile, to make the glaze, combine the onion, broth, the remaining ¼ cup of tangerine juice and ¼ cup of vinegar, the tangerine zest, salt, and pepper in a medium nonstick saucepan; bring to a boil. Reduce the heat and simmer, stirring occasionally, until the mixture is syrupy and reduced by half, about 15 minutes. Remove the saucepan from the heat.

4 Place the duck on the grill rack. Grill, turning once and basting with the glaze during the first 5 minutes of grilling, until cooked through, 8–10 minutes. Transfer the duck to a cutting board; let stand about 5 minutes. Cut the duck, on the diagonal, into ¼-inch-thick slices. Place a mound of spinach on each of 8 plates and arrange the duck, slightly overlapping the slices, around the spinach. Drizzle any leftover glaze over the duck and sprinkle with the parsley.

PER SERVING (1 duck breast and about ⅔ cup spinach): 155 Cal, 2 g Fat, 1 g Sat Fat, 0 g Trans Fat, 122 mg Chol, 272 mg Sod, 9 g Carb, 2 g Fib, 25 g Prot, 46 mg Calc.
POINTS value: 3.

HOW WE DID IT

Perfectly cooked duck breasts are slightly pink in the center. To eliminate the guesswork when checking for doneness, grill the duck until an instant-read thermometer registers 155°F when inserted in the thickest part of a breast. When tangerines aren't in season, use an orange.

Hoisin Duck and Vegetable Stir-Fry

HANDS-ON PREP 15 MIN ■ COOK 10 MIN ■ SERVES 4

$^2/_3$ cup reduced-sodium chicken broth

$^1/_4$ cup hoisin sauce

2 tablespoons reduced-sodium soy sauce

3 teaspoons cornstarch

4 teaspoons Asian (dark) sesame oil

1 pound skinless boneless duck breast halves, cut crosswise into thin strips

3 scallions, chopped

1 tablespoon grated peeled fresh ginger

$^1/_2$ pound fresh green beans, trimmed

1 small yellow bell pepper, seeded and cut into strips

1 cup grape tomatoes, halved

1 Whisk together the broth, hoisin sauce, soy sauce, and cornstarch in a small bowl until smooth; set aside.

2 Heat 2 teaspoons of the Asian sesame oil in a large nonstick skillet or wok set over medium-high heat until a drop of water sizzles in it. Add the duck and stir-fry until browned and cooked through, about 4 minutes. Transfer the duck to a plate; set aside.

3 Heat the remaining 2 teaspoons of sesame oil in the same skillet. Add the scallions and ginger; stir-fry until fragrant, about 30 seconds. Add the green beans and bell pepper; stir-fry until crisp-tender, about 3 minutes. Add the tomatoes and stir-fry 1 minute. Return the duck along with the broth mixture to the skillet. Cook, stirring constantly, until the mixture bubbles and thickens, about 1 minute longer.

PER SERVING (1 cup): 232 Cal, 7 g Fat, 1 g Sat Fat, 0 g Trans Fat, 66 mg Chol, 659 mg Sod, 16 g Carb, 3 g Fib, 27 g Prot, 61 mg Calc.
POINTS value: 5.

FOOD NOTE

The majority of duck breasts are sold frozen, so you'll need to plan ahead to prepare this dish. To reduce the risk of foodborne illness, thaw the duck overnight in the refrigerator, not at room temperature.

CHAPTER SIX

Savory Meats

Beef Tenderloin with Red Wine and Mushrooms

HANDS-ON PREP 20 MIN ■ COOK 45 MIN ■ SERVES 8

1 (2-pound) beef tenderloin, trimmed

1 cup dry red wine

1/4 cup chopped flat-leaf parsley

1 tablespoon balsamic vinegar

1/2 teaspoon dried thyme

1/2 teaspoon salt

1/2 teaspoon freshly ground pepper

2 teaspoons extra-virgin olive oil

3/4 pound mixed fresh wild mushrooms, such as shiitake (stemmed), cremini, and oyster, halved if large

1 small onion, thinly sliced

1/2 cup reduced-sodium beef broth

1 Remove the beef from the refrigerator and let stand at cool room temperature 1 hour.

2 Place an oven rack in the bottom third of the oven and preheat the oven to 450°F.

3 Combine 1/2 cup of the wine, the parsley, vinegar, and thyme in a small bowl. Place the meat on a rack in a roasting pan. Brush with the wine mixture and sprinkle with 1/4 teaspoon of the salt and 1/4 teaspoon of the pepper. Roast until an instant-read thermometer inserted into the center of the meat registers 140°F for medium, about 45 minutes. Transfer the beef to a cutting board; cover loosely with foil and let stand.

4 Meanwhile, heat the oil in a large nonstick skillet set over medium-high heat. Add the mushrooms, onion, the remaining 1/4 teaspoon of salt and 1/4 teaspoon of pepper; cook, stirring frequently, until the mushrooms release some of their liquid and the onion is softened, about 10 minutes. Add the remaining 1/2 cup of wine and the broth. Cook until the liquid is reduced by half. Remove the skillet from the heat.

5 Cut the beef into 16 slices and serve with the mushroom mixture.

PER SERVING (2 slices beef and 2 tablespoons mushroom mixture): 207 Cal, 9 g Fat, 3 g Sat Fat, 1 g Trans Fat, 64 mg Chol, 182 mg Sod, 4 g Carb, 1 g Fib, 26 g Prot, 22 mg Calc.
POINTS value: 5.

MAKE IT CORE

To fit this recipe into the **Core Plan**, substitute reduced-sodium beef broth for the dry red wine.

Mini Beef Wellingtons

HANDS-ON PREP 25 MIN ■ COOK 20 MIN ■ SERVES 6

6 (¼-pound) filets mignons, trimmed

¼ teaspoon salt

¾ teaspoon freshly ground pepper

1 teaspoon olive oil

¾ pound sliced fresh cremini mushrooms (about 3 cups)

1 onion, chopped

2 garlic cloves, minced

1½ teaspoons chopped fresh thyme

⅔ cup dry sherry

6 (12 x 17-inch) sheets frozen phyllo dough, thawed

1 Preheat the oven to 400°F. Spray a large baking sheet with nonstick spray.

2 Sprinkle the filets with the salt and pepper. Heat the oil in a large nonstick skillet set over medium-high heat. Add the filets and cook until browned, about 2 minutes on each side. Transfer to a plate; keep warm.

3 Add the mushrooms, onion, garlic, and thyme to the skillet; cook, stirring until the mushrooms are softened, about 6 minutes. Add the sherry and cook until the liquid is evaporated, about 3 minutes. Remove the skillet from heat; let cool 5 minutes.

4 Place 1 phyllo sheet on the work surface with a long side facing you. Cover the remaining phyllo with a damp paper towel and plastic wrap to prevent it from drying out. Spray the phyllo with nonstick spray. Top with another phyllo sheet; spray with nonstick spray, then cut the phyllo crosswise in half. Place 1 filet in the center of the lower third of one of the phyllo stacks. Top with ¼ cup of the mushroom mixture. Fold the short sides of the phyllo over the filet and roll up, jelly-roll style. Transfer the Wellington, seam side down, to the baking sheet. Repeat with the remaining phyllo, filets, and mushroom mixture to make 6 Wellingtons in all.

5 Spray the Wellingtons with nonstick spray. Bake until the phyllo is golden and an instant-read thermometer inserted into the side of a Wellington registers 145°F for medium, 10–12 minutes.

PER SERVING (1 Wellington): 243 Cal, 10 g Fat, 3 g Sat Fat, 1 g Trans Fat, 57 mg Chol, 429 mg Sod, 15 g Carb, 2 g Fib, 23 g Prot, 19 mg Calc.
POINTS value: 5.

GOOD IDEA

It's best to thaw frozen phyllo in the refrigerator according to the package directions, a process that can take up to 24 hours. Quick-thawing methods (such as in a microwave) are less reliable, often resulting in gooey areas that stick together.

Japanese Beef Hot Pot

HANDS-ON PREP 15 MIN ■ COOK 20 MIN ■ SERVES 8

½ (16-ounce) box thin spaghetti

1 tablespoon canola oil

2 tablespoons sugar

1 (1-pound) beef tenderloin, trimmed, cut in half lengthwise then thinly sliced crosswise

½ pound Savoy cabbage, cut into 1-inch pieces

1 bunch scallions, cut into 1-inch pieces

1 red bell pepper, seeded and thinly sliced

½ pound fresh shiitake mushrooms, stemmed, caps halved

1 (14½-ounce) can reduced-sodium chicken broth

¼ cup reduced-sodium soy sauce

½ pound reduced-fat firm tofu, diced

1 (6-ounce) package baby spinach

1 Cook the thin spaghetti according to the package directions, omitting the salt if desired. Drain and rinse under cold water; drain again.

2 Meanwhile, heat the oil in a nonstick Dutch oven set over medium heat. Add the sugar and cook, stirring frequently, until caramel-colored, about 2 minutes. Add half of the beef and cook, stirring constantly, until just cooked through, about 2 minutes. Transfer the beef to a plate. Repeat with the remaining beef, leaving it in the Dutch oven.

3 Return the reserved beef to the Dutch oven. Stir in the pasta, cabbage, scallions, bell pepper, mushrooms, broth, and soy sauce; bring to a boil. Reduce the heat and simmer, covered, stirring occasionally, until the vegetables are tender, about 5 minutes. Stir in the tofu and spinach; cook until the spinach wilts, about 1 minute.

PER SERVING (generous 1 cup): **258 Cal, 7 g Fat, 2 g Sat Fat, 1 g Trans Fat, 29 mg Chol, 472 mg Sod, 31 g Carb, 4 g Fib, 19 g Prot, 52 mg Calc.**
POINTS value: **5.**

FOOD NOTE

If the sugar becomes too dark while caramelizing it in step **2**, simply reduce the heat to medium.

Zesty Steak Fajitas

HANDS-ON PREP 10 MIN ■ COOK 10 MIN ■ SERVES 4

3 tablespoons fresh lime juice

3 garlic cloves, minced

2 teaspoons chili powder

¾ pound beef top round steak, trimmed and thinly sliced

1 large onion, thinly sliced

1 red bell pepper, seeded and sliced into thin strips

1 serrano pepper, seeded and chopped (wear gloves to prevent irritation)

1½ tablespoons reduced-sodium soy sauce

1 tablespoon Worcestershire sauce

4 (8-inch) whole-wheat flour tortillas, warmed

½ cup fat-free sour cream

½ cup prepared tomato salsa

1 Combine the lime juice, garlic, and chili powder in a large zip-close plastic bag; add the steak. Squeeze out the air and seal the bag; turn to coat the steak. Refrigerate, turning the bag occasionally, 20 minutes. Drain the beef; discard the marinade.

2 Spray a large nonstick skillet with nonstick spray and set over medium-high heat. Add the onion, bell pepper, and serrano; cook, stirring occasionally, until softened, about 5 minutes. Add the steak and cook until lightly browned but still barely red in the center, 3–4 minutes. Add the soy sauce and Worcestershire sauce; cook 1 minute.

3 Place the tortillas on a work surface; spoon 1 cup of the beef mixture in a strip in the middle of each tortilla, leaving a 1½-inch border on each side. Fold the bottom of each tortilla over the filling, then fold the sides in and roll up, jelly-roll style, to form a neat package. Serve at once with the sour cream and salsa.

PER SERVING (1 fajita, 2 tablespoons sour cream, and 2 tablespoons salsa): 285 Cal, 6 g Fat, 1 g Sat Fat, 1 g Trans Fat, 52 mg Chol, 566 mg Sod, 36 g Carb, 4 g Fib, 24 g Prot, 165 mg Calc. *POINTS* value: 5.

FOOD NOTE

These fajitas are also delicious prepared with flank steak. If you enjoy your Tex-Mex food on the milder side, substitute a jalapeño pepper for the serrano.

Cowboy Beef Stew

HANDS-ON PREP 15 MIN ■ COOK 1 HR 30 MIN ■ SERVES 6

2 slices reduced-sodium bacon

1 pound beef top round steak, trimmed and cut into ³/₄-inch chunks

³/₄ teaspoon salt

¹/₄ teaspoon freshly ground pepper

1 tablespoon all-purpose flour

¹/₂ pound frozen small white onions

4 carrots, cut into 1¹/₂-inch pieces

2 celery stalks, cut into 1¹/₂-inch pieces

3 garlic cloves, finely chopped

1 (12-ounce) bottle dark beer

1 cup strong brewed coffee

2 tablespoons ketchup

1 tablespoon dark molasses

¹/₄ teaspoon crushed red pepper

1 pound Yukon Gold potatoes, peeled and cut into ³/₄-inch chunks

¹/₂ pound green beans, trimmed and halved

1 Cook the bacon in a nonstick Dutch oven set over medium heat until crisp. With a slotted spoon, transfer to a paper towel to drain. Remove all but 2 teaspoons of the drippings from the Dutch oven.

2 Meanwhile, pat the beef chunks dry with paper towels; sprinkle with the salt and ¹/₈ teaspoon of the ground pepper. Put the beef and flour in a large zip-close plastic bag. Shake the bag until the beef is evenly coated with the flour.

3 Heat the drippings in the Dutch oven over medium-high heat. Add half of the beef and cook until browned on all sides, about 5 minutes. Transfer to a plate. Repeat with the remaining beef. Crumble the bacon; set aside.

4 Add the onions, carrots, celery, and garlic to the Dutch oven. Cook, stirring frequently to scrape up the browned bits from the bottom of the pot, until the onions are golden, about 3 minutes. Stir in the beef, bacon, beer, coffee, ketchup, molasses, crushed red pepper, and the remaining ¹/₈ teaspoon of ground pepper; bring to a boil. Reduce the heat and simmer, covered, 1 hour. Add the potatoes and green beans; simmer, covered, until the beef and potatoes are fork-tender, about 20 minutes.

PER SERVING (about 1²/₃ cups): 242 Cal, 3 g Fat, 1 g Sat Fat, 1 g Trans Fat, 41 mg Chol, 452 mg Sod, 32 g Carb, 5 g Fib, 21 g Prot, 60 mg Calc.
POINTS value: 4.

FOOD NOTE

As the story goes, out on the range, cowboys sometimes tossed leftover coffee into the stew that was always bubbling over the fire so as not to waste it. Coffee adds an enticing richness and is especially good in combination with the dark beer.

Meatloaf with Bell Pepper and Onion

HANDS-ON PREP 15 MIN ■ COOK 50 MIN ■ SERVES 8

1 onion, finely chopped

1 red bell pepper, seeded and finely chopped

3 garlic cloves, minced

2 pounds ground lean beef (7% fat or less)

1 cup ketchup

$\frac{1}{2}$ cup Italian-seasoned dried bread crumbs

1 egg white

2 tablespoons Dijon mustard

1 teaspoon Worcestershire sauce

$\frac{1}{4}$ teaspoon salt

$\frac{1}{4}$ teaspoon freshly ground pepper

1 Preheat the oven to 400°F. Spray a large rimmed baking sheet with nonstick spray.

2 Spray a large nonstick skillet with nonstick spray and set over medium-high heat. Add the onion and bell pepper; cook, stirring occasionally, until softened, about 5 minutes. Add the garlic and cook, stirring constantly, until fragrant, about 30 seconds. Remove the skillet from the heat; let cool 10 minutes.

3 Combine the beef, onion mixture, $\frac{1}{2}$ cup of the ketchup, the bread crumbs, egg white, mustard, Worcestershire sauce, salt, and ground pepper in a large bowl. Transfer the mixture to the baking sheet and form into a 5 x 10-inch loaf. Spread the remaining $\frac{1}{2}$ cup of ketchup over the top of the meatloaf. Bake until an instant-read thermometer inserted into the center of the meatloaf registers 160°F, 45–50 minutes. Transfer the meatloaf to a cutting board and let stand 10 minutes. Cut into 8 slices.

PER SERVING (1 slice): 224 Cal, 6 g Fat, 2 g Sat Fat, 1 g Trans Fat, 62 mg Chol, 695 mg Sod, 16 g Carb, 1 g Fib, 26 g Prot, 37 mg Calc.
POINTS value: 5.

GOOD IDEA

Meatloaf makes great leftovers, especially in a sandwich. Completely cool any leftover slices, then wrap and refrigerate up to 3 days. Place a slice of meatloaf on a split ciabatta roll that has been spread with 1 tablespoon of your favorite mustard or fat-free mayonnaise. Top with salad greens, thinly sliced tomato, and red onion. This will increase the per-serving *POINTS* value by *3.*

Cuban-Style Picadillo

HANDS-ON PREP 10 MIN ■ COOK 25 MIN ■ SERVES 6

2 teaspoons olive oil

1 large green bell pepper, seeded and chopped

1 onion, chopped

3 garlic cloves, minced

1/2 teaspoon crushed red pepper

1 pound ground lean beef (7% fat or less)

1 (14 1/2-ounce) can fire-roasted crushed tomatoes

1 cup frozen peas

1/4 cup currants

2 tablespoons chopped pimiento-stuffed green olives

1 teaspoon ground cumin

1 teaspoon unsweetened cocoa powder

1/2 teaspoon salt

2 cups hot cooked brown rice

1/4 cup slivered almonds (optional)

1 Heat the oil in a large nonstick skillet set over medium heat. Add the bell pepper, onion, garlic, and crushed red pepper. Cook, stirring, until the onion is golden, 7–10 minutes. Add the beef and cook, breaking it apart with a wooden spoon, until browned, about 6 minutes.

2 Stir in the tomatoes, peas, currants, olives, cumin, cocoa, and salt; bring to a boil. Reduce the heat and simmer, covered, until the flavors are blended, about 10 minutes. Serve with the rice and sprinkle with the almonds, if using.

PER SERVING (scant 1 cup picadillo and 1/3 cup rice without almonds): **259 Cal, 7 g Fat, 2 g Sat Fat, 0 g Trans Fat, 41 mg Chol, 520 mg Sod, 30 g Carb, 5 g Fib, 20 g Prot, 41 mg Calc.** *POINTS* value: **5**.

GOOD IDEA

Enjoy this delicious dish as they do in Cuba: with a side of black beans or pinto beans (1/2 cup cooked beans will increase the per-serving **POINTS** value by **2**).

Texas-Style Meatloaf ☑

HANDS-ON PREP 10 MIN ■ COOK 1 HR 5 MIN ■ SERVES 6

3/4 pound ground lean beef (7% fat or less)

3/4 pound ground lean pork loin

1/2 cup prepared fat-free chunky salsa

1 egg white, lightly beaten

2 teaspoons ancho chile powder

2 teaspoons ground cumin

1 teaspoon dried oregano

3/4 teaspoon salt

1 cup shredded fat-free Monterey Jack cheese

1 Preheat the oven to 350°F. Spray a 4 x 8-inch loaf pan with canola oil nonstick spray.

2 Combine the beef, pork, 1/4 cup of the salsa, the egg white, ancho chile powder, cumin, oregano, and salt in a large bowl, mixing just until blended. Pack half of the mixture into the loaf pan. Sprinkle with the cheese, leaving a 1/2-inch border all around. Top with the remaining meat mixture. Spread the remaining 1/4 cup of salsa over the meat. Bake until an instant-read thermometer inserted into the center of the meatloaf registers 160°F, 65–70 minutes.

3 Transfer the meatloaf to a cutting board and let stand 5 minutes. Cut into 6 slices.

PER SERVING (1 slice): 184 Cal, 5 g Fat, 2 g Sat Fat, 0 g Trans Fat, 65 mg Chol, 653 mg Sod, 3 g Carb, 1 g Fib, 30 g Prot, 284 mg Calc.
POINTS value: 4.

TRY IT

For an Italian-style meatloaf, use fat-free tomato sauce instead of the salsa; substitute 2 teaspoons Italian seasoning for the ancho chile powder, cumin, and oregano; and use fat-free mozzarella instead of the Monterey Jack cheese.

Smoky Roast Pork with Peaches and Plums ☑

2 teaspoons smoked paprika

1 teaspoon dried thyme

3/4 teaspoon salt

1/4 teaspoon freshly ground pepper

1 (1-pound) pork tenderloin, trimmed

2 teaspoons olive oil

2 shallots, finely chopped

1 garlic clove, minced

3 peaches, halved, pitted, and cut into 1/2-inch-thick wedges

2 plums, halved, pitted, and cut into 1/2-inch-thick wedges

1 Preheat the oven to 450°F. Spray a large rimmed baking pan with olive oil nonstick spray.

2 Combine the smoked paprika, thyme, 1/2 teaspoon of the salt, and the pepper in a small bowl. Rub the spice mixture all over the pork. Put the pork in the pan and roast until an instant-read thermometer inserted into the center of the pork registers 160°F for medium, 30–35 minutes.

3 Meanwhile, heat the oil in a large nonstick skillet set over medium-high heat. Add the shallots and garlic; cook, stirring, until softened, 1–2 minutes. Add the peaches, plums, and the remaining 1/4 teaspoon of salt. Cook, stirring occasionally, until the fruit softens slightly, about 4 minutes. Remove the skillet from the heat.

4 Transfer the pork to a cutting board and cut into 8 slices. Arrange on a platter; spoon the fruit alongside.

PER SERVING (2 slices pork and 1/2 cup fruit): 229 Cal, 7 g Fat, 2 g Sat Fat, 0 g Trans Fat, 63 mg Chol, 483 mg Sod, 18 g Carb, 3 g Fib, 24 g Prot, 22 mg Calc.
POINTS value: 5.

GOOD IDEA

Complete the meal by serving with steamed green beans and mashed potatoes (1/2 cup each cooked green beans and mashed potatoes will increase the per-serving **POINTS** value by **2**).

Chuck Wagon Chili ☑

HANDS-ON PREP 10 MIN ■ COOK 45 MIN ■ SERVES 6

2 teaspoons canola oil

½ pound ground lean beef (7% fat or less)

½ pound ground lean pork

1 red bell pepper, seeded and chopped

1 onion, chopped

2 garlic cloves, minced

1 (14½-ounce) can fire-roasted crushed tomatoes

¼ cup water

2 tablespoons seeded and finely chopped jalapeño peppers (wear gloves to prevent irritation)

1 tablespoon chili powder

1 teaspoon ground cumin

1 teaspoon salt

½ teaspoon dried oregano

1 (15½-ounce) can red kidney beans, rinsed and drained

6 tablespoons fat-free shredded cheddar cheese

3 scallions, thinly sliced

Fat-free sour cream (optional)

1 Heat the oil in a large nonstick skillet set over medium heat. Add the beef and pork; cook, breaking it up with a wooden spoon, until no longer pink, about 6 minutes. Add the bell pepper, onion, and garlic; cook, stirring, until softened, 3–5 minutes.

2 Stir in the tomatoes, water, jalapeño peppers, chili powder, cumin, salt, and oregano; bring to a boil. Reduce the heat and simmer, covered, stirring occasionally, 30 minutes. Stir in the beans and cook until heated through, about 5 minutes. Serve with the cheese, scallions, and sour cream, if using.

PER SERVING (1½ cups chili, 1 tablespoon cheese, and 1 tablespoon scallion without sour cream): 225 Cal, 6 g Fat, 2 g Sat Fat, 0 g Trans Fat, 47 mg Chol, 887 mg Sod, 20 g Carb, 6 g Fib, 24 g Prot, 131 mg Calc.
POINTS value: 4.

GOOD IDEA

If you like, sprinkle 6 crushed baked low-fat tortilla chips on top of each serving (the per-serving *POINTS* value will increase by *1*). Be sure to deduct it from your **weekly POINTS Allowance**.

Herb-Grilled Pork Chops with Vegetables ☑

HANDS-ON PREP 15 MIN ■ COOK 55 MIN ■ SERVES 4

1 large lemon

1 tablespoon chopped fresh rosemary

1 tablespoon chopped fresh thyme

3 garlic cloves, crushed with a garlic press

2 teaspoons olive oil

4 ($\frac{1}{4}$-pound) boneless center-cut pork loin chops, trimmed

1 teaspoon salt

$\frac{1}{2}$ teaspoon freshly ground pepper

1 pound baby red potatoes, scrubbed and halved

1 zucchini, cut lengthwise into 8 slices

1 yellow squash, cut lengthwise into 8 slices

1 Finely grate the zest from the lemon. Juice the lemon; reserve. Combine the lemon zest, rosemary, thyme, garlic, and oil in a small bowl. Sprinkle the pork with $\frac{1}{2}$ teaspoon of the salt and $\frac{1}{4}$ teaspoon of the pepper. Rub half of the lemon mixture over both sides of the pork chops; reserve the remaining lemon mixture. Put the pork on a plate; cover and refrigerate at least 1 hour or up to 4 hours.

2 Spray the grill rack with olive oil nonstick spray and preheat the grill to medium or prepare a medium fire.

3 Toss together the potatoes, the remaining lemon mixture, $\frac{1}{4}$ teaspoon of the remaining salt, and $\frac{1}{8}$ teaspoon of the remaining pepper in a medium bowl. Lightly spray the potatoes with olive oil nonstick spray; place on the grill rack, cut side down. Grill, turning once, until tender, about 45 minutes. Transfer the potatoes to a bowl; keep warm.

4 Sprinkle the zucchini and yellow squash with the remaining $\frac{1}{4}$ teaspoon of salt and $\frac{1}{8}$ teaspoon of pepper; lightly spray the vegetables with olive oil nonstick spray. Place the pork and vegetables on the grill rack. Grill the pork until an instant-read thermometer inserted into the side of a chop registers 160°F, about 4 minutes on each side. Grill the vegetables until tender, about 4 minutes on each side. Transfer the pork and vegetables to a platter; drizzle the lemon juice over the vegetables. Add the potatoes to the platter.

PER SERVING (1 pork chop, 4 squash slices, and about $\frac{1}{2}$ cup potatoes): 277 Cal, 9 g Fat, 3 g Sat Fat, 0 g Trans Fat, 65 mg Chol, 635 mg Sod, 20 g Carb, 4 g Fib, 28 g Prot, 56 mg Calc. *POINTS* value: 5.

GOOD IDEA

If you like, use all zucchini or yellow squash. Or substitute a different vegetable, such as eggplant (cut into small pieces), broccoli (use medium florets), or whole green beans.

Pork Chops with Rosemary-Wine Sauce

HANDS-ON PREP 10 MIN ■ COOK 15 MIN ■ SERVES 4

4 (1/4-pound) boneless center-cut pork loin chops, trimmed

1/4 teaspoon salt

1/4 teaspoon freshly ground pepper

3 tablespoons all-purpose flour

2 teaspoons olive oil

1 1/2 tablespoons chopped fresh rosemary

1/2 cup dry red wine

1   Season the pork with the salt and pepper. Spread the flour on a sheet of wax paper. Coat the pork with the flour, shaking off the excess; discard any leftover flour.

2   Heat the oil a large nonstick skillet set over medium-high heat. Add the pork and rosemary; cook until the pork is golden brown and until an instant-read thermometer inserted into the side of a chop registers 160°F, 4–5 minutes on each side. Transfer the pork to a platter; keep warm.

3   Add the wine to the skillet; bring to a boil. Cook, stirring with a wooden spoon to scrape up the browned bits from the bottom of the skillet, until reduced to 1/4 cup, 2–3 minutes; pour over the pork.

PER SERVING (1 chop and 1 tablespoon sauce): 203 Cal, 9 g Fat, 3 g Sat Fat, 0 g Trans Fat, 66 mg Chol, 194 mg Sod, 5 g Carb, 0 g Fib, 24 g Prot, 24 mg Calc.

POINTS value: 5.

HOW WE DID IT

Coating the pork chops with flour serves two purposes: it makes the chops nice and crusty, and it gives the wine sauce body.

Pork and Rice–Stuffed Cabbage ✓

HANDS-ON PREP 20 MIN ■ COOK I HR I5 MIN ■ SERVES 6

6 large green cabbage leaves	³/₄ pound ground lean pork
I tablespoon olive oil	2 cups cooked brown rice
I onion, finely chopped	2 egg whites, lightly beaten
3 garlic cloves, minced	³/₄ teaspoon salt
I teaspoon dried Italian seasoning	¹/₄ teaspoon freshly ground pepper
I zucchini or yellow squash, finely chopped	I (15-ounce) can tomato sauce

1 Preheat the oven to 350°F. Lightly spray a 7 x 11-inch baking dish with olive oil nonstick spray.

2 Bring a large pot of water to a boil. Add the cabbage and cook until tender, 3–4 minutes; drain in a colander. Rinse under cold running water, then drain again. Trim the thick ribs from the base of the leaves; set the leaves aside.

3 Meanwhile, to make the filling, heat the oil in a medium nonstick skillet set over medium-high heat. Add the onion, garlic, and Italian seasoning; cook, stirring occasionally, until softened, about 2 minutes. Add the zucchini or squash and cook, stirring occasionally, until tender, about 5 minutes. Transfer to a large bowl; let cool 5 minutes. Add the pork, rice, egg whites, salt, and pepper; mix well.

4 Spread ¹/₄ cup of the tomato sauce in the bottom of the baking dish. Arrange the cabbage leaves on the work surface. Place a rounded ¹/₂ cupful of the filling in the center of each cabbage leaf. Fold the two sides of each leaf over the filling and roll up, jelly-roll style, starting at the base of the leaf. Place the rolls, seam side down, in the baking dish; pour the remaining tomato sauce on top. Bake until an instant-read thermometer inserted into the center of a roll registers 160°F, about 50 minutes.

PER SERVING (I roll and about ¹/₂ cup sauce): **207 Cal, 5 g Fat, I g Sat Fat, 0 g Trans Fat, 32 mg Chol, 771 mg Sod, 25 g Carb, 4 g Fib, 16 g Prot, 53 mg Calc.**
POINTS value: 4.

FOOD NOTE

If you don't have cooked brown rice handy, a speedy alternative is to cook I (5¹/₄-ounce) package of boil-in-the-bag brown rice according to the package directions. Let the rice cool slightly before combining it with the remaining filling ingredients in step **3**.

Thai Pork and Rice Bowl

HANDS-ON PREP 15 MIN ■ COOK 25 MIN ■ SERVES 6

2 teaspoons canola oil

1 pound ground lean pork

2 assorted color bell peppers, seeded and cut into strips

1/2 pound fresh white mushrooms, thickly sliced

1/4 pound baby bok choy, cut into 1/4-inch-wide strips

2 cups reduced-sodium chicken broth

1 cup brown basmati rice

1 tablespoon reduced-sodium soy sauce

3/4 teaspoon Thai green or red curry paste

4 scallions, thinly sliced

1/2 cup coarsely chopped fresh cilantro

2 tablespoons fresh lime juice

1   Heat the oil in a large nonstick skillet or wok set over medium-high heat until a drop of water sizzles in it. Add the pork and stir-fry until the pork almost loses its pink color, about 4 minutes. Add the bell peppers, mushrooms, and bok choy; stir-fry 1 minute.

2   Add the broth, rice, soy sauce, and curry paste to the skillet; bring to a boil, stirring. Reduce the heat and simmer, covered, until the rice is tender and the broth is absorbed, about 20 minutes.

3   Remove the skillet from the heat; stir in the scallions and cilantro. Drizzle with the lime juice and serve at once.

PER SERVING (1 1/2 cups): 247 Cal, 5 g Fat, 1 g Sat Fat, 0 g Trans Fat, 42 mg Chol, 363 mg Sod, 30 g Carb, 3 g Fib, 20 g Prot, 24 mg Calc.
POINTS value: 5.

TRY IT

Thai curry paste, a concentrated mixture of fiery green or red chiles and spices, is traditionally used in Thai curry dishes that are laden with high-fat coconut milk. You can also add it to low-fat stir-fries, soups, and marinades for a bit of exotic flavor. Look for Thai curry paste in the ethnic foods section at the supermarket.

Ham, Mushroom, and Ginger Fried Rice ☑

HANDS-ON PREP 15 MIN ■ COOK 15 MIN ■ SERVES 6

4 teaspoons canola oil

6 thin slices peeled fresh ginger, cut into very thin strips

2 garlic cloves, finely chopped

1/2 pound fresh shiitake mushrooms, stemmed and sliced

1 red bell pepper, seeded and cut into 1/4-inch dice

1 cup very small broccoli florets

2 large eggs, beaten

2 cups cold cooked brown rice

1 (1/4-pound) piece lean baked ham, cut into 1/4-inch dice

1 cup bean sprouts

1 cup frozen shelled edamame (green soybeans)

4 scallions, thinly sliced

1/2 teaspoon salt

1/4 teaspoon freshly ground pepper

1 Heat 2 teaspoons of the oil in a large nonstick skillet or wok set over medium-high heat until a drop of water sizzles in it. Add the ginger and garlic; stir-fry until fragrant, about 30 seconds. Add the mushrooms, bell pepper, and broccoli; stir-fry until the vegetables are crisp-tender and the mushrooms begin to brown, about 5 minutes. Transfer to a medium bowl.

2 Heat 1 teaspoon of the oil in the skillet. Add the eggs and stir-fry until softly scrambled, about 2 minutes. Break the eggs into small pieces and add to the vegetables in the bowl.

3 Heat the remaining 1 teaspoon of oil in the skillet. Add the rice, ham, bean sprouts, edamame, and scallions; stir-fry until heated through, about 3 minutes. Return the vegetables and eggs to the skillet; sprinkle with the salt and pepper. Stir-fry until heated through, about 1 minute.

PER SERVING (1 1/3 cups): 196 Cal, 6 g Fat, 1 g Sat Fat, 0 g Trans Fat, 44 mg Chol, 465 mg Sod, 24 g Carb, 4 g Fib, 11 g Prot, 49 mg Calc.
POINTS value: 4.

FOOD NOTE

Frozen shelled edamame are now available in most large supermarkets, but if you can't find them, just substitute an equal amount of frozen peas (the cooking time will remain the same).

Lamb and Vegetable Skewers ☑

HANDS-ON PREP 20 MIN ■ COOK 10 MIN ■ SERVES 4

1/4 cup reduced-sodium chicken broth

Grated zest of 1 orange

3 tablespoons fresh lemon juice

2 teaspoons dried oregano

1 teaspoon dried rosemary

1 teaspoon dried thyme

1 tablespoon extra-virgin olive oil

2 garlic cloves, minced

1/8 teaspoon hot pepper sauce

1 pound boneless leg of lamb, trimmed and cut into 1-inch chunks

1 medium red onion, cut into 8 wedges

1 yellow bell pepper, seeded and cut into 8 squares

1 zucchini, cut into 8 rounds

8 large cherry tomatoes

1/2 teaspoon salt

1   Put the broth, zest, lemon juice, oregano, rosemary, thyme, oil, garlic, and pepper sauce in a food processor and puree. Place the mixture in a large zip-close plastic bag; add the lamb. Squeeze out the air and seal the bag; turn to coat the lamb. Refrigerate, turning the bag occasionally, at least 1 hour or up to overnight. Drain; discard the marinade.

2   Spray the grill rack with olive oil nonstick spray and preheat the grill to medium or prepare a medium fire.

3   Alternately thread the red onion wedges, bell pepper, zucchini, tomatoes, and lamb on 4 (12-inch) metal skewers, beginning and ending with the onion. Sprinkle the kebabs with the salt and place on the grill rack. Grill, turning, until the vegetables are charred along the edges and an instant-read thermometer inserted into the center of a chunk of lamb registers 145°F for medium, about 10 minutes.

PER SERVING (1 kebab): 174 Cal, 6 g Fat, 2 g Sat Fat, 0 g Trans Fat, 71 mg Chol, 330 mg Sod, 8 g Carb, 2 g Fib, 21 g Prot, 29 mg Calc.
POINTS value: 4.

GOOD IDEA

Complete the meal by serving the lamb and vegetables on a bed of cooked mixed wild rice, brown rice, and black lentils sprinkled with chopped fresh chives (1/2 cup combination of cooked wild rice, brown rice, and lentils will increase the per-serving **POINTS** value by about 2).

Grilled Lamb Chops with Herb Pesto

HANDS-ON PREP 10 MIN ■ COOK 10 MIN ■ SERVES 6

1 cup packed flat-leaf parsley

1 cup packed fresh mint leaves

1/4 cup reduced-sodium chicken broth

2 tablespoons slivered almonds

2 tablespoons grated Romano cheese

1 tablespoon olive oil

1 garlic clove, chopped

1/4 teaspoon salt

1/4 teaspoon freshly ground pepper

1 lemon, halved

6 (1/4-pound) boneless loin lamb chops,
1 inch thick, trimmed

1 To make the pesto, put the parsley, mint, broth, almonds, Romano, oil, garlic, salt, and pepper in a food processor; pulse, scraping down the sides of the bowl several times, until the mixture forms a coarse paste.

2 Squeeze the lemon halves over the lamb chops. Spray a large ridged grill pan with olive oil nonstick spray and set over medium-high heat. Add the lamb and cook until an instant-read thermometer inserted into the side of a chop registers 145°F for medium, about 3 1/2 minutes on each side. Serve each chop with a dollop of the pesto.

PER SERVING (1 lamb chop and about 1 tablespoon pesto): 178 Cal, 9 g Fat, 3 g Sat Fat, 0 g Trans Fat, 74 mg Chol, 184 mg Sod, 4 g Carb, 2 g Fib, 21 g Prot, 78 mg Calc.
POINTS value: 4.

GOOD IDEA

These tasty chops are excellent served with a side of whole-wheat couscous (2/3 cup cooked couscous for each serving will increase the **POINTS** value by **2**).

Spring Lamb with Artichoke Hearts ☑

2 teaspoons olive oil

2 garlic cloves, finely chopped

2 teaspoons chopped fresh rosemary

1 teaspoon chopped fresh thyme

1 (14-ounce) can quartered artichoke hearts, drained

1 teaspoon grated orange zest

1/2 teaspoon salt

1/8 teaspoon freshly ground pepper

4 (5-ounce) bone-in rib lamb chops, about 1 inch thick, trimmed

1 Heat the oil in a medium nonstick skillet set over medium heat. Add the garlic, 1 teaspoon of the rosemary, and the thyme; cook, stirring occasionally, until fragrant, about 1 minute. Add the artichokes; increase the heat and cook, stirring until lightly browned, 3–4 minutes. Remove the skillet from the heat and stir in the orange zest; set aside.

2 Spray the broiler rack with nonstick spray and preheat the broiler.

3 Combine the remaining 1 teaspoon of rosemary, the salt, and pepper in a bowl. Rub the herb mixture on both sides of the lamb chops. Place the lamb on the broiler rack and broil 4 inches from the heat until an instant-read thermometer inserted into the side of a chop registers 145°F for medium, about 5 minutes on each side. Serve with the artichokes.

PER SERVING (1 lamb chop and 1/4 cup artichoke hearts): 182 Cal, 8 g Fat, 2 g Sat Fat, 0 g Trans Fat, 57 mg Chol, 519 mg Sod, 6 g Carb, 0 g Fib, 20 g Prot, 16 mg Calc.
POINTS value: 4.

GOOD IDEA

Serve these savory lamb chops with a side of wild rice (2/3 cup cooked wild rice will increase the per-serving **POINTS** value by **2**).

Harvest Shepherd's Pie

HANDS-ON PREP 20 MIN ■ COOK 50 MIN ■ SERVES 6

1 ³/₄ pounds sweet potatoes, peeled and cut into 1-inch chunks

²/₃ cup fat-free milk

1 tablespoon butter

1 teaspoon salt

¹/₄ teaspoon freshly ground pepper

1 pound ground lean lamb loin

1 onion, chopped

4 garlic cloves, minced

2 teaspoons curry powder

1 ¹/₂ cups reduced-sodium beef broth

2 tablespoons tomato paste

1 (10-ounce) package frozen peas and carrots

1 Preheat the oven to 350°F. Spray a 2-quart baking dish with nonstick spray.

2 To make the topping, place the sweet potatoes in a large pot with enough cold water to cover; bring to a boil. Cook until the sweet potatoes are fork-tender, 10–12 minutes; drain. Return the sweet potatoes to the pot; add the milk, butter, ¹/₂ teaspoon of the salt, and ¹/₈ teaspoon of the pepper. Mash the sweet potatoes until creamy; set aside.

3 To make the filling, put the lamb in a large nonstick skillet and set over medium-high heat. Cook, breaking it apart with a wooden spoon, until browned, about 5 minutes. Transfer to a medium bowl; set aside.

4 Add the onion, garlic, and curry powder; cook, stirring occasionally, until the onion is lightly browned, about 5 minutes. Add ¹/₂ cup of the broth and the tomato paste; cook, stirring occasionally, until the mixture is slightly thickened, 1–2 minutes. Add the peas and carrots; cook, stirring occasionally, until thawed, 1–2 minutes. Stir in the remaining 1 cup of broth; cook until the mixture is slightly thickened, 3–4 minutes. Stir in the reserved lamb and the remaining ¹/₂ teaspoon of salt and ¹/₈ teaspoon of pepper.

5 Transfer the lamb mixture to the baking dish. Spread the potato topping evenly on top and bake until the filling is bubbly around the edges, about 20 minutes. Remove the pie from the oven.

6 Preheat the broiler. Broil the shepherd's pie, 5 inches from the heat, until the topping is lightly browned, 1–2 minutes. Let stand 5 minutes before serving.

PER SERVING (1¹/₃ cups): 272 Cal, 6 g Fat, 3 g Sat Fat, 0 g Trans Fat, 49 mg Chol, 603 mg Sod, 35 g Carb, 4 g Fib, 20 g Prot, 83 mg Calc.
POINTS value: 5.

MAKE IT CORE

To make this recipe fit the **Core Plan,** substitute canola oil for the butter.

Veal Scaloppine Marsala

HANDS-ON PREP 15 MIN ■ COOK 10 MIN ■ SERVES 4

4 (1/4-pound) veal scaloppine

1/2 teaspoon salt

1/4 teaspoon freshly ground pepper

3 teaspoons extra-virgin olive oil

1 onion, chopped

1 tablespoon all-purpose flour

1/2 pound fresh cremini mushrooms, sliced

1/2 cup dry marsala wine

1/2 cup reduced-sodium chicken broth

1 cup cherry tomatoes, halved

2 tablespoons chopped fresh basil

1   Sprinkle the veal with 1/4 teaspoon of the salt and 1/8 teaspoon of the pepper. Heat 2 teaspoons of the oil in a large nonstick skillet set over medium-high heat. Add the veal and cook until lightly browned, about 1 1/2 minutes on each side. Transfer the veal to a plate; keep warm.

2   Heat the remaining 1 teaspoon of oil in the skillet. Add the onion and flour; cook, stirring constantly, 30 seconds. Add the mushrooms and the remaining 1/4 teaspoon of salt and 1/8 teaspoon of pepper. Cook, stirring frequently, until the mushrooms are softened, about 4 minutes. Add the marsala, broth, tomatoes, and basil; bring to a boil and cook, stirring occasionally, until slightly thickened, about 2 minutes. Return the veal to the skillet and cook until heated through, about 1 minute.

PER SERVING (1 scaloppine and about 1/3 cup vegetables with sauce): 205 Cal, 8 g Fat, 2 g Sat Fat, 1 g Trans Fat, 74 mg Chol, 381 mg Sod, 12 g Carb, 2 g Fib, 20 g Prot, 38 mg Calc. POINTS value: 4.

GOOD IDEA

This elegantly simple dish pairs beautifully with tiny steamed red potatoes (1 cup cooked potatoes will increase the per-serving **POINTS** value by **2**).

Flavorful Fish

Salmon with Tabbouleh Salad ☑

HANDS-ON PREP 15 MIN ■ COOK 6 MIN ■ SERVES 4

3 cups boiling water

1 cup bulgur

4 (1/4-pound) skinless thick salmon fillets

1 teaspoon salt

1/2 teaspoon coarsely ground pepper

1 small red onion, thinly sliced

2 tablespoons white-wine vinegar

1 tablespoon extra-virgin olive oil

1 cup mixed baby salad greens

4 plum tomatoes, quartered

1/3 cup chopped fresh basil

8 pitted black olives, halved

1 Pour the boiling water over the bulgur in a large bowl. Cover and set aside until the bulgur is softened, about 30 minutes. Drain well in a colander, shaking the colander several times to remove all the excess water.

2 Meanwhile, sprinkle the salmon with 1/2 teaspoon of the salt and the pepper. Spray a nonstick skillet with nonstick spray and set over medium-high heat. Add the salmon and cook until just opaque in the center, about 3 minutes on each side. Transfer the salmon to a plate and let cool to room temperature.

3 Combine the red onion, vinegar, oil, and the remaining 1/2 teaspoon of salt in a large bowl. Add the bulgur, salad greens, tomatoes, basil, and olives; toss to coat well. Spoon the salad onto a large platter and top with the salmon.

PER SERVING (1 salmon fillet and 1 1/4 cups salad): 335 Cal, 10 g Fat, 2 g Sat Fat, 0 g Trans Fat, 65 mg Chol, 805 mg Sod, 32 g Carb, 8 g Fib, 30 g Prot, 52 mg Calc.
POINTS value: 7.

FOOD NOTE

Bulgur, a staple grain in the Middle East, is made of wheat kernels that have been steamed, dried, and crushed. It comes in fine, medium, and coarse grain. For tabbouleh, we prefer medium- or coarse-grain.

Salmon and Vegetable Packets

HANDS-ON PREP 15 MIN ■ COOK 20 MIN ■ SERVES 4

4 carrots, cut into matchstick strips

1 red bell pepper, seeded and cut into very thin strips

1 leek (white and light green parts only), cleaned and thinly sliced

2 (5-ounce) Yukon Gold potatoes, peeled and cut into matchstick strips

4 (1/4-pound) skinless salmon fillets

1/2 cup reduced-sodium vegetable broth, heated

4 tablespoons dry white wine

4 teaspoons olive oil

2 tablespoons chopped fresh basil

1 teaspoon ground ginger

1/2 teaspoon salt

1/4 teaspoon freshly ground pepper

4 lemon slices

1   Preheat the oven to 425°F.

2   Combine the carrots, bell pepper, leek, and potatoes in a steamer basket; place in a saucepan filled with 1 inch of boiling water. Cover tightly and steam until the vegetables are crisp-tender, about 2 minutes. Remove the steamer basket from the saucepan.

3   Tear off 4 (16-inch) squares of foil. Place one-eighth of the vegetable mixture in the center of each foil square. Top each mound of vegetables with a salmon fillet, then cover with the remaining vegetable mixture. Spoon 2 tablespoons of the hot broth over each portion; drizzle with 1 tablespoon of the wine and 1 teaspoon of the oil. Sprinkle each with the basil, ginger, salt, and pepper; top with a lemon slice.

4   To close the packets, bring the 2 opposite long sides of the foil up to meet in the center; fold the edges over twice to make a tight seal. Double fold the open sides to seal the packets. Place the packets on a baking sheet and bake just until the salmon is opaque in the center, about 15 minutes. To serve, carefully open the packets, avoiding the steam that is released; slide the fish and vegetables onto plates. Serve drizzled with any juices.

PER SERVING (1 salmon fillet and 1 cup vegetables): 323 Cal, 11 g Fat, 3 g Sat Fat, 0 g Trans Fat, 75 mg Chol, 454 mg Sod, 28 g Carb, 6 g Fib, 27 g Prot, 89 mg Calc.
POINTS value: 7.

MAKE IT CORE

To fit this dish into the **Core Plan,** substitute vegetable broth for the wine.

Sesame-Lime Grilled Tuna

HANDS-ON PREP 5 MIN ▪ COOK 12 MIN ▪ SERVES 4

2 tablespoons reduced-sodium soy
   sauce

¼ cup fresh lime juice

2 teaspoons Asian (dark) sesame oil

3 garlic cloves, minced

¼ teaspoon freshly ground pepper

4 (6-ounce) tuna steaks (about 1½
   inches thick)

1 Combine the soy sauce, lime juice, sesame oil, garlic, and pepper in a large zip-close plastic bag; add the tuna. Squeeze out the air and seal the bag; turn to coat the tuna. Refrigerate, turning the bag occasionally, 30 minutes. Remove the tuna from the marinade; discard the marinade.

2 Spray the grill rack with nonstick spray; preheat the grill to medium-high or prepare a medium-high fire.

3 Place the tuna on the grill rack. Grill until browned but still pink in the center, about 6 minutes on each side for medium-rare.

PER SERVING (1 tuna steak): 226 Cal, 9 g Fat, 3 g Sat Fat, 0 g Trans Fat, 101 mg Chol, 167 mg Sod, 1 g Carb, 0 g Fib, 33 g Prot, 20 mg Calc.
POINTS value: 5.

EXPRESS LANE

No time to prepare the grill? Broil the tuna instead. Spray a broiler rack with nonstick spray and preheat the broiler. Place the tuna on the rack and broil 5 inches from the heat until barely pink in the center, about 6 minutes on each side.

Tuna and Vegetable Bake

HANDS-ON PREP 20 MIN ■ COOK 45 MIN ■ SERVES 6

6 cups extra-wide egg noodles

1 (10 ¾-ounce) can reduced-fat condensed cream of celery soup

1 cup low-fat (1%) milk

3 teaspoons olive oil

1 small onion, chopped

2 garlic cloves, minced

½ pound fresh white or cremini mushrooms, sliced

1 cup frozen peas and carrots

½ teaspoon dried thyme

2 (6-ounce) cans solid white tuna in water, drained and flaked

½ cup jarred roasted red peppers, drained and chopped

¼ cup chopped fresh parsley

½ cup fresh bread crumbs

1 Preheat the oven to 350°F. Spray an 8-inch-square baking dish with nonstick spray. Cook the noodles according to the package directions; drain and keep warm.

2 Meanwhile, whisk together the soup and milk in a large bowl; set aside.

3 Heat 2 teaspoons of the oil in a large nonstick skillet set over medium heat. Add the onion and garlic; cook, stirring frequently, until slightly softened, about 3 minutes. Stir in the mushrooms, peas and carrots, and thyme; cook, stirring occasionally, until the mushrooms are softened, about 5 minutes. Stir into the soup mixture. Add the noodles, tuna, roasted peppers, and parsley; toss well.

4 Spoon the tuna-noodle mixture into the baking dish. Toss together the bread crumbs and the remaining 1 teaspoon of oil; sprinkle over the casserole. Bake until hot and bubbling, 30–35 minutes.

PER SERVING (1 generous cup): 294 Cal, 7 g Fat, 2 g Sat Fat, 0 g Trans Fat, 54 mg Chol, 481 mg Sod, 39 g Carb, 3 g Fib, 20 g Prot, 150 mg Calc.
POINTS value: 6.

PLAN AHEAD

Stock your freezer with bags of your favorite frozen vegetables, such as the peas and carrots used in this recipe, to make cooking easier. Frozen vegetables sold in bags are individually quick-frozen and the bags are resealable, so you can take out only as much as you need and return the rest to the freezer.

Tuna and Bell Pepper Soft Tacos

HANDS-ON PREP 15 MIN ■ COOK 10 MIN ■ SERVES 4

2 tablespoons fresh lime juice

1 teaspoon ground cumin

1 teaspoon chili powder

3/4 teaspoon salt

1 pound tuna steak, cut into 1/2-inch-
   thick strips

1 tablespoon olive oil

2 red bell peppers, seeded and cut into
   thin strips

1 large onion, sliced

1 jalapeño pepper, seeded and minced
   (wear gloves to prevent irritation)

2 tablespoons chopped fresh cilantro

4 (8-inch) fat-free flour tortillas, warmed

8 tablespoons prepared tomato salsa

4 tablespoons fat-free sour cream

Lime wedges

1 Combine the lime juice, cumin, chili powder, and 1/4 teaspoon of the salt in a large zip-close plastic bag; add the tuna. Squeeze out the air and seal the bag; turn to coat the tuna. Refrigerate about 10 minutes.

2 Heat the oil in a large nonstick skillet set over medium-high heat. Add the bell peppers, onion, jalapeño, and the remaining 1/2 teaspoon of salt; cook, stirring occasionally, until softened, about 5 minutes. Remove the tuna from the marinade; add to the skillet and cook, stirring occasionally, until just opaque in the center, 3–4 minutes. Stir in the cilantro.

3 Top each tortilla with 1 cup of the tuna mixture, 2 tablespoons of the salsa, and 1 tablespoon of the sour cream. Fold each tortilla in half and serve at once with lime wedges.

PER SERVING (1 taco): 356 Cal, 10 g Fat, 2 g Sat Fat, 0 g Trans Fat, 44 mg Chol, 793 mg Sod, 33 g Carb, 4 g Fib, 33 g Prot, 129 mg Calc.
POINTS value: 7.

ZAP IT

To heat the tortillas in a flash, stack them on a small plate, cover loosely with wax paper, and microwave on High for 50 seconds.

Cod with Tarragon-Lemon Bread Crumbs

HANDS-ON PREP 10 MIN ■ COOK 15 MIN ■ SERVES 4

4 (1/4-pound) cod fillets

4 teaspoons canola oil

1/4 cup fresh lemon juice

2 tablespoons plain dried bread crumbs

2 tablespoons drained capers

1 tablespoon grated lemon zest

1/4 teaspoon salt

1/8 teaspoon freshly ground pepper

2 tablespoons chopped fresh tarragon

1 Preheat the oven to 350°F. Spray a 9 x 13-inch baking dish with nonstick spray.

2 Place the cod fillets in the baking dish; brush the fish with the oil, then drizzle with the lemon juice. Combine the bread crumbs, capers, lemon zest, salt, and pepper in a small bowl; sprinkle evenly over the fish. Bake just until the fish is opaque in the center, 15–20 minutes. Spoon any pan juices over the fillets and sprinkle with the tarragon.

PER SERVING (1 fillet): 168 Cal, 6 g Fat, 1 g Sat Fat, 0 g Trans Fat, 60 mg Chol, 388 mg Sod, 5 g Carb, 1 g Fib, 22 g Prot, 40 mg Calc.
POINTS value: 4.

HOW WE DID IT

When a recipe calls for grated citrus zest and fresh citrus juice, remember to grate the zest before squeezing the juice; it's much easier to grate zest from a whole piece of fruit.

Creole-Seasoned Tilapia

HANDS-ON PREP 10 MIN ■ COOK 6 MIN ■ SERVES 4

1/4 cup all-purpose flour

1/4 cup chopped flat-leaf parsley

1 tablespoon Creole seasoning

1/4 cup fat-free egg substitute

4 (6-ounce) tilapia fillets

4 teaspoons canola oil

Lemon wedges

1 Combine the flour, parsley, and Creole seasoning on a sheet of wax paper. Pour the egg substitute into a shallow bowl.

2 Dip the fillets, one at a time, in the egg substitute, then coat with the flour mixture. Place the fillets on a platter; cover and refrigerate 30 minutes.

3 Heat the oil in a large nonstick skillet set over medium-high heat. Add the tilapia and cook until browned and just opaque in the center, about 3 minutes on each side. Serve with lemon wedges.

PER SERVING (1 fillet): 261 Cal, 7 g Fat, 1 g Sat Fat, 0 g Trans Fat, 104 mg Chol, 330 mg Sod, 7 g Carb, 1 g Fib, 39 g Prot, 55 mg Calc.
POINTS value: 6.

GOOD IDEA

Different brands of Creole seasoning vary widely in the amount of cayenne they contain. We recommend that you taste a tiny bit of the seasoning and, if necessary, adjust the amount called for in our recipe.

Halibut with Moroccan Tomato Sauce and Couscous ☑

HANDS-ON PREP 15 MIN ■ COOK 15 MIN ■ SERVES 4

1 cup whole-wheat couscous	1 garlic clove, minced
1/2 teaspoon salt	1 teaspoon ground coriander
4 (5-ounce) halibut fillets	1/2 teaspoon turmeric
1/4 teaspoon freshly ground pepper	1 (14 1/2-ounce) can diced tomatoes
4 teaspoons olive oil	1/2 cup bottled clam juice or fish broth
1 yellow bell pepper, seeded and chopped	3 tablespoons fresh lemon juice
4 shallots, chopped	1/2 cup chopped flat-leaf parsley

1 Prepare the couscous according to package directions, adding 1/4 teaspoon of the salt. Fluff with a fork.

2 Meanwhile, sprinkle the halibut with the remaining 1/4 teaspoon of salt and the pepper. Heat 2 teaspoons of the oil in a large nonstick skillet set over medium-high heat. Add the halibut and cook until browned, about 2 minutes on each side. Transfer the halibut to a plate; set aside.

3 Heat the remaining 2 teaspoons of oil in the same skillet set over medium heat. Add the bell pepper, shallots, and garlic; cook, stirring frequently, until softened, about 4 minutes. Stir in the coriander and turmeric. Add the tomatoes, clam juice, and lemon juice; bring to a boil, stirring occasionally. Add the halibut; reduce the heat and simmer, covered, until the fish is just opaque in the center, about 5 minutes. Stir in the parsley.

4 Divide the couscous evenly among 4 plates; top with the halibut and sauce.

PER SERVING (1 fillet, 3/4 cup couscous, and about 1/2 cup sauce): 452 Cal, 9 g Fat, 1 g Sat Fat, 0 g Trans Fat, 48 mg Chol, 575 mg Sod, 57 g Carb, 10 g Fib, 41 g Prot, 122 mg Calc.
POINTS value: 9.

FOOD NOTE

Couscous, a staple of North African and Middle Eastern cuisines, is a type of pasta—not a grain, as is often thought. The tiny couscous granules are made from semolina flour, which comes from durum wheat. Whole-wheat couscous contains more nutrients and fiber than regular couscous and requires a few more minutes of cooking time.

Red Snapper with Jalapeño Tartar Sauce ☑

HANDS-ON PREP 15 MIN ■ COOK 6 MIN ■ SERVES 4

1/4 cup fat-free mayonnaise

2 scallions, thinly sliced

1 jalapeño pepper, seeded and minced
(wear gloves to prevent irritation)

2 tablespoons chopped fresh cilantro

1 tablespoon fresh lime juice

1/4 teaspoon + 1 tablespoon fajita
seasoning

4 (6-ounce) red snapper fillets

2 teaspoons canola oil

1 To make the tartar sauce, combine the mayonnaise, scallions, jalapeño, cilantro, lime juice, and 1/4 teaspoon of the fajita seasoning in a serving bowl; set aside.

2 Sprinkle both sides of the snapper fillets with the remaining 1 tablespoon fajita seasoning. Heat the oil in a large nonstick skillet set over medium-high heat. Add the fish and cook until browned and just opaque in the center, about 3 minutes on each side. Serve with the tartar sauce.

PER SERVING (1 fillet and 2 tablespoons tartar sauce): 204 Cal, 5 g Fat, 1 g Sat Fat, 0 g Trans Fat, 62 mg Chol, 357 mg Sod, 4 g Carb, 1 g Fib, 34 g Prot, 57 mg Calc.
POINTS value: 4.

TRY IT

Make use of versatile fajita seasoning to punch up the flavor of other foods, including chicken breasts, pork chops, and shrimp.

Mussels in Spicy Tomato Broth

HANDS-ON PREP 15 MIN ■ COOK 15 MIN ■ SERVES 4

2 teaspoons olive oil

1/2 onion, chopped

4 garlic cloves, minced

1/4 cup dry white wine or
   reduced-sodium chicken broth

2 plum tomatoes, chopped

1/4 teaspoon crushed red pepper

4 pounds mussels, scrubbed and
   debearded

2 tablespoons chopped flat-leaf parsley

4 (1-ounce) slices French or Italian
   bread, toasted

1 Heat the oil in a nonstick Dutch oven set over medium-high heat. Add the onion and garlic; cook, stirring occasionally, until golden, about 7 minutes. Add the wine, tomatoes, and crushed red pepper; bring to a boil. Reduce the heat and simmer about 2 minutes.

2 Add the mussels and simmer, covered, until they open, about 5 minutes. Discard any mussels that do not open.

3 Stir in the parsley. Divide the mussels evenly among 4 bowls; ladle the broth over the mussels. Serve with the toasted bread.

PER SERVING (about 30 mussels, 1/4 cup broth, and 1 slice of bread): 203 Cal, 5 g Fat, 1 g Sat Fat, 0 g Trans Fat, 45 mg Chol, 543 mg Sod, 19 g Carb, 1 g Fib, 20 g Prot, 97 mg Calc.
POINTS value: 4.

MAKE IT CORE

To fit this recipe into the **Core Plan,** use the chicken broth instead of the wine and omit the toasted bread.

Maryland Crab Cakes with Lemon Rémoulade ☑

HANDS-ON PREP 20 MIN ▪ COOK 6 MIN ▪ SERVES 4

5 tablespoons fat-free mayonnaise

2 tablespoons chopped fresh parsley

2 tablespoons minced shallots

1 tablespoon drained capers

2 teaspoons grated lemon zest

Dash hot pepper sauce

1 large egg, lightly beaten

1 teaspoon Dijon mustard

1 teaspoon Chesapeake Bay seasoning

1/2 teaspoon Worcestershire sauce

1 pound fresh, canned, or thawed frozen lump crabmeat, picked over

1 To make the rémoulade, combine 3 tablespoons of the mayonnaise, the parsley, shallots, capers, lemon zest, and pepper sauce in a small bowl; cover and refrigerate.

2 Combine the remaining 2 tablespoons of mayonnaise, the egg, mustard, Bay seasoning, and Worcestershire sauce in a large bowl; gently stir in the crabmeat. Shape mixture into 8 patties. Place on a plate; cover and refrigerate 30 minutes.

3 Spray a large nonstick skillet with canola nonstick spray and set over medium-high heat. Add the crab cakes and cook until heated through and well-browned, about 3 minutes on each side. Serve with the rémoulade.

PER SERVING (2 crab cakes and 2 tablespoons sauce): 156 Cal, 4 g Fat, 1 g Sat Fat, 0 g Trans Fat, 169 mg Chol, 794 mg Sod, 4 g Carb, 1 g Fib, 25 g Prot, 134 mg Calc.
POINTS value: 3.

FOOD NOTE

Chesapeake Bay seasoning, a unique blend of celery seeds, paprika, allspice, cayenne, and other spices, gives these crab cakes the authentic flavor prized by crab-cake connoisseurs in the Chesapeake Bay region. Look for it in the spice aisle of your supermarket; Old Bay is the best-known brand. A side serving of steamed asparagus will add no additional **POINTS** value.

If you serve this with wine, remember to deduct it from your **Weekly POINTS Allowance**. A 4-ounce glass has a **POINTS** value of **2**.

Ham-Wrapped Scallops with Tangerine-Balsamic Sauce

HANDS-ON PREP 15 MIN ■ COOK 15 MIN ■ SERVES 4

1 cup tangerine or orange-tangerine juice

1/4 cup balsamic vinegar

1 teaspoon sugar

1 teaspoon grated tangerine or orange zest

5 thin slices baked Virginia ham (about 2 1/2 ounces)

1 pound sea scallops (about 20)

1 Preheat the oven to 450°F. Spray a baking sheet with nonstick spray.

2 Combine the tangerine juice, vinegar, and sugar in a medium saucepan and set over high heat. Cook until thickened, about 8 minutes. Remove the saucepan from the heat and stir in the tangerine zest.

3 Meanwhile, cut each slice of ham into 4 long strips. Wrap each scallop in a strip of ham and place, seam side down, on the baking sheet. Bake 5 minutes; brush with the tangerine-juice mixture. Continue to bake until just opaque in the center, 2–3 minutes longer. Drizzle the scallops with any remaining tangerine juice mixture.

PER SERVING (5 scallops): 148 Cal, 2 g Fat, 1 g Sat Fat, 0 g Trans Fat, 33 mg Chol, 425 mg Sod, 11 g Carb, 0 g Fib, 21 g Prot, 94 mg Calc.
POINTS value: 3.

FOOD NOTE

Choose scallops that are creamy white or slightly pink for the best flavor and guaranteed freshness. They are sometimes labeled "dry." Scallops that are bright white have been soaked in a solution to preserve them and should be avoided.

Chipotle-Lime Shrimp

HANDS-ON PREP 10 MIN ■ COOK 8 MIN ■ SERVES 4

4 teaspoons olive oil

2 teaspoons grated lime zest

1 tablespoon fresh lime juice

1 teaspoon minced canned chipotles en adobo

2 garlic cloves, minced

1/4 teaspoon salt

1 pound jumbo shrimp, peeled and deveined

Lime wedges

1 Spray the broiler rack with nonstick spray. Preheat the broiler.

2 Combine the oil, lime zest and juice, chipotles en adobo, garlic, and salt in a large bowl; add the shrimp and toss to coat. Arrange the shrimp on the broiler rack; broil 5 inches from the heat until just opaque in the center, about 4 minutes on each side. Serve with lime wedges.

PER SERVING (4–5 shrimp): 116 Cal, 5 g Fat, 1 g Sat Fat, 0 g Trans Fat, 65 mg Chol, 349 mg Sod, 3 g Carb, 1 g Fib, 14 g Prot, 59 mg Calc.
POINTS value: 3.

TRY IT

Chipotle chiles en adobo are smoked jalapeño peppers that have been canned in a sauce of ground chiles, herbs, and vinegar. Look for them in the Mexican food section of well-stocked supermarkets. If you can't find chipotles en adobo, substitute the same amount of chipotle pepper sauce.

Shrimp and Sausage Paella

HANDS-ON PREP 15 MIN ■ COOK 35 MIN ■ SERVES 6

6 ounces turkey kielbasa, cut into 1/4-inch-thick slices

2 red bell peppers, seeded and chopped

1 onion, chopped

4 garlic cloves, chopped

1 (8-ounce) bottle clam juice or 1 cup reduced-sodium chicken broth

1/2 teaspoon saffron threads, crushed

3/4 cup long-grain white rice

1 pound large shrimp, peeled and deveined

1 (15-ounce) can artichoke hearts, drained and quartered

1/2 cup frozen peas

1 Spray a large nonstick skillet with nonstick spray and set over medium-high heat. Add the kielbasa and cook, turning frequently, until lightly browned, about 6 minutes. Add the bell peppers, onion, and garlic; cook, stirring often, until softened, about 5 minutes.

2 Stir in the clam juice and saffron. Bring to a boil and stir in the rice. Reduce the heat and simmer, covered, 15 minutes. Add the shrimp, artichoke hearts, and peas; cook, covered, until the shrimp are just opaque, about 10 minutes longer.

PER SERVING (about 1 1/2 cups): 243 Cal, 3 g Fat, 1 g Sat Fat, 0 g Trans Fat, 132 mg Chol, 597 mg Sod, 31 g Carb, 2 g Fib, 21 g Prot, 54 mg Calc.

POINTS value: 5.

HOW WE DID IT

Here is the easiest—and neatest—way to seed and chop a bell pepper: Cut the pepper lengthwise in half. With your fingers, remove the core and stem and shake out any loose seeds. Place the pepper on the counter, skin side down (to make it easier to cut). With a large knife, cut a pepper half lengthwise into 1/4-inch-wide strips, then gather the strips into a pile and cut crosswise into 1/4-inch pieces.

Shrimp and Vegetable Sushi Rolls

HANDS-ON PREP 20 MIN ■ COOK 20 MIN ■ SERVES 8

2 cups water

1 1/2 cups short-grain white rice

3 tablespoons rice vinegar

1 tablespoon sugar

1/4 teaspoon salt

8 sheets nori (seaweed)

1 teaspoon prepared wasabi paste

3/4 pound large shrimp (about 36), peeled, deveined, cooked, and cut crosswise in half

1 Hass avocado, halved, pitted, peeled, and cut lengthwise into 16 slices

1 cucumber, peeled, halved, seeded, and cut lengthwise into matchstick strips

2 carrots, cut lengthwise into matchstick strips

2 teaspoons toasted sesame seeds

Reduced-sodium soy sauce (optional)

Pickled ginger slices (optional)

1 Combine the water and rice in a medium saucepan; bring to a boil. Reduce the heat and simmer, covered, until the liquid is absorbed and the rice is tender, about 20 minutes. Remove the saucepan from the heat and let stand 10 minutes.

2 Combine the vinegar, sugar, and salt in a small bowl; stir into the rice. Let cool to room temperature.

3 Place 1 nori sheet, shiny side down, on a sushi mat with a long side facing you. With moistened hands, pat one-eighth (about 1/2 cup) of the rice mixture over the nori, leaving a 1-inch border along the long edge farthest away from you. Spread 1/8 teaspoon of the wasabi paste over the rice. Arrange one-eighth of the shrimp, avocado, cucumber, and carrot along the bottom third of the rice. Sprinkle with 1/4 teaspoon of the sesame seeds.

4 Lift the nori edge closest to you and fold over the filling. Lift the bottom edge of the sushi mat and roll toward the top edge, pressing firmly on the sushi roll. Sprinkle a few drops of water on the edge of the nori; press the seam closed. Repeat to make 8 rolls in all. The rolls may be covered and refrigerated up to 6 hours. Just before serving, slice each roll crosswise into 6 pieces. Serve with soy sauce and pickled ginger, if using.

PER SERVING (6 pieces without soy sauce or ginger): 182 Cal, 4 g Fat, 1 g Sat Fat, 0 g Trans Fat, 48 mg Chol, 152 mg Sod, 28 g Carb, 3 g Fib, 8 g Prot, 22 mg Calc.
POINTS value: 3.

HOW WE DID IT

To make an easy, clean cut when slicing sushi, use a serrated knife and dip it in hot water after cutting each slice.

Eggplant-Mushroom Lasagna

HANDS-ON PREP 20 MIN ■ COOK 1 HR ■ SERVES 4

1 (1-pound) eggplant, peeled and cut crosswise into $1/4$-inch-thick slices

1 zucchini, cut lengthwise into $1/4$-inch-thick slices

$1/2$ teaspoon salt

$1/4$ teaspoon freshly ground pepper

1 tablespoon olive oil

2 garlic cloves, finely chopped

1 (28-ounce) can petite diced tomatoes

1 (10-ounce) package fresh cremini mushrooms, sliced

1 large red bell pepper, seeded and chopped

8 fresh basil leaves, torn

$1/8$ teaspoon crushed red pepper

5 ($6^{1}/_{2}$ x 7-inch) sheets no-boil lasagna noodles

4 tablespoons grated Parmesan cheese

1 Preheat the oven to 400°F. Spray 2 baking sheets and an 8-inch square baking dish with nonstick spray.

2 Place the eggplant and zucchini slices on the baking sheets, overlapping them if necessary. Spray the vegetables with nonstick spray; sprinkle with the salt and $1/8$ teaspoon of the ground pepper. Bake until tender, about 15 minutes; set aside.

3 Meanwhile, heat the oil in a large nonstick skillet set over medium-high heat. Add the garlic and cook, stirring, until fragrant, about 30 seconds. Add the tomatoes with their juice, the mushrooms, bell pepper, basil, crushed red pepper, and the remaining $1/8$ teaspoon ground pepper. Reduce the heat and simmer until the sauce is bubbly but not thickened, about 10 minutes.

4 Spread $1/2$ cup of the sauce in the baking dish and cover with 1 lasagna noodle. Top with one-fourth of the eggplant and zucchini slices, then top with $1/2$ cup of sauce. Sprinkle with 1 tablespoon of the cheese. Repeat to make 4 more layers, ending with a layer of noodles and the remaining sauce. Cover the dish with foil and bake until bubbly, about 35 minutes. Uncover and bake until all the sauce has been absorbed, 10–15 minutes longer. Let stand 5 minutes; then cut into four portions.

PER SERVING ($1/4$ of lasagna): 365 Cal, 8 g Fat, 2 g Sat Fat, 0 g Trans Fat, 5 mg Chol, 599 mg Sod, 62 g Carb, 9 g Fib, 15 g Prot, 182 mg Calc.
POINTS value: 7.

TRY IT

Petite diced tomatoes are a great convenience for the cook. The tomato pieces are a bit smaller than regular diced tomatoes, which you can use here also. If you prefer irregular pieces of tomato in your sauce, use whole tomatoes packed in juice and break them up with your fingers.

Spaghetti with Spring Vegetables

HANDS-ON PREP 25 MIN ■ COOK 20 MIN ■ SERVES 6

³/₄ (16-ounce) box thin spaghetti

¹/₂ pound asparagus, trimmed and cut into 1¹/₂-inch pieces

2 tablespoons extra-virgin olive oil

3 shallots, thinly sliced

2 garlic cloves, finely chopped

¹/₂ pound mixed fresh mushrooms, such as cremini, shiitake (stemmed), oyster, and black trumpet, halved or quartered if large

1 pint grape tomatoes, halved

1 cup frozen peas, thawed

¹/₂ teaspoon salt

¹/₄ teaspoon freshly ground pepper

¹/₂ cup chopped fresh parsley

¹/₄ cup chopped fresh basil

¹/₂ cup grated Parmesan cheese

1 Cook the pasta according to the package directions, omitting the salt if desired. Drain and keep warm.

2 Meanwhile, bring a large saucepan of water to a boil. Add the asparagus and cook 3 minutes. Drain, then plunge into a bowl of ice water to stop the cooking. Drain again and set aside.

3 Heat the oil in a large nonstick skillet set over medium-high heat. Add the shallots and garlic; cook, stirring, until fragrant, about 30 seconds. Add the mushrooms and cook, stirring, until golden, about 4 minutes. Reduce the heat to medium. Add the asparagus, tomatoes, peas, salt, and pepper; cook, stirring, until the tomatoes just begin to soften, about 3 minutes. Stir in the parsley and basil. Remove the skillet from the heat. Add the pasta and cheese; toss to coat. Serve hot or at room temperature.

PER SERVING (generous 1 cup): 322 Cal, 8 g Fat, 2 g Sat Fat, 0 g Trans Fat, 5 mg Chol, 354 mg Sod, 50 g Carb, 5 g Fib, 13 g Prot, 126 mg Calc.
POINTS value: 6.

GOOD IDEA

You can include almost any fresh herb or combination of herbs to complement the vegetables here: fresh oregano, marjoram, chives, thyme, and chervil would all work well. This popular pasta dish, often called *pasta primavera*, was invented in the 1970s at New York's swanky Le Cirque restaurant to showcase spring vegetables.

Pasta with Mixed-Vegetable Ragu ☑

HANDS-ON PREP 20 MIN ■ COOK 45 MIN ■ SERVES 8

2 tablespoons extra-virgin olive oil

1 onion, chopped

3 garlic cloves, finely chopped

1 carrot, finely chopped

1 zucchini, finely chopped

1/2 red bell pepper, seeded and finely chopped

6 fresh white or cremini mushrooms, chopped

1 (28-ounce) can crushed tomatoes

1/2 cup chopped flat-leaf parsley

1/4 cup chopped fresh basil

1 tablespoon chopped fresh oregano or 1 teaspoon dried

1/2 teaspoon salt

1/4 teaspoon freshly ground pepper

1 (16-ounce) box whole-wheat spaghetti

1 Heat the oil in a large nonstick saucepan set over medium heat. Add the onion and half the garlic; cook, stirring, until softened, about 5 minutes. Add the carrot and cook until crisp-tender, about 5 minutes. Add the zucchini, bell pepper, and mushrooms; cook stirring frequently, until the mushroom juices are evaporated, about 6 minutes.

2 Add the tomatoes, parsley, basil, oregano, remaining garlic, salt, and ground pepper to the saucepan. Simmer, stirring occasionally, until the vegetables are very tender and the sauce is thickened, about 30 minutes.

3 Meanwhile, cook the spaghetti according to the package directions, omitting the salt if desired; drain. Divide the pasta evenly among 8 plates and top with the ragu.

PER SERVING (1 1/2 cups): 278 Cal, 5 g Fat, 1 g Sat Fat, 0 g Trans Fat, 0 mg Chol, 290 mg Sod, 54 g Carb, 10 g Fib, 11 g Prot, 81 mg Calc.
POINTS value: 5.

TRY IT

Ragus, rich and delicious ground-meat-and-tomato pasta sauces, are famous in the Emilia-Romagna region of northern Italy, where they are commonly made with a combination of beef, pork, and veal. Our no-meat version is lighter but every bit as satisfying. The pasta can also be spooned into a warm serving bowl and topped with the ragu. Toss to coat, then serve. To stay in the **Core Plan**, serve with chilled water instead of the red wine.

Ricotta Cheese Ravioli with Butternut Squash Sauce

HANDS-ON PREP 25 MIN ■ COOK 25 MIN ■ SERVES 4

2 teaspoons olive oil

1 small onion, chopped

1 garlic clove, finely chopped

2 cups fresh or thawed frozen butternut squash chunks

1 (14½-ounce) can reduced-sodium chicken broth

1½ teaspoons chopped fresh sage

½ teaspoon ground pepper

¼ teaspoon salt

⅛ teaspoon + pinch nutmeg

½ cup part-skim ricotta cheese

5 tablespoons grated Parmesan cheese

1 egg white

1 (12-ounce) package wonton wrappers (24 wrappers)

Sage leaves

1 Heat the oil in a large nonstick skillet set over medium heat. Add the onion and garlic; cook until fragrant, about 1 minute. Add the squash, broth, chopped sage, ¼ teaspoon of the pepper, the salt, and the ⅛ teaspoon of the nutmeg; cook, stirring until the squash is very tender and the liquid is evaporated, about 15 minutes. Remove the skillet from the heat; let cool 15 minutes.

2 Meanwhile, to make the ravioli, combine the ricotta, 3 tablespoons of the Parmesan, the egg white, and the remaining ¼ teaspoon of pepper in a small bowl. Lightly dust a work surface with flour. Place 12 wonton wrappers on the surface and put 1½ teaspoons of the cheese mixture in the center of each wrapper. With a pastry brush that has been dipped in water, dampen the edges of the wrappers, then place another wrapper on top, pressing out the air as you pinch the edges together to seal them. Cover lightly with a damp towel; set aside.

3 Puree the squash mixture in a food processor. If too thick, add water, 1 tablespoon at a time, until the mixture has a saucelike consistency. Pour into a medium saucepan and set over medium heat. Bring to a gentle simmer, stirring frequently; keep warm.

4 Meanwhile, bring a large pot of water to a boil. Reduce the heat to a gentle boil; slip half of the ravioli into the water and cook until they float to the surface, about 4 minutes. With a slotted spoon, transfer the ravioli to a colander. Drain well, then transfer to a bowl and keep warm. Cook and drain the remaining ravioli. Spoon the sauce evenly into each of 4 shallow bowls and top with the ravioli. Sprinkle the ravioli with the remaining 2 tablespoons of Parmesan and a pinch of nutmeg. Garnish with sage leaves and serve at once.

PER SERVING (6 Parmesan-dusted ravioli and ¼ cup sauce): **289 Cal, 8 g Fat, 3 g Sat Fat, 0 g Trans Fat, 19 mg Chol, 865 mg Sod, 42 g Carb, 4 g Fib, 14 g Prot, 242 mg Calc.** POINTS value: **6.**

PLAY IT SAFE

It is best to allow the butternut squash to cool a bit before pureeing it in a food processor. This will prevent the hot squash from spurting as a result of the steam that builds up in the machine.

Bow Ties with Tomato-Vodka Sauce

HANDS-ON PREP 10 MIN ■ COOK 25 MIN ■ SERVES 4

2 cups bow ties (farfalle)

1 tablespoon olive oil

1/2 small onion, finely chopped

1 plum tomato, chopped

1/4 cup reduced-sodium vegetable broth

1 tablespoon tomato paste

1/4 teaspoon crushed red pepper

1/4 cup heavy cream

2 tablespoons vodka or reduced-sodium vegetable broth

2 tablespoons grated Parmesan cheese

2 tablespoons chopped fresh basil

1 Cook the bow ties according to the package directions, omitting the salt if desired. Drain and transfer to a large bowl; keep warm.

2 Meanwhile, heat the oil in a medium nonstick skillet set over medium-high heat. Add the onion and tomato; cook, stirring frequently, until softened, about 5 minutes. Stir in the broth, tomato paste, and crushed red pepper; bring to a boil. Reduce the heat to medium; add the heavy cream and vodka. Cook, stirring constantly, until heated through (do not let boil). Pour the sauce over the pasta and toss to coat well. Sprinkle with the Parmesan and basil.

PER SERVING (3/4 cup): 174 Cal, 10 g Fat, 5 g Sat Fat, 0 g Trans Fat, 22 mg Chol, 91 mg Sod, 17 g Carb, 1 g Fib, 4 g Prot, 54 mg Calc.
POINTS value: 4.

TRY IT

Adding vodka to tomato sauce might seem strange, but this Italian-American specialty is simply delicious. You can't taste the vodka, but it adds a special something that makes the dish delectable. Hearty, chewy bow ties are the perfect complement to the rich sauce.

Grits with Goat Cheese and Scallions

HANDS-ON PREP 5 MIN ■ COOK 15 MIN ■ SERVES 4

1³/₄ cups water

¹/₄ teaspoon salt

¹/₂ cup quick-cooking grits

2 ounces fresh (mild) goat cheese

3 tablespoons grated Parmesan cheese

¹/₄ teaspoon freshly ground pepper

2 scallions, chopped

Bring the water and salt to a boil in a medium saucepan. Slowly whisk in the grits. Reduce the heat and simmer, covered, stirring occasionally, until thickened, about 8 minutes. Remove the saucepan from the heat and stir in the goat cheese, Parmesan cheese, and pepper. Spoon into a serving bowl and sprinkle with the scallions.

PER SERVING (¹/₂ cup): 138 Cal, 4 g Fat, 2 g Sat Fat, 0 g Trans Fat, 11 mg Chol, 310 mg Sod, 17 g Carb, 1 g Fib, 8 g Prot, 182 mg Calc.
POINTS value: 3.

FOOD NOTE

Native Americans introduced the early European settlers to hominy—hulled and dried kernels of corn, which when ground became grits. The grits were then simmered in water or milk until very thick and porridge-like, a dish that has become a true Southern tradition.

Mediterranean Ratatouille Casserole

HANDS-ON PREP 20 MIN ■ COOK 25 MIN ■ SERVES 4

4 teaspoons olive oil

1 large onion, chopped

2 garlic cloves, finely chopped

1 (1 1/4-pound) eggplant, peeled and diced

2 red bell peppers, seeded and cut into 1/2-inch dice

1 zucchini, diced

1 1/2 teaspoons herbes de Provence

1/2 teaspoon salt

1/4 teaspoon freshly ground pepper

1 (14 1/2-ounce) can diced tomatoes, drained

1 (3-inch-long) strip orange zest, removed with a vegetable peeler

1/4 cup grated Parmesan cheese

1/4 cup plain dried bread crumbs

1 Heat the oil in a large nonstick skillet set over medium heat. Add the onion and garlic; cook, stirring, until softened, about 4 minutes. Add the eggplant, bell peppers, zucchini, herbes de Provence, salt, and pepper; cook, stirring, until the eggplant begins to soften, about 4 minutes. Stir in the tomatoes and orange zest; cook, stirring occasionally, until the vegetables are softened, about 15 minutes.

2 Meanwhile, preheat the broiler. Spray four 1-cup baking dishes with nonstick spray.

3 Spoon the ratatouille into the baking dishes. Combine the Parmesan and bread crumbs in a small bowl; sprinkle evenly over the vegetable mixture. Broil 5 inches from the heat until golden brown, about 2 minutes.

PER SERVING (1 cup): 182 Cal, 7 g Fat, 2 g Sat Fat, 0 g Trans Fat, 4 mg Chol, 576 mg Sod, 27 g Carb, 8 g Fib, 7 g Prot, 146 mg Calc.
POINTS value: 3.

PLAN AHEAD

Ratatouille, a classic vegetable dish from southern France, pays homage to the vegetables and herbs grown there. This casserole, which can be put together several hours ahead and placed under the broiler just before serving, is as delicious hot as it is warm or at room temperature. Ratatouille also makes a great filling for a hearty vegetarian sandwich on ciabatta or other crusty country-style bread.

Vegetable–Jack Cheese Quesadillas

HANDS-ON PREP 20 MIN ■ COOK 20 MIN ■ SERVES 4

1 teaspoon olive oil

1 onion, thinly sliced

1 large red bell pepper, seeded and thinly sliced

2 garlic cloves, finely chopped

1 cup frozen corn kernels, thawed

1 teaspoon ground cumin

3/4 teaspoon dried oregano

2 scallions, chopped

1/4 cup chopped fresh cilantro

8 (6-inch) flour tortillas

1 cup shredded reduced-fat Monterey Jack cheese

Hot pepper sauce

1 Heat the oil in a large nonstick skillet set over medium heat. Add the onion, bell pepper, and garlic; cook, stirring, until softened, about 5 minutes. Stir in the corn, cumin, and oregano; cook until heated through, about 2 minutes. Remove the skillet from the heat; stir in the scallions and cilantro.

2 Place 4 of the tortillas on a work surface. Sprinkle 1/4 cup of the Monterey Jack over each tortilla. Spoon the vegetable mixture on top, dividing it evenly; dot with pepper sauce. Cover with the remaining 4 tortillas, pressing down lightly.

3 Wipe the skillet clean. Spray with nonstick spray and set over medium-high heat. Add 1 quesadilla and cook until crispy and toasted in spots, about 2 minutes. Lightly spray the quesadilla with nonstick spray; turn and cook until the tortilla is crispy and the cheese is melted, about 1½ minutes longer. Transfer to a cutting board; keep warm. Repeat with the remaining quesadillas. Cut each quesadilla into 4 wedges and serve at once.

PER SERVING (1 quesadilla): 363 Cal, 12 g Fat, 5 g Sat Fat, 0 g Trans Fat, 20 mg Chol, 551 mg Sod, 52 g Carb, 5 g Fib, 15 g Prot, 303 mg Calc.
POINTS value: 7.

GOOD IDEA

Quesadillas are easy to prepare and delicious to eat. Perhaps best of all is that they are versatile. You can cook up almost any favorite vegetables for the filling; consider mushrooms, broccoli, plum tomatoes, or spinach. As for the cheese, pepperjack, cheddar, and goat cheese are all tasty alternatives to Monterey Jack.

Risotto-Style Barley with Shiitake Mushrooms ☑

HANDS-ON PREP 15 MIN ■ COOK 1 HR 10 MIN ■ SERVES 6

2 tablespoons olive oil

3 shallots, finely chopped

1/2 pound fresh shiitake mushrooms, stemmed, caps sliced

2 garlic cloves, finely chopped

2 teaspoons chopped fresh thyme or 1/2 teaspoon dried

1 cup pearl barley

2 (14 1/2-ounce) cans reduced-sodium vegetable broth

1/2 teaspoon salt

1/4 teaspoon freshly ground pepper

1 Heat the oil in a large nonstick saucepan set over medium heat. Add the shallots and cook, stirring, until beginning to soften, 4–5 minutes. Add the shiitakes and cook, stirring, until golden, about 6 minutes. Stir in the garlic and thyme; cook until fragrant, about 1 minute. Add the barley and cook, stirring, 1 minute.

2 Add enough water to the broth to equal 4 1/2 cups. Add 3 1/2 cups of the broth, the salt, and pepper to the saucepan. Bring to a boil, reduce the heat and simmer, covered, until the liquid is almost absorbed and the barley is almost tender, about 30 minutes. Add the remaining 1 cup of broth and the mushroom mixture; cook, uncovered, stirring occasionally, until the barley is tender, 12–15 minutes longer.

PER SERVING (3/4 cup): 186 Cal, 5 g Fat, 1 g Sat Fat, 0 g Trans Fat, 0 mg Chol, 460 mg Sod, 30 g Carb, 6 g Fib, 7 g Prot, 17 mg Calc.
POINTS value: 3.

FOOD NOTE

When shopping for barley, you are likely to find several types. Hulled barley has the outer husk removed and is very nutritious. Scotch barley is husked and coarsely ground, while pearl barley has the bran removed and has also been steamed and polished. It is available coarse, medium, and fine and is good in soups and stews.

Asparagus and Pea Risotto

HANDS-ON PREP 15 MIN ■ COOK 35 MIN ■ SERVES 8

1 (1-pound) bunch asparagus, trimmed and cut into 1 1/2-inch pieces

1 teaspoon salt

3 (14 1/2-ounce) cans reduced-sodium vegetable broth

1 tablespoon olive oil

2 leeks (white and pale green parts only), cleaned and chopped

3 garlic cloves, finely chopped

1 1/2 cups Arborio rice

1/3 cup dry white wine

1 cup frozen baby peas

2 teaspoons grated orange zest

1/2 cup grated Parmesan cheese

1/4 teaspoon freshly ground pepper

Chopped fresh chives

1 Bring a large saucepan of water to a boil. Add the asparagus and salt; cook 3 minutes. Drain, then plunge into a bowl of ice water to stop the cooking. Drain; set aside.

2 Meanwhile, bring the broth to a simmer in a large saucepan set over medium heat; reduce the heat and keep at a gentle simmer.

3 Heat the oil in a large nonstick skillet set over medium heat. Add the leeks and garlic; cook until softened, about 3 minutes. Add the rice and cook, stirring, until coated with the oil, about 1 minute. Stir in the wine and cook, stirring constantly, until it is absorbed. Add the broth, 1/2 cup at a time, stirring until it is absorbed before adding more, until the rice is tender but firm in the center, about 20 minutes in all. Reduce the heat if the risotto bubbles too quickly. Stir in the asparagus, peas, and orange zest with the last addition of broth. Stir in the Parmesan and pepper; sprinkle with chives and serve at once.

PER SERVING (1 cup): 241 Cal, 5 g Fat, 2 g Sat Fat, 0 g Trans Fat, 5 mg Chol, 532 mg Sod, 37 g Carb, 3 g Fib, 11 g Prot, 134 mg Calc.
POINTS value: 5.

GOOD IDEA

This risotto is the perfect way to welcome spring, especially with fresh asparagus and baby peas. As with most risottos, the recipe is flexible. So substitute lemon zest for the orange zest if you like, and use a medium onion instead of the leeks if you prefer. The risotto will be just as delicious.

Double-Cheese Polenta with Mushroom Sauce

HANDS-ON PREP 15 MIN ■ COOK 20 MIN ■ SERVES 6

1 tablespoon olive oil

2 shallots, finely chopped

1 pound mixed fresh mushrooms, such as oyster, shiitake (stemmed), white, and cremini, sliced

1 tablespoon chopped fresh thyme or 1 teaspoon dried

1/2 cup reduced-sodium vegetable broth

1 tablespoon reduced-sodium soy sauce

3 cups low-fat (1%) milk

2 cups water

1/2 teaspoon salt

1/4 teaspoon freshly ground pepper

1 cup instant polenta

2 ounces fresh (mild) goat cheese

1/2 cup shredded fontina cheese

1/4 cup chopped fresh parsley

1 Heat the oil in a large nonstick skillet set over medium-high heat. Add the shallots and cook, stirring, 1 minute. Add the mushrooms and thyme; cook, stirring, until the mushroom juices have evaporated, about 6 minutes. Add the broth and soy sauce; cook until slightly reduced, 2–3 minutes. Remove the skillet from the heat; keep warm.

2 Combine the milk, water, salt, and pepper in a large saucepan and set over medium-high heat. Bring to a boil, then whisk in the polenta in a slow, steady stream. Reduce the heat to medium and cook, stirring constantly, until the polenta is thick and creamy, about 5 minutes. Remove the saucepan from the heat and stir in the goat cheese and fontina until melted. Divide the polenta evenly among 6 shallow bowls; top with the mushroom sauce and sprinkle with the parsley. Serve at once.

PER SERVING (2/3 cup polenta and 1/3 cup mushroom sauce): 275 Cal, 10 g Fat, 5 g Sat Fat, 0 g Trans Fat, 23 mg Chol, 535 mg Sod, 35 g Carb, 4 g Fib, 14 g Prot, 240 mg Calc. POINTS value: 6.

EXPRESS LANE

Save time by using pre-sliced mushrooms. You can also use pre-sliced portobello mushrooms, but cut the slices in half or in thirds so they aren't too large.

Grilled Portobello Mushroom and Onion "Burgers"

HANDS-ON PREP 10 MIN ■ COOK 15 MIN ■ SERVES 4

4 large portobello mushrooms (about 1 pound), stemmed

2 tablespoons + 2 teaspoons fat-free Italian dressing

1/4 teaspoon salt

1/4 teaspoon freshly ground pepper

4 (1/2-inch-thick) slices onion

4 multigrain hamburger rolls, split

1 cup baby arugula

4 thick slices tomato

2 ounces fresh (mild) goat cheese

1   Spray the grill rack with nonstick spray. Preheat the grill to high or prepare a hot fire.

2   Brush the portobellos with 2 tablespoons of the dressing, then sprinkle with the salt and pepper. Place the mushrooms and onions on the grill rack. Grill, turning once, until softened, about 12 minutes.

3   Line the bottoms of the rolls with the arugula. Top each with a mushroom, stem side up, a slice of onion, and a slice of tomato. Drizzle with the remaining 2 teaspoons of dressing. Spread one-fourth of the goat cheese on the cut side of each roll top and place on top.

PER SERVING (1 burger): 220 Cal, 6 g Fat, 3 g Sat Fat, 0 g Trans Fat, 13 mg Chol, 664 mg Sod, 36 g Carb, 5 g Fib, 9 g Prot, 142 mg Calc.
POINTS value: 4.

HOW WE DID IT

To prevent the onion slices from falling apart on the grill, we suggest using narrow metal skewers to hold them together. Push a skewer through the side of each onion so the rings stay together. Use a medium onion that is slightly smaller in diameter than the portobellos.

Cheddar, Corn, and Tortilla Casserole

HANDS-ON PREP 20 MIN ■ COOK 50 MIN ■ SERVES 4

4 (6-inch) corn tortillas

1 red bell pepper, seeded and cut into thin strips

1 large onion, thinly sliced

2 garlic cloves, finely chopped

1/2 teaspoon ancho chile powder

1/2 teaspoon dried oregano

1/2 teaspoon salt

1 (15-ounce) can creamed corn

2 large eggs

3 egg whites

2/3 cup shredded reduced-fat Monterey Jack cheese

1 teaspoon hot pepper sauce

1 Preheat the oven to 375°F. Spray a 1½-quart baking dish with nonstick spray. Stack the tortillas and cut into 1½-inch-wide strips. Place the strips on a baking sheet in one layer. Bake until lightly golden, about 6 minutes; set aside.

2 Spray a large nonstick skillet with nonstick spray and set over medium heat. Add the bell pepper, onion, garlic, ancho chile powder, oregano, and salt; cook, stirring, until softened, about 6 minutes. Remove the skillet from the heat and let cool.

3 Meanwhile, combine the creamed corn, eggs, egg whites, 1/3 cup of the Monterey Jack cheese, and the pepper sauce in a large bowl. Stir in the vegetable mixture. Spoon about half the mixture into the baking dish. Arrange half the tortilla strips on top. Spoon the remaining vegetable mixture on top and cover with the remaining tortilla strips. Sprinkle with the remaining 1/3 cup of Monterey Jack. Bake until golden and set in the center, 35–40 minutes.

PER SERVING (1/4 of casserole): 261 Cal, 8 g Fat, 4 g Sat Fat, 0 g Trans Fat, 120 mg Chol, 909 mg Sod, 36 g Carb, 4 g Fib, 14 g Prot, 210 mg Calc.
POINTS value: 5.

PLAN AHEAD

The tortilla strips can be baked up to 2 days ahead and stored (when cool) in a zip-close plastic bag. The vegetable mixture can be cooked up to 6 hours ahead and set aside. The cheese can be shredded and stored in the refrigerator in a zip-close plastic bag up to 2 days.

Indian-Style Mixed Vegetable Stew ✓

HANDS-ON PREP 15 MIN ■ COOK 35 MIN ■ SERVES 6

2 tablespoons canola oil

1 large onion, chopped

1 tablespoon minced peeled fresh ginger

3 garlic cloves, finely chopped

1 tablespoon curry powder

1 (14 1/2-ounce) can diced tomatoes

1 (14 1/2-ounce) can reduced-sodium vegetable broth

1 (1 1/4-pound) eggplant, peeled and cut into 1-inch chunks

1 large zucchini, cut into 1-inch chunks

3 large carrots, sliced on the diagonal

1/2 pound Yukon Gold potatoes, peeled and cut into 1-inch chunks

1/2 teaspoon salt

1/4 teaspoon freshly ground pepper

1 (10-ounce) box frozen cauliflower florets, thawed

1 (15 1/2-ounce) can chickpeas, rinsed and drained

2 teaspoons dried mint

1 Heat the oil in a nonstick Dutch oven or pot set over medium heat. Add the onion, ginger, and garlic; cook, stirring, until softened, about 4 minutes. Stir in the curry powder and cook until fragrant, about 1 minute.

2 Add the tomatoes and broth and bring to a simmer. Add the eggplant, zucchini, carrots, potatoes, salt, and pepper. Simmer, covered, stirring occasionally, until softened, about 20 minutes. Stir in the cauliflower and chickpeas; simmer, covered, until heated through, about 3 minutes. Sprinkle with the mint.

PER SERVING (1 1/4 cups): 131 Cal, 2 g Fat, 0 g Sat Fat, 0 g Trans Fat, 0 mg Chol, 480 mg Sod, 25 g Carb, 7 g Fib, 6 g Prot, 58 mg Calc.
POINTS value: 2.

TRY IT

Sprinkling the stew with refreshing, crispy dried mint leaves adds an additional flavor dimension and an enticing aroma to this stew.

Dried Apricot, Chickpea, and Bulgur Pilaf

HANDS-ON PREP 15 MIN ■ COOK 25 MIN ■ SERVES 6

1 tablespoon olive oil

1 onion, chopped

1 1/2 teaspoons ground cumin

1/4 teaspoon cinnamon

1 cup bulgur

1 (15 1/2-ounce) can chickpeas, rinsed and drained

1 (14 1/2-ounce) can reduced-sodium vegetable broth

8 dried apricots, cut into 1/4-inch pieces

1/2 teaspoon salt

1/4 teaspoon freshly ground pepper

2 scallions, chopped

1 Heat the oil in a medium nonstick saucepan set over medium heat. Add the onion and cook, stirring, until softened, about 4 minutes. Add the cumin and cinnamon; cook, stirring, until fragrant, about 1 minute. Stir in the bulgur and cook, stirring, 2 minutes.

2 Stir in the chickpeas, broth, apricots, salt, and pepper. Reduce the heat and simmer, covered, until the liquid is absorbed, 15–18 minutes. Remove the saucepan from the heat and let stand 5 minutes; fluff the pilaf with a fork. Sprinkle with the scallions and serve.

PER SERVING (3/4 cup): 246 Cal, 4 g Fat, 1 g Sat Fat, 0 g Trans Fat, 0 mg Chol, 449 mg Sod, 4 g Carb, 9 g Fib, 9 g Prot, 78 mg Calc.
POINTS value: 4.

FOOD NOTE

Pilaf (also known as *pilau*) is a grain-based dish that originated in the Middle East and is now also very popular in India. All pilafs begin the same way: onion is cooked in oil, then the pilaf grain is added and cooked until toasted before the liquid and/or vegetables, meat, poultry, or seafood and seasonings are added. A classic pilaf is rice-based, but bulgur makes a fine pilaf as well.

Quinoa, Fennel, and Sun-Dried Tomato Pilaf ☑

HANDS-ON PREP 15 MIN ■ COOK 20 MIN ■ SERVES 4

2 teaspoons olive oil

1 fennel bulb, cored and chopped, fronds reserved

1 onion, finely chopped

1 celery stalk, finely chopped

1 carrot, finely chopped

2 garlic cloves, finely chopped

1/2 teaspoon dried thyme

1 cup quinoa, well rinsed

1 1/2 cups reduced-sodium vegetable broth

1/2 teaspoon salt

1/8 teaspoon freshly ground pepper

6 sun-dried tomatoes (not oil-packed), cut into 1/4-inch pieces

6 pitted brine-cured kalamata olives, chopped

1 Heat the oil in a large nonstick saucepan set over medium heat. Add the fennel, onion, celery, carrot, garlic, and thyme; cook, stirring, until softened, about 5 minutes.

2 Stir in the quinoa and cook, stirring, 2 minutes. Add the broth, salt, and pepper; bring to a boil. Reduce the heat and simmer, covered, 10 minutes. Stir in the sun-dried tomatoes and olives; simmer, covered, until the liquid is absorbed, about 5 minutes longer. Remove the saucepan from the heat; let stand 5 minutes. Fluff with a fork. Spoon into a serving bowl and garnish with the reserved fennel fronds.

PER SERVING (about 1 1/3 cups): 232 Cal, 6 g Fat, 1 g Sat Fat, 0 g Trans Fat, 0 mg Chol, 779 mg Sod, 39 g Carb, 6 g Fib, 8 g Prot, 80 mg Calc.
POINTS value: 4.

FOOD NOTE

To the Incas, quinoa (KEEN-wah) was considered the "mother grain." Today it is sometimes called a super-grain, as it contains more protein than any other grain. But more important, quinoa is a complete protein because it has all eight essential amino acids. Don't be fooled by the tininess of the grains; when cooked, they swell to four times their original size.

Spicy Black Bean Cakes with Tomato Salsa

HANDS-ON PREP 20 MIN ■ COOK 15 MIN ■ SERVES 6

1 cup canned black beans, rinsed and drained

1/2 red bell pepper, seeded and chopped

2 scallions, finely chopped

1/4 cup chopped fresh cilantro

1/2 jalapeño pepper, seeded and minced (wear gloves to prevent irritation)

1 cup all-purpose flour

1 teaspoon baking powder

1/2 teaspoon ground cumin

1/2 teaspoon salt

3/4 cup low-fat (1%) milk

3 large eggs

1 tablespoon canola oil

3/4 cup prepared tomato salsa

6 tablespoons Greek-style fat-free yogurt

1 Combine the black beans, bell pepper, scallions, cilantro, and jalapeño in a medium bowl. Whisk together the flour, baking powder, cumin, and salt in a large bowl. Beat the milk, eggs, and oil in a medium bowl; stir into the flour mixture until moistened. Add the bean mixture and stir until well combined.

2 Spray a large nonstick skillet with nonstick spray and set over medium heat until a drop of water sizzles in it. Spoon the batter into the skillet by 1/4 cupfuls. Cook until the tops of the cakes are covered with bubbles and the edges look dry, 2–3 minutes. Turn and cook until lightly browned, about 1 1/2 minutes longer. Transfer to a plate; keep warm while cooking the remaining cakes. Serve with the salsa and yogurt.

PER SERVING (2 cakes, 2 tablespoons salsa, and 1 tablespoon yogurt): 230 Cal, 6 g Fat, 1 g Sat Fat, 0 g Trans Fat, 108 mg Chol, 493 mg Sod, 35 g Carb, 4 g Fib, 11 g Prot, 170 mg Calc. *POINTS* value: 4.

PLAN AHEAD

Why not cook up a double batch of these lusciously tasty cakes to enjoy at another time? After cooking up the cakes, set them on a wire rack and let cool completely. Stack them between sheets of wax paper and place in a zip-close plastic freezer bag. Press out all the air and seal the bag, then date and label. Freeze up to 3 months. Take out as many cakes as you like, place them in a single layer on a rack in the oven or toaster oven and heat through.

Spinach and Lentils ☑

HANDS-ON PREP 10 MIN ■ COOK 30 MIN ■ SERVES 4

3 cups water

1 cup brown lentils

1/2 pound flat-leaf spinach, trimmed

1 teaspoon olive oil

1 onion, chopped

3 garlic cloves, finely chopped

1/4 cup reduced-sodium vegetable broth

2 tablespoons apple-cider vinegar

1/2 teaspoon salt

1/4 teaspoon freshly ground pepper

1 Bring the water and lentils to a boil in a medium saucepan set over medium-high heat. Reduce the heat and simmer, covered, until the lentils are tender but retain their shape, 15–20 minutes. Drain, then transfer to a serving bowl; keep warm.

2 Meanwhile, spray a large nonstick skillet with nonstick spray and set over medium-high heat. Shake the spinach to remove some of the excess water; add the spinach to the skillet and cook, covered, until wilted, 3–4 minutes; drain off any water. Add the spinach to the lentils.

3 Wipe the skillet dry with paper towels; add the oil and set over medium heat. Add the onion and garlic; cook, stirring until softened, about 4 minutes. Add the broth, vinegar, salt, and pepper; bring to a simmer. Add the lentil mixture to the skillet and cook, stirring, just until heated through, about 2 minutes.

PER SERVING (about 3/4 cup): 196 Cal, 2 g Fat, 0 g Sat Fat, 0 g Trans Fat, 0 mg Chol, 341 mg Sod, 33 g Carb, 13 g Fib, 14 g Prot, 66 mg Calc.
POINTS value: 3.

GOOD IDEA

There are several leafy greens that you can use in this recipe besides spinach. Escarole, broccolini, kale, and mustard greens are all tasty possibilities. You can also use almost any vinegar you have on hand, including red-wine, white-wine, or sherry.

Potato, Gruyère, and Tofu Casserole

HANDS-ON PREP 10 MIN ■ COOK 1 HR 20 MIN ■ SERVES 4

½ pound reduced-fat firm tofu, cut into ½-inch-thick slices

2 teaspoons olive oil

1 large onion, sliced

2 garlic cloves, finely chopped

1¾ pounds red potatoes, peeled and cut into ¼-inch-thick slices

2 teaspoons finely chopped fresh rosemary

1 teaspoon chopped fresh thyme

½ teaspoon salt

¼ teaspoon freshly ground pepper

½ cup shredded Gruyère cheese

1¼ cups reduced-sodium vegetable broth

1 Line a baking sheet with a double layer of paper towels. Place the tofu on top and cover with another double layer of paper towels. Cover with another baking sheet and weight with 2 large food cans, such as cans of tomatoes. Let stand 15 minutes; then pat the tofu dry with more paper towels.

2 Preheat the oven to 375°F. Spray a 2-quart shallow baking dish with nonstick spray.

3 Meanwhile, heat the oil in a large nonstick skillet set over medium heat. Add the onion and garlic; cook, stirring, until golden, about 8 minutes.

4 Toss together the potatoes, onion mixture, rosemary, thyme, salt, and pepper in a large bowl. Spoon half of the potato mixture in the baking dish, pressing down lightly. Top with the tofu and ¼ cup of the Gruyère. Top with the remaining potato mixture; pour in the broth, then sprinkle with the remaining ¼ cup of Gruyère.

5 Cover tightly with foil and bake 45 minutes. Uncover and bake until the potatoes are tender and the cheese is melted and golden, about 15 minutes longer.

PER SERVING (¼ of casserole): 224 Cal, 7 g Fat, 3 g Sat Fat, 0 g Trans Fat, 15 mg Chol, 584 mg Sod, 26 g Carb, 4 g Fib, 13 g Prot, 175 mg Calc.
POINTS value: 4.

ZAP IT

Any leftovers can be quickly heated in the microwave. Heat one portion (about ½ cup) on High until heated through, 2–3 minutes.

Barley Salad with Apples, Grapes, and Walnuts

HANDS-ON PREP 15 MIN ■ COOK 35 MIN ■ SERVES 6

3 cups water

2/3 cup pearl barley

3/4 teaspoon salt

1/4 cup low-fat sour cream

2 tablespoons reduced-fat mayonnaise

1 tablespoon fresh lemon juice

1 teaspoon honey

1 large unpeeled apple, such as Braeburn, Gala, or Empire, cored, and cut into 1/2-inch dice

1 cup seedless red grapes, halved

1/3 cup walnuts, toasted and chopped

1 Combine the water, barley, and salt in a medium saucepan and bring to a boil over medium-high heat. Reduce the heat and simmer, covered, until tender, about 30 minutes. Drain in a colander, then rinse under cold running water to stop the cooking; set aside.

2 Stir together the sour cream, mayonnaise, lemon juice, and honey in a serving bowl. Add the barley, apple, grapes, and walnuts; toss gently to coat evenly.

PER SERVING (generous 3/4 cup): 205 Cal, 6 g Fat, 1 g Sat Fat, 0 g Trans Fat, 1 mg Chol, 85 mg Sod, 35 g Carb, 6 g Fib, 4 g Prot, 37 mg Calc.

POINTS value: 4.

FOOD NOTE

This salad is a grain-based rendition of the traditional Waldorf salad, which was created at the Waldorf-Astoria Hotel in 1896 by maître d'hotel Oscar Tschirky. The original salad contained only three ingredients—apples, celery, and mayonnaise—but by 1928 walnuts had been included. For a bit of sweetness, we've added grapes and left out the celery, which you can add if you like.

CHAPTER NINE

Simple Sides

Roasted Asparagus with Lemon and Chives ☑

HANDS-ON PREP 15 MIN ■ COOK 20 MIN ■ SERVES 4

1 (1-pound) bunch asparagus, trimmed

2 teaspoons olive oil

1/4 teaspoon salt

1/8 teaspoon freshly ground pepper

1 tablespoon fresh lemon juice

2 tablespoons chopped fresh chives

1 Preheat the oven to 425°F.

2 Put the asparagus in a shallow roasting pan. Drizzle with the oil and sprinkle with the salt and pepper; toss to coat evenly. Spread in a single layer and bake, shaking the pan occasionally, until tender and browned in spots, about 20 minutes. Transfer the asparagus to a platter; sprinkle with the lemon juice and chives.

PER SERVING (4–6 spears): 37 Cal, 3 g Fat, 0 g Sat Fat, 0 g Trans Fat, 0 mg Chol, 148 mg Sod, 3 g Carb, 1 g Fib, 2 g Prot, 15 mg Calc.
POINTS value: 1.

GOOD IDEA

Give the asparagus even more flavor by grating fresh Parmesan cheese on top just before serving. For a special occasion, use a vegetable peeler to make Parmesan shavings (2 tablespoons of grated Parmesan cheese will increase the per-serving **POINTS** by *1*). Be sure to deduct it from your **weekly POINTS Allowance.**

Beet Greens with Golden Onion ☑

HANDS-ON PREP 10 MIN ■ COOK 15 MIN ■ SERVES 4

4 teaspoons olive oil

1 onion, thinly sliced

1 bunch beet greens or red Swiss chard, stems thinly sliced and greens thickly sliced

¼ teaspoon salt

⅛ teaspoon freshly ground pepper

Heat the oil in a large nonstick skillet set over medium heat. Add the onion and cook until deep golden, 8–10 minutes. Stir in the beet greens, salt, and pepper; cook, stirring occasionally, until tender, about 5 minutes.

PER SERVING (½ cup): 68 Cal, 5 g Fat, 1 g Sat Fat, 0 g Trans Fat, 0 mg Chol, 299 mg Sod, 6 g Carb, 2 g Fib, 2 g Prot, 56 mg Calc.
POINTS value: 1.

FOOD NOTE

Beet greens are the leafy tops of beets. They are sweet, tasty, and chock-full of vitamins and minerals. They are available in farmers' markets in early summer and in some supermarkets. Red or green Swiss chard is a good substitute.

Stir-Fried Bok Choy with Shiitake Mushrooms

HANDS-ON PREP 20 MIN ■ COOK 10 MIN ■ SERVES 4

2 teaspoons canola oil

4 (¹/₄-pound) heads baby bok choy, trimmed and sliced

¹/₂ cup reduced-sodium chicken broth

12 fresh shiitake mushrooms, stemmed, caps thickly sliced

1 large red bell pepper, seeded and thinly sliced

6 scallions, cut into 1¹/₂-inch pieces

1 tablespoon reduced-sodium soy sauce

1 teaspoon Asian (dark) sesame oil

1 teaspoon minced peeled fresh ginger

2 garlic cloves, finely chopped

¹/₂ teaspoon crushed red pepper

1 teaspoon sesame seeds, toasted (optional)

Heat the canola oil in a large nonstick skillet or wok set over high heat until a drop of water sizzles in it. Add the bok choy and broth; cook, covered, 1 minute. Add the mushrooms; stir-fry until softened, 2–3 minutes. Add all the remaining ingredients except the sesame seeds; stir-fry, until the bell pepper is softened and the liquid is evaporated, 3–4 minutes. Sprinkle with the sesame seeds if using and serve at once.

PER SERVING (1 cup without sesame seeds): 110 Cal, 4 g Fat, 0 g Sat Fat, 0 g Trans Fat, 0 mg Chol, 271 mg Sod, 15 g Carb, 5 g Fib, 7 g Prot, 124 mg Calc.
POINTS value: 2.

MAKE IT CORE

To fit this recipe into the **Core Plan,** omit the sesame oil and sesame seeds.

Broccoli Rabe with Garlic and Parmesan

HANDS-ON PREP 10 MIN ■ COOK 20 MIN ■ SERVES 4

1 (1¼-pound) bunch broccoli rabe,
   trimmed and coarsely chopped

2 teaspoons olive oil

4 garlic cloves, minced

½ teaspoon salt

¼ teaspoon crushed red pepper

¼ cup grated Parmesan cheese

1 Bring a large pot of water to a boil over medium-high heat. Add the broccoli rabe and cook until the thickest stems are tender, about 3 minutes. Drain; set aside.

2 Heat the oil in a large nonstick skillet set over medium heat. Add the garlic and cook, stirring, until fragrant, about 1 minute. Add the broccoli rabe and sprinkle with the salt and crushed red pepper; cook, stirring, until coated with the oil and heated through, about 2 minutes. Spoon into a serving bowl and sprinkle with the Parmesan.

PER SERVING (1 cup): 162 Cal, 4 g Fat, 1 g Sat Fat, 0 g Trans Fat, 4 mg Chol, 418 mg Sod, 7 g Carb, 3 g Fib, 6 g Prot, 128 mg Calc.
POINTS value: 3.

TRY IT

Broccoli rabe, also known as *broccoli di rape,* is a slightly bitter green that is greatly appreciated by Italian families. Boiling it in lots of water tames its bitterness and tenderizes the tough stems, while sautéing it with garlic and crushed red pepper makes it delicious. Look for leaves that are firm with small green (not yellowing) bud clusters.

Brussels Sprouts with Raisins

HANDS-ON PREP 10 MIN ■ COOK 8 MIN ■ SERVES 4

1 (10-ounce) container Brussels sprouts, trimmed and cut lengthwise in half

½ cup raisins

2 teaspoons grated lemon zest

2 tablespoons fresh lemon juice

4 teaspoons olive oil

¼ teaspoon salt

¼ teaspoon freshly ground pepper

1 Bring 2 inches of water to a boil in a large saucepan set over medium-high heat. Put the Brussels sprouts in a steamer basket and set in the saucepan. Cook, covered, until tender, 8–12 minutes.

2 Meanwhile, combine the raisins, lemon zest and juice, oil, salt, and pepper in a serving bowl. Add the Brussels sprouts and toss to coat. Serve hot or at room temperature.

PER SERVING (¾ cup): 118 Cal, 5 g Fat, 1 g Sat Fat, 0 g Trans Fat, 0 mg Chol, 163 mg Sod, 19 g Carb, 4 g Fib, 3 g Prot, 19 mg Calc.
POINTS value: 2.

MAKE IT CORE

To fit this recipe into the **Core Plan** substitute ½ cup finely diced apple for the raisins.

Red Cabbage Slaw

HANDS-ON PREP 20 MIN ■ COOK NONE ■ SERVES 4

3 tablespoons fat-free sour cream

1 tablespoon + 1 teaspoon reduced-fat mayonnaise

1/3 cup red-wine vinegar

3 tablespoons sugar

1 tablespoon canola oil

1 teaspoon Dijon mustard

1/2 teaspoon celery seeds

1/4 teaspoon salt

1/8 teaspoon freshly ground pepper

1 small red cabbage (about 1 pound), cored and shredded

2 carrots, shredded

2 scallions, chopped

Whisk together the sour cream, mayonnaise, vinegar, sugar, oil, mustard, celery seeds, salt, and pepper in a large bowl. Add the cabbage, carrots, and scallions; toss well to coat evenly. Serve at once or cover and refrigerate to serve later.

PER SERVING (1 1/2 cups): 133 Cal, 6 g Fat, 1 g Sat Fat, 0 g Trans Fat, 0 mg Chol, 237 mg Sod, 21 g Carb, 3 g Fib, 3 g Prot, 84 mg Calc.
POINTS value: 3.

FOOD NOTE

If you like coleslaw on the crisp side, serve it within 1 hour. And if you prefer it on the soft side, refrigerate up to 4 hours.

Cinnamon-Scented Red Cabbage and Apple

HANDS-ON PREP 15 MIN ■ COOK 1 HR ■ SERVES 4

2 teaspoons canola oil

1 onion, thinly sliced

3 tablespoons packed brown sugar

1 Granny Smith apple, peeled, halved, cored, and sliced

1/2 cup water

1/2 cup orange juice

1 (3-inch) cinnamon stick

1 small red cabbage (about 1 1/2 pounds), cored and shredded

3 tablespoons red-wine vinegar

1/4 teaspoon salt

1/8 teaspoon freshly ground pepper

1 Heat the oil in a Dutch oven set over medium heat. Add the onion and cook until softened, about 4 minutes. Add the brown sugar and cook, stirring, until deep golden, about 8 minutes. Stir in the apple, water, orange juice, and cinnamon stick; cook, stirring, 2 minutes.

2 Stir in the cabbage, vinegar, salt, and pepper; bring to a boil. Reduce the heat to low. Cook, covered, stirring occasionally, until the cabbage is very tender, about 45 minutes. Remove the cinnamon stick before serving.

PER SERVING (1 cup): 140 Cal, 3 g Fat, 0 g Sat Fat, 0 g Trans Fat, 0 mg Chol, 167 mg Sod, 29 g Carb, 4 g Fib, 3 g Prot, 90 mg Calc.

POINTS value: 2.

EXPRESS LANE

Save on your prep time by buying preshredded cabbage, which is available in the produce section of supermarkets. You will need about 8 cups of either green or red cabbage.

Carrots with Ginger-Honey Dressing

HANDS-ON PREP 20 MIN ■ COOK 12 MIN ■ SERVES 4

8 large carrots (about 2 pounds), cut into matchstick strips

1/2 cup water

2 tablespoons unseasoned rice vinegar

1 tablespoon canola oil

2 teaspoons minced peeled fresh ginger

1 teaspoon Asian (dark) sesame oil

1 teaspoon ground cumin

1/2 teaspoon honey

1/2 teaspoon salt

1/4 teaspoon freshly ground pepper

1 tablespoon black sesame seeds (optional)

1 Bring 2 inches of water to a boil in a large pot. Put the carrots in a large steamer basket and set in the pot. Cook, covered, until crisp-tender, about 6 minutes. Drain in a colander, then hold under cold running water to stop the cooking; set aside.

2 To make the dressing, put 1/2 cup of the carrots, the water, vinegar, canola oil, ginger, sesame oil, cumin, honey, salt, and pepper in a blender; puree.

3 Put the remaining carrots in a serving bowl; pour the dressing over and toss to coat evenly. Sprinkle with the sesame seeds if using and serve at once.

PER SERVING (1 cup without sesame seeds): 109 Cal, 5 g Fat, 1 g Sat Fat, 0 g Trans Fat, 0 mg Chol, 342 mg Sod, 16 g Carb, 5 g Fib, 2 g Prot, 44 mg Calc.
POINTS value: 2.

TRY IT

The classic Japanese-style ginger dressing in this recipe is also delicious tossed with a crisp salad of mixed greens, cucumber, and tomatoes. You can prepare a double recipe and store the extra dressing in a covered jar in the refrigerator up to 4 days.

Cauliflower Parmesan

HANDS-ON PREP 15 MIN ■ COOK 40 MIN ■ SERVES 4

1 (2-pound) cauliflower, cut into florets

2 cups prepared fat-free tomato-basil sauce

½ teaspoon dried oregano

⅛ teaspoon freshly ground pepper

Pinch crushed red pepper

¼ cup plain dried bread crumbs

1 cup shredded part-skim mozzarella cheese

2 tablespoons grated Parmesan cheese

1 Preheat the oven to 375°F.

2 Meanwhile, bring a large pot of water to a boil. Add the cauliflower and cook until tender, 8–10 minutes; drain well.

3 Spread 1 cup of the tomato sauce in a 2-quart baking dish; sprinkle with the oregano, ground pepper, and crushed red pepper. Top with the cauliflower and sprinkle evenly with the bread crumbs. Pour the remaining 1 cup of sauce evenly over the crumbs, then sprinkle with the mozzarella and Parmesan. Bake until heated through and the mozzarella is melted, about 20 minutes.

PER SERVING (about 1 cup): 176 Cal, 6 g Fat, 4 g Sat Fat, 0 g Trans Fat, 18 mg Chol, 431 mg Sod, 20 g Carb, 4 g Fib, 12 g Prot, 338 mg Calc.

POINTS value: 3.

GOOD IDEA

Shredding mozzarella is not easy to do, as its soft texture makes the cheese difficult to run neatly across a grater. But there is a way to do it quickly and easily. Pop the chunk of cheese into the freezer until very cold and firmed up, about 30 minutes, then it will shred easily.

Cauliflower with Golden Raisins and Pecans

HANDS-ON PREP 15 MIN ■ COOK 20 MIN ■ SERVES 4

1 (2-pound) cauliflower, cut into florets

2 tablespoons chopped pecans

4 teaspoons olive oil

2 garlic cloves, minced

$\frac{1}{3}$ cup golden raisins

2 tablespoons chopped fresh parsley

$\frac{1}{4}$ teaspoon salt

$\frac{1}{8}$ teaspoon freshly ground pepper

1 Bring a large pot of water to a boil. Add the cauliflower and cook until tender, 8–10 minutes; drain and keep warm.

2 Meanwhile, spread the pecans in a large nonstick skillet and set over medium heat; cook, shaking the pan occasionally, until toasted, about 5 minutes. Transfer to a small bowl; set aside.

3 Heat the oil in the same skillet set over medium heat. Add the garlic and cook, stirring, until golden, about 2 minutes. Add the cauliflower, raisins, pecans, parsley, salt, and pepper; cook, stirring, until heated through, about 2 minutes.

PER SERVING (1$\frac{1}{4}$ cups): 133 Cal, 7 g Fat, 1 g Sat Fat, 0 g Trans Fat, 0 mg Chol, 176 mg Sod, 16 g Carb, 3 g Fib, 3 g Prot, 32 mg Calc.
POINTS value: 3.

PLAN AHEAD

Here's an easy way to keep chopped parsley fresh for several days: Briefly rinse the parsley under cold running water and pat dry with paper towels. Chop the parsley and place in a sieve; hold under cold running water about 30 seconds. Wrap the parsley in a triple layer of paper towels and squeeze until thoroughly dry and fluffy. Transfer the parsley to a paper towel–lined container and refrigerate.

Warm Chile-Spiced Edamame ☑

HANDS-ON PREP 5 MIN ■ COOK 20 MIN ■ SERVES 6

1 (16-ounce) package frozen unshelled edamame (green soybeans)

1 teaspoon canola oil

1 teaspoon salt

1/2 teaspoon chipotle chile powder

1/4 teaspoon freshly ground pepper

1/8 teaspoon cayenne

1 Cook the edamame according to the package directions; drain.

2 Heat the oil in a large nonstick skillet set over medium-high heat. Add the edamame, salt, chipotle chile powder, pepper, and cayenne; cook, stirring frequently, until fragrant, about 1 minute. Serve at once.

PER SERVING (about 1/3 cup): 108 Cal, 4 g Fat, 0 g Sat Fat, 0 g Trans Fat, 0 mg Chol, 418 mg Sod, 9 g Carb, 4 g Fib, 8 g Prot, 52 mg Calc.
POINTS value: 2.

ZAP IT

Leftovers of this dish reheat well in the microwave. Just before serving, microwave on High until heated through, about 40 seconds for each 1/3 cup serving.

Green Beans Oreganato ☑

HANDS-ON PREP 15 MIN ■ COOK 20 MIN ■ SERVES 4

1 pound green beans, trimmed and cut in 1½-inch pieces

4 teaspoons olive oil

3 large shallots, finely chopped (about ½ cup)

2 garlic cloves, finely chopped

1 large tomato, cut into ½-inch dice

½ teaspoon dried oregano

½ teaspoon salt

¼ teaspoon freshly ground pepper

¼ cup packed flat-leaf parsley leaves

1 Bring ½ inch of water to a boil in a large nonstick skillet set over medium-high heat. Add the green beans and cook, covered, until tender, 6–7 minutes; drain in a colander. Rinse under cold running water to stop the cooking; set aside.

2 Wipe the skillet dry. Heat the oil in the skillet set over medium heat. Add the shallots and garlic; cook, stirring, until softened, about 4 minutes. Add the tomato and oregano; cook until the tomato begins to release its juice, about 2 minutes.

3 Add the green beans, salt, and pepper to the skillet; cook, stirring, until heated through, about 2 minutes. Spoon into a serving bowl and sprinkle with the parsley.

PER SERVING (1½ cups): **89 Cal, 5 g Fat, 1 g Sat Fat, 0 g Trans Fat, 0 mg Chol, 160 mg Sod, 11 g Carb, 4 g Fib, 2 g Prot, 59 mg Calc.**
POINTS value: 1.

GOOD IDEA

You can substitute 1 cup of halved cherry tomatoes for the large tomato if you like. And if you have a medium onion on hand, you can use it instead of the shallots.

Creamy Garlic Mashed Potatoes

HANDS-ON PREP 20 MIN ■ COOK 25 MIN ■ SERVES 5

1 1/2 pounds Russet potatoes, peeled and
   cut into 1-inch chunks

4 large garlic cloves, peeled

1/3 cup low-fat (1%) milk

2 tablespoons unsalted butter, cut into
   4 pieces

3/4 teaspoon salt

1/4 teaspoon freshly ground pepper

1 Put the potatoes and garlic in a large saucepan; add enough cold water to cover and bring to a boil. Reduce the heat and simmer, partially covered, until the potatoes are fork-tender, about 15 minutes.

2 Meanwhile, combine the milk, butter, salt, and pepper in a small saucepan and set over medium heat; bring just to a boil. Remove the saucepan from the heat; set aside.

3 Drain the potatoes and garlic; return them to the pot and mash until smooth. With a wooden spoon, gradually stir in the milk mixture until creamy. Serve at once.

PER SERVING (about 2/3 cup): 131 **Cal, 4 g Fat, 3 g Sat Fat, 0 g Trans Fat, 11 mg Chol, 303 mg Sod, 22 g Carb, 2 g Fib, 3 g Prot, 30 mg Calc.**
POINTS value: 3.

PLAN AHEAD

Although mashed potatoes are at their best when freshly made, it is possible to partially prepare them up to 6 hours ahead. Cook the potatoes and garlic as directed, then drain and press through a food mill or potato ricer into a large microwavable bowl. Cover with plastic wrap. To serve, vent the plastic wrap and microwave on High until heated through, about 5 minutes. Meanwhile, heat the milk mixture as directed in step 2. Stir into the hot potatoes as directed in step 3.

German Potato Salad with Turkey Bacon

HANDS-ON PREP 20 MIN ■ COOK 35 MIN ■ SERVES 4

1 1/2 pounds red potatoes, peeled, halved if large

4 slices turkey bacon

Olive oil

1 small onion, chopped

1/4 cup reduced-sodium chicken broth

3 tablespoons white-wine vinegar

1 tablespoon coarse-grained mustard

1 teaspoon sugar

1 teaspoon paprika

1/2 teaspoon mustard powder

2 tablespoons chopped fresh parsley

1 Put the potatoes in a large saucepan; add enough water to cover. Bring to a boil. Reduce the heat and cook, partially covered, until fork-tender, about 20 minutes. When cool enough to handle, cut the potatoes into bite-size chunks and put in a large bowl.

2 Meanwhile, cook the bacon in a medium nonstick skillet until crisp. Drain on paper towels and coarsely crumble over the potatoes. Add enough olive oil to the bacon drippings to equal 2 teaspoons.

3 Heat the oil mixture in the same skillet set over medium heat. Add the onion and cook, stirring, until softened, about 4 minutes. Stir in the broth, vinegar, coarse-grained mustard, sugar, paprika, and mustard powder; bring to a simmer. Pour the hot dressing over the potatoes; toss gently and let stand, covered, until some of the dressing is absorbed, 2–3 minutes. Sprinkle with the parsley and serve hot or warm.

PER SERVING (1 cup): 156 Cal, 2 g Fat, 0 g Sat Fat, 0 g Trans Fat, 10 mg Chol, 277 mg Sod, 24 g Carb, 3 g Fib, 8 g Prot, 15 mg Calc.
POINTS value: 3.

MAKE IT CORE

To fit this tasty salad into the **Core Plan,** substitute 2 or 3 slices of Canadian bacon for the turkey bacon, omit the sugar, and add the full 2 teaspoons of olive oil called for in step 2.

Warm Potato Salad with Lemon-Scallion Dressing

HANDS-ON PREP 20 MIN ■ COOK 15 MIN ■ SERVES 6

1 ³/₄ pounds small red potatoes, scrubbed and quartered

2 tablespoons fresh lemon juice

4 teaspoons olive oil

1 tablespoon dry white wine

³/₄ teaspoon salt

¹/₄ teaspoon freshly ground pepper

3 scallions, chopped

2 tablespoons chopped fresh parsley

1 Put the potatoes in a large saucepan and add enough water to cover. Bring to a boil. Reduce the heat and cook, partially covered, until fork-tender, about 10 minutes. Drain; set aside.

2 Meanwhile, whisk together the lemon juice, oil, wine, salt, and pepper in a large bowl; add the still-warm potatoes and toss to coat well. Add the scallions and parsley; toss to mix.

3 Cover and let stand at least 30 minutes or up to 3 hours to allow the flavors to blend.

PER SERVING (¹/₂ cup): 133 Cal, 3 g Fat, 0 g Sat Fat, 0 g Trans Fat, 0 mg Chol, 329 mg Sod, 25 g Carb, 2 g Fib, 2 g Prot, 16 mg Calc.
POINTS value: 3.

HOW WE DID IT

Combining warm potatoes with dressing is a classic French technique. It allows the potatoes to thoroughly absorb the dressing, making them especially tasty.

Sweet Potato Pancakes

HANDS-ON PREP 15 MIN ■ COOK 15 MIN ■ SERVES 4

2 ($\frac{1}{2}$-pound) sweet potatoes

$\frac{1}{4}$ cup low-fat (1%) milk

1 large egg, separated

4 teaspoons maple syrup + additional
for serving (optional)

$\frac{1}{4}$ teaspoon salt

$\frac{1}{8}$ teaspoon cinnamon

Pinch nutmeg

$\frac{1}{4}$ cup all-purpose flour

$\frac{1}{2}$ teaspoon baking powder

1   Preheat the oven to 425°F. Line a baking sheet with foil. With a fork, pierce the potatoes several times and place on the baking sheet. Bake until soft, about 40 minutes. When cool enough to handle, peel off and discard the skins.

2   Mash the potatoes in a medium bowl. Add the milk, egg yolk, the 4 teaspoons of maple syrup, the salt, cinnamon, and nutmeg, stirring until blended. Whisk together the flour and baking powder in a small bowl; stir into the potato mixture until blended.

3   With an electric mixer on medium speed or with a whisk, beat the egg white in a medium bowl until soft peaks form. With a rubber spatula, gently fold into the potato mixture.

4   Spray a large nonstick skillet with nonstick spray and set over medium heat. Drop the batter into the skillet by slightly rounded tablespoonfuls, flattening slightly to form 6 (2-inch) patties. Cook until golden and set, about $1\frac{1}{2}$ minutes on each side. Transfer to a warm plate; keep warm. Repeat with the remaining potato mixture to make 24 pancakes in all. Serve at once with the additional maple syrup if using.

PER SERVING (6 pancakes without additional maple syrup): 147 Cal, 2 g Fat, 1 g Sat Fat, 0 g Trans Fat, 54 mg Chol, 237 mg Sod, 28 g Carb, 2 g Fib, 4 g Prot, 80 mg Calc.
POINTS value: 3.

GOOD IDEA

These miniature pancakes make a tasty side dish for grilled pork tenderloin, roast turkey, or broiled chicken. Alternatively, make them part of a light vegetarian supper by serving them with a mixed greens salad.

Rice Salad with Bell Peppers and Edamame

HANDS-ON PREP 10 MIN ■ COOK 45 MIN ■ SERVES 4

1 cup brown rice

2 cups water

3 teaspoons olive oil

½ cup frozen shelled edamame (from a 16-ounce package)

1 large red bell pepper, seeded and chopped

2 scallions, thinly sliced

2 tablespoons distilled white vinegar

½ teaspoon sugar

1 Rinse the rice under cold running water; drain. Combine the rice, water, and 1 teaspoon of the oil in a medium saucepan; bring to a boil. Reduce the heat and simmer, covered, until the rice is tender and the liquid is absorbed, about 45 minutes. Remove the saucepan from the heat and let stand, covered, 30 minutes. Fluff the rice with a fork to separate the grains.

2 Meanwhile, cook the edamame according to the package directions.

3 Combine the edamame, bell pepper, scallions, vinegar, the remaining 2 teaspoons of oil, and the sugar in a serving bowl; add the rice and toss to mix well.

PER SERVING (generous 1 cup): 237 Cal, 5 g Fat, 1 g Sat Fat, 0 g Trans Fat, 0 mg Chol, 10 mg Sod, 41 g Carb, 5 g Fib, 6 g Prot, 36 mg Calc.
POINTS value: 4.

FOOD NOTE

Edamame (eh-duh-MAH-may) is Japanese for "beans on branches." These green soybeans are sold in bags, shelled and unshelled, in the frozen vegetable section in supermarkets.

Vegetable Stir-Fried Rice ☑

3 tablespoons reduced-sodium soy sauce

1 tablespoon rice vinegar

1 tablespoon canola oil

1 red bell pepper, seeded and diced

$\frac{1}{4}$ pound fresh shiitake mushrooms, stemmed and sliced

2 teaspoons grated peeled fresh ginger

2 $\frac{1}{2}$ cups cold cooked brown rice

$\frac{1}{3}$ cup thinly sliced scallion

1 cup frozen peas, thawed

$\frac{1}{4}$ teaspoon crushed red pepper

1 Combine the soy sauce and vinegar in a small bowl; set aside.

2 Heat the oil in a large nonstick skillet or wok set over high heat until a drop of water sizzles in it. Add the bell pepper, mushrooms, and ginger; stir-fry until softened, about 3 minutes. Add the rice, stirring well to break up any clumps; stir-fry until heated through, 3–4 minutes.

3 Sprinkle the soy sauce mixture over the rice. Add the scallions, peas, and crushed red pepper; stir-fry 1 minute. Serve at once.

PER SERVING (about $\frac{2}{3}$ cup): 155 Cal, 3 g Fat, 0 g Sat Fat, 0 g Trans Fat, 0 mg Chol, 332 mg Sod, 28 g Carb, 4 g Fib, 5 g Prot, 21 mg Calc.
POINTS value: 3.

HOW WE DID IT

It is traditional to use cold cooked rice for fried rice. The cold rice separates more easily into individual grains than hot rice, and it doesn't readily absorb oil. To chill cooked rice, spread it thinly on a baking sheet and refrigerate until cold, about 1 hour. The chilled rice can then be refrigerated in a covered container up to several days, if you like.

Oven-Roasted Root Vegetables ☑

HANDS-ON PREP 20 MIN ■ COOK 40 MIN ■ SERVES 4

2 carrots, halved or quartered lengthwise and cut into 3-inch pieces

2 parsnips, cut into 1-inch pieces

10 ounces baby potatoes (such as
fingerling and red-skinned),
unpeeled, halved

1 large shallot, thinly sliced

4 teaspoons olive oil

1 tablespoon chopped fresh thyme

¼ teaspoon salt

⅛ teaspoon freshly ground pepper

1 Preheat the oven to 400°F.

2 Combine the carrots, parsnips, potatoes, and shallot in a large nonstick roasting pan; drizzle with the oil and sprinkle with the thyme, salt, and pepper; toss to coat. Spread the vegetables in an even layer. Roast, stirring occasionally, until the vegetables are browned in spots and tender, about 40 minutes.

PER SERVING (½ cup): 119 Cal, 5 g Fat, 1 g Sat Fat, 0 g Trans Fat, 0 mg Chol, 177 mg Sod, 19 g Carb, 3 g Fib, 2 g Prot, 32 mg Calc.
POINTS value: 2.

GOOD IDEA

Use our simple roasting technique for other vegetables: turnips, Brussels sprouts, green beans, cauliflower, and broccoli all take on a tempting sweet flavor when oven-roasted.

Red Cherry, Grape, and Apple Mold

HANDS-ON PREP 15 MIN ■ COOK NONE ■ SERVES 8

2 cups boiling water

2 (3-ounce) packages red cherry– or raspberry-flavored gelatin

1 1/2 cups chilled mandarin orange–flavored sparkling water

1 1/2 cups seedless green or red grapes, halved

1 Gala or Golden Delicious apple, peeled, cored, and cut into 1/2-inch dice

1/3 cup pecans, chopped

1   Lightly spray a 6-cup ring mold with nonstick spray.

2   Pour the boiling water over the gelatin in a medium bowl; stir until the gelatin is completely dissolved. Add the sparkling water. Refrigerate just until thickened, 1 1/2–2 hours. Stir in the grapes, apple, and pecans. Pour the mixture into the ring mold; refrigerate until set, at least 4 hours or up to overnight.

3   To unmold, dip the ring mold in a large bowl of warm (not hot) water for about 10 seconds. Shake the mold back and forth to help loosen the gelatin from the sides of the pan. Invert a flat serving plate on top of the pan and invert. Gently shake the pan to help release the gelatin, then slowly lift off the pan.

PER SERVING (3/4 cup): 128 Cal, 3 g Fat, 0 g Sat Fat, 0 g Trans Fat, 0 mg Chol, 64 mg Sod, 24 g Carb, 1 g Fib, 3 g Prot, 12 mg Calc.
POINTS value: 3.

HOW WE DID IT

A beautiful gelatin mold is clear and contains no bubbles. The key is not to agitate the gelatin more than is necessary. When combining the gelatin and water, stir very slowly and gently with a rubber spatula to avoid creating bubbles. Then carefully stir in the fruit and nuts.

CHAPTER TEN

Slow-Cooker Specials

Mustardy Pot Roast with Vegetables

HANDS-ON PREP 10 MIN ■ COOK 5 HRS 10 MIN ■ SERVES 8

3 tablespoons all-purpose flour

1 teaspoon salt

½ teaspoon freshly ground pepper

1 (2½-pound) beef eye-round roast

1 teaspoon canola oil

1 (24-ounce) bag frozen vegetables
for stew

1 (10¾-ounce) can reduced-sodium
reduced-fat condensed cream of
mushroom soup

1 tablespoon coarse-grained mustard

½ teaspoon Italian seasoning

1 Combine the flour, salt, and pepper in a small bowl. Sprinkle 1 tablespoon of the mixture all over the beef. Heat the oil in a large nonstick skillet set over medium-high heat. Add the beef and cook, turning frequently, until browned, 6–8 minutes.

2 Meanwhile, combine the frozen vegetables and remaining flour mixture in a 5- or 6-quart slow cooker; mix well. Place the beef on top of the vegetables. Combine the soup, mustard, and Italian seasoning in a small bowl; pour over the beef. Cook, covered, until the beef and vegetables are fork-tender, 5–6 hours on high or 10–12 hours on low.

3 Transfer the beef to a cutting board; keep warm. With a slotted spoon, transfer the vegetables to a bowl; keep warm. Pour the sauce into a medium saucepan and bring to a boil over medium-high heat. Continue to boil, stirring occasionally, until reduced to 1½ cups, 6–8 minutes. Cut the beef into 24 slices; arrange on a platter. Spoon the vegetables around the beef and serve with the sauce.

PER SERVING (3 slices beef, ½ cup vegetables, and 3 tablespoons sauce): 252 Cal, 9 g Fat,
3 g Sat Fat, 1 g Trans Fat, 66 mg Chol, 556 mg Sod, 12 g Carb, 1 g Fib, 29 g Prot, 10 mg Calc.
POINTS value: 6.

PLAN AHEAD

Here's how to make a tasty beef stroganoff dinner for 4 later on in the week. Place half of the beef, vegetables, and sauce in separate containers and refrigerate up to 2 days. To prepare the stroganoff, cut the beef into cubes, then combine it with the vegetables and sauce in a medium saucepan. Set over medium heat and cook until heated through. Remove the saucepan from the heat and stir in 6 tablespoons light sour cream. Do not let boil.

Tuscan Beef with Tomatoes ☑

HANDS-ON PREP 10 MIN ■ COOK 4 HR 45 MIN ■ SERVES 8

1 (2½-pound) beef eye-round roast

1 teaspoon salt

½ teaspoon freshly ground pepper

1 teaspoon olive oil

2 onions, sliced

½ pound fresh cremini mushrooms, sliced

4 garlic cloves, minced

1 (28-ounce) can Italian-style crushed tomatoes

½ cup reduced-sodium beef or chicken broth

1 Sprinkle the beef with ½ teaspoon of the salt and ¼ teaspoon of the pepper. Heat the oil in a large nonstick skillet set over medium-high heat. Add the beef and cook until browned on all sides, about 6 minutes.

2 Transfer the beef to a 5- or 6-quart slow cooker. Add the onions, mushrooms, and garlic to the skillet; cook, stirring occasionally, until beginning to brown and soften, 6–7 minutes. Add the tomatoes, broth, the remaining ½ teaspoon of salt, and ¼ teaspoon of pepper; cook, stirring occasionally, until the mixture begins to thicken, 5–6 minutes; pour over the beef. Cook, covered, until the beef is fork-tender, 4–5 hours on high or 8–10 hours on low.

3 Transfer the beef to a cutting board; keep warm. Pour the sauce into a large saucepan and bring to a boil over medium-high heat. Boil, stirring occasionally to prevent the bottom from scorching, until reduced by about one-third, 15–18 minutes. Cut the beef into 16 slices; transfer to a platter. Serve with the sauce.

PER SERVING (2 slices beef and about ½ cup sauce with vegetables): 220 Cal, 5 g Fat, 2 g Sat Fat, 0 g Trans Fat, 65 mg Chol, 689 mg Sod, 11 g Carb, 2 g Fib, 30 g Prot, 15 mg Calc. *POINTS* value: 4.

FOOD NOTE

Beef eye-round roast is cut from the leg eye-round muscle. It is a somewhat elongated piece of boneless meat with a very thin covering of fat. The eye round is naturally very lean, so it benefits greatly from long, slow, moist cooking.

Italian-Style Beef Rolls

HANDS-ON PREP 20 MIN ■ COOK 3 HR 10 MIN ■ SERVES 6

$^1/_2$ cup currants

$^1/_2$ cup hot water

1 cup Italian-seasoned dried bread crumbs

$^1/_2$ cup chopped fresh parsley

$^1/_2$ cup grated Romano cheese

1 tablespoon olive oil

6 ($^1/_4$-pound) beef top round steaks (about $^1/_4$ inch thick)

$^1/_4$ teaspoon freshly ground pepper

1 $^1/_2$ cups fat-free marinara sauce

1 Soak the currants in the hot water in a small bowl about 10 minutes. Drain, reserving 3 tablespoons of the water.

2 Combine the currants, bread crumbs, parsley, Romano, and oil in a medium bowl. Add enough of the reserved water, 1 tablespoon at a time, to bind the filling.

3 Place 1 steak between 2 sheets of wax paper. With a meat mallet or the bottom of a heavy saucepan, pound to $^1/_8$-inch thickness. Repeat with the remaining steaks. Remove and discard the top sheets of wax paper; sprinkle the steaks with the pepper. Press $^1/_4$ cup of the filling onto each pounded steak so it adheres, leaving a $^1/_2$-inch border. From a short end, roll up jelly-roll style. Tie each roll securely with kitchen string.

4 Spray a large nonstick skillet with nonstick spray and set over medium-high heat. Add the steak rolls and cook, turning occasionally, until well browned on all sides, about 8 minutes. Transfer the rolls to a 5- or 6-quart slow cooker. Add the marinara sauce; mix well. Cook, covered, until the beef rolls are fork-tender, 3–4 hours on high or 6–8 hours on low. Remove the strings before serving; serve with the sauce.

PER SERVING (1 roll and $^1/_4$ cup sauce): 310 Cal, 8 g Fat, 3 g Sat Fat, 1 g Trans Fat, 65 mg Chol, 772 mg Sod, 28 g Carb, 2 g Fib, 31 g Prot, 173 mg Calc.
POINTS value: 6.

GOOD IDEA

Serve these savory beef rolls with a side of penne or fusilli ($^1/_2$ cup cooked pasta per serving will increase the **POINTS** value by **2**).

Swiss Steak

HANDS-ON PREP 15 MIN ■ COOK 4 HR 10 MIN ■ SERVES 4

1 (1-pound) beef top round steak

1 teaspoon paprika

1/4 teaspoon salt

1/4 teaspoon freshly ground pepper

3 onions, sliced

3 garlic cloves, minced

1/2 cup reduced-sodium beef or chicken broth

2 tablespoons reduced-sodium soy sauce

1 tablespoon quick-cooking tapioca

1 Sprinkle the steak with the paprika, salt, and pepper. Spray a large nonstick skillet with nonstick spray and set over medium-high heat. Add the steak and cook until browned, about 3 minutes on each side.

2 Combine the onions, garlic, broth, soy sauce, and tapioca in a 5- or 6-quart slow cooker. Place the steak on top of the onion mixture. Cook, covered, until the steak and vegetables are fork-tender, 4–5 hours on high or 8–10 hours on low.

3 Transfer the steak to a cutting board and cut into 8 slices. Serve with the onion mixture.

PER SERVING (2 slices steak and 1/2 cup onion mixture): 216 Cal, 9 g Fat, 4 g Sat Fat, 0 g Trans Fat, 48 mg Chol, 556 mg Sod, 12 g Carb, 2 g Fib, 21 g Prot, 27 mg Calc.
POINTS value: 5.

GOOD IDEA

Swiss steak is defined as a steak that is smothered in moist ingredients. Our version is also tasty prepared with lean flank steak. Serve with a side of mashed potatoes to soak up all the delicious juices (1/2 cup cooked potatoes will increase the per-serving *POINTS* value by *2*).

220   Weight Watchers All-Time Favorites

Classic New England Dinner ☑

HANDS-ON PREP 10 MIN ■ COOK 4 HRS ■ SERVES 6

1 (³/₄-pound) beef top round steak

3 (¹/₄-pound) skinless boneless chicken breast halves

1 (20-ounce) package fresh vegetables and herbs for soup

3 cups water

1 (1.4-ounce) package vegetable soup mix

¹/₂ small head green cabbage (about ¹/₂ pound), cut into 6 wedges

2 (¹/₄-pound) Yukon Gold potatoes, peeled, each cut into 6 wedges

6 tablespoons prepared horseradish, drained

1 Put the steak, chicken, the herbs from the soup package, the water, and vegetable soup mix in a 5- or 6-quart slow cooker. Cook, covered, until the steak and chicken are fork-tender, 3–4 hours on high or 6–8 hours on low.

2 Meanwhile, chop the vegetables from the soup package. Remove the steak and chicken from the slow cooker; set aside. Layer the cabbage, potatoes, and chopped vegetables in the slow cooker. Place the steak and chicken on top of the vegetables. Cook, covered, until the vegetables are fork-tender, 1–2 hours on high or 3–4 hours on low.

3 Transfer the steak and chicken to a cutting board. Cut the steak into 12 slices and each chicken breast half crosswise in half. Discard the herbs; divide the broth and vegetables among 6 large soup bowls. Top with the steak and chicken. Serve with the horseradish.

PER SERVING (2 slices steak, 1 piece chicken, 1¹/₃ cups vegetables, ¹/₂ cup broth, and 1 tablespoon horseradish): 247 Cal, 6 g Fat, 2 g Sat Fat, 0 g Trans Fat, 57 mg Chol, 338 mg Sod, 21 g Carb, 5 g Fib, 27 g Prot, 63 mg Calc.
POINTS value: 5.

FOOD NOTE

You'll find packages of fresh vegetables and herbs for soup in the produce aisle of the supermarket. Most mixes include onions or leeks, carrots, celery, turnips or parsnips, parsley, and sometimes dill. Package sizes vary—you'll need a little over a pound for this recipe. Peel any of the vegetables if necessary.

Favorite Slow-Cooker Meatloaf

HANDS-ON PREP 15 MIN ■ COOK 3 HR ■ SERVES 8

1 1/2 pounds ground unseasoned meat-loaf mix

1 onion, chopped

1 green bell pepper, seeded and chopped

1 egg white

3/4 cup ketchup

1/2 cup Italian-seasoned dried bread crumbs

1 tablespoon Dijon mustard

1/4 teaspoon salt

1/4 teaspoon freshly ground pepper

1 Cover a wire rack small enough to fit in the slow cooker with foil; spray the foil with nonstick spray. Combine the meatloaf mix, onion, bell pepper, egg white, 1/4 cup of the ketchup, the bread crumbs, mustard, salt, and ground pepper in a large bowl; mix well. Shape the mixture into a 5 x 9-inch loaf.

2 Place the meatloaf on the rack in a 5- or 6-quart slow cooker. Spread the remaining 1/2 cup of ketchup over the top of the meatloaf. Cook, covered, until an instant-read thermometer inserted into the center of the meatloaf registers 160°F, 3–4 hours on high or 6–8 hours on low. Transfer to a cutting board and cut into 8 slices.

PER SERVING (1 slice): 192 Cal, 8 g Fat, 3 g Sat Fat, 0 g Trans Fat, 52 mg Chol, 494 mg Sod, 14 g Carb, 2 g Fib, 17 g Prot, 38 mg Calc.

POINTS value: 4.

TRY IT

Look for meatloaf mix—a convenient combination of lean ground beef, pork, and veal—in the meat case at the supermarket. Or use half lean ground beef (7% fat or less) and half ground skinless turkey.

Pork with Cherry-Mustard Glaze

HANDS-ON PREP 15 MIN ■ COOK 4 HR 10 MIN ■ SERVES 10

1 (2½-pound) boneless pork loin

1 teaspoon salt

½ teaspoon freshly ground pepper

1 teaspoon extra-virgin olive oil

1 onion, chopped

1 tablespoon minced peeled fresh ginger

3 garlic cloves, minced

1 (12-ounce) jar cherry preserves

1 tablespoon honey Dijon mustard

1 Sprinkle the pork with the salt and pepper. Heat the oil in a large nonstick skillet set over medium-high heat. Add the pork and cook until browned on all sides, about 6 minutes. Transfer the pork to a 5- or 6-quart slow cooker.

2 Add the onion, ginger, and garlic to the skillet; cook, stirring frequently, until the ginger and garlic begin to brown, about 1 minute. Remove the skillet from the heat; stir in the preserves and mustard. Pour over the pork. Cook, covered, until the pork is fork-tender, 4–5 hours on high or 8–10 hours on low.

3 Transfer the pork to a cutting board and cut into 10 slices. Serve with the sauce.

PER SERVING (1 slice pork and ¼ cup sauce): 258 Cal, 8 g Fat, 3 g Sat Fat, 0 g Trans Fat, 63 mg Chol, 324 mg Sod, 24 g Carb, 0 g Fib, 22 g Prot, 28 mg Calc.
POINTS value: **6**.

HOW WE DID IT

Here is the easiest—and most professional—way to chop an onion: Cut the onion in half through the root end. Place one half, cut side down, on a cutting board. With a large knife, cut lengthwise (straight down) into ¼-inch-thick slices, cutting up to the root end. Cut horizontally (across) to make ¼-inch-thick strips, cutting up to the root end. Slice the onion crosswise to make ¼-inch pieces. Repeat with the remaining onion half.

Fruited Pork Tenderloin

HANDS-ON PREP 15 MIN ■ COOK 3 HR 10 MIN ■ SERVES 4

1 (1-pound) pork tenderloin

3/4 teaspoon salt

1/4 teaspoon freshly ground pepper

1 teaspoon canola oil

1 cup canned cranberry sauce

1/2 cup dried apricots, cut into thin strips

1 tablespoon cornstarch

1/4 teaspoon ground allspice

2 teaspoons grated orange zest

1 Sprinkle the pork with 1/2 teaspoon of the salt and 1/8 teaspoon of the pepper. Heat the oil in a large nonstick skillet set over medium-high heat. Add the pork and cook until browned on all sides, about 6 minutes. Transfer to a 5- or 6-quart slow cooker.

2 Combine the cranberry sauce, apricots, cornstarch, allspice, and the remaining 1/4 teaspoon of salt and 1/8 teaspoon of pepper in a small bowl; pour over the pork, turning to coat. Cook, covered, until the pork is fork-tender, 3–4 hours on high or 6–8 hours on low.

3 Transfer the pork to a cutting board and cut into 8 slices. Stir the orange zest into the sauce and serve with the pork.

PER SERVING (2 slices pork and about 1/4 cup sauce): 295 Cal, 5 g Fat, 2 g Sat Fat, 0 g Trans Fat, 63 mg Chol, 503 mg Sod, 40 g Carb, 2 g Fib, 23 g Prot, 23 mg Calc.
POINTS value: 6.

GOOD IDEA

An arugula or watercress salad makes the perfect accompaniment to this pleasantly sweet and tangy dish (2 cups greens tossed with 1 tablespoon reduced-calorie creamy salad dressing will increase the per-serving **POINTS** value by 1).

Teriyaki Pork

HANDS-ON PREP 15 MIN ■ COOK 3 HR 10 MIN ■ SERVES 4

1 (1-pound) pork tenderloin

¼ cup reduced-sodium soy sauce

1 tablespoon minced peeled fresh ginger

2 garlic cloves, minced

1 tablespoon rice-wine vinegar

1 tablespoon packed light brown sugar

1 tablespoon cornstarch

2 scallions, thinly sliced

1 Spray a large nonstick skillet with nonstick spray and set over medium-high heat. Add the pork and cook until browned on all sides, about 6 minutes. Transfer the pork to a 5- or 6-quart slow cooker.

2 Combine the soy sauce, ginger, garlic, vinegar, brown sugar, and cornstarch in a small bowl; pour over the pork. Cook, covered, until the pork is fork-tender, 3–4 hours on high or 6–8 hours on low. Transfer the pork to a cutting board and cut into 8 slices. Serve sprinkled with the scallions.

PER SERVING (2 slices pork and 2 tablespoons sauce): 167 Cal, 4 g Fat, 1 g Sat Fat, 0 g Trans Fat, 63 mg Chol, 726 mg Sod, 8 g Carb, 0 g Fib, 27 g Prot, 11 mg Calc.
POINTS value: 4.

GOOD IDEA

Leftovers make a tasty filling for Asian-style wraps. Fill a warm 7-inch whole-wheat flour tortilla with 2 slices of warmed-up pork and 2 tablespoons sauce, sprinkle with thinly sliced scallions, and roll up. The **POINTS** value will increase by **1**.

Pork Barbecue Sandwiches

HANDS-ON PREP 10 MIN ■ COOK 3 HR 10 MIN ■ SERVES 6

1½ pounds pork tenderloin

1 cup prepared barbecue sauce

1 onion, minced

1½ teaspoons ancho chile powder

6 kaiser or soft sandwich rolls, split

6 pickle wedges

1 Spray a large nonstick ridged grill pan with nonstick spray and set over medium-high heat. Add the pork and cook until browned on all sides, about 6 minutes. Transfer the pork to a cutting board. When cool enough to handle, cut the pork into ¾-inch chunks and transfer to a 5- or 6-quart slow cooker.

2 Stir together the barbecue sauce, onion, and ancho chile powder in a small bowl; add to the pork and mix well. Cook, covered, until the pork is fork-tender, 3–4 hours on high or 6–8 hours on low.

3 With two forks or with your finger, shred the pork. Spoon ½ cup of the pork mixture onto each roll; serve with the wedge.

PER SERVING (1 sandwich and 1 pickle wedge): 299 Cal, 7 g Fat, 2 g Sat Fat, 0 g Trans Fat, 63 mg Chol, 722 mg Sod, 30 g Carb, 2 g Fib, 27 g Prot, 80 mg Calc.

POINTS value: 6.

FOOD NOTE

Pulled pork is the traditional barbecue of North Carolina, where it is often made from a whole hog. The pork is slow-cooked over hickory wood for up to 16 hours or until meltingly tender. Our slow-cooker version is surprisingly delicious—and so much easier—and the pork makes great leftovers. Let it cool, then refrigerate in an airtight container up to 3 days. Reheat on the stovetop or in a microwave.

Pork Chops with Cremini Mushrooms

HANDS-ON PREP 15 MIN ■ COOK 3 HR 5 MIN ■ SERVES 4

4 (1/4-pound) boneless pork loin chops

1/2 teaspoon salt

1/4 teaspoon freshly ground pepper

1 (10 3/4-ounce) can reduced-sodium reduced-fat condensed cream of mushroom soup

1/4 cup water

4 carrots, chopped

1/4 pound fresh cremini mushrooms, sliced

1 teaspoon Worcestershire sauce

1 teaspoon dried oregano

1/2 teaspoon dried thyme

1 Sprinkle the pork chops with the salt and pepper. Spray a large nonstick skillet with nonstick spray and set over medium-high heat. Add the pork and cook until browned, about 2 minutes on each side.

2 Combine the soup, water, carrots, mushrooms, Worcestershire sauce, oregano, and thyme in a 5- or 6-quart slow cooker; mix well. Place the pork chops on top of the vegetable mixture. Cook, covered, until the pork and vegetables are fork-tender, 3–4 hours on high or 6–8 hours on low.

PER SERVING (1 pork chop and 1/2 cup vegetables): 230 Cal, 8 g Fat, 3 g Sat Fat, 0 g Trans Fat, 64 mg Chol, 637 mg Sod, 14 g Carb, 3 g Fib, 25 g Prot, 41 mg Calc.

POINTS value: 5.

GOOD IDEA

Serve this classic family fare with a side of steamed red potatoes (1/2 cup cooked potatoes will increase the per-serving **POINTS** value by 1).

Braised Pork Chops with Dates and Thyme

HANDS-ON PREP 15 MIN ■ COOK 3 HR 20 MIN ■ SERVES 4

4 ($\frac{1}{4}$-pound) boneless pork loin chops

$\frac{3}{4}$ teaspoon salt

$\frac{1}{4}$ teaspoon freshly ground pepper

2 teaspoons olive oil

3 onions, thinly sliced

$\frac{1}{2}$ teaspoon dried thyme

24 pitted dates

$\frac{3}{4}$ cup unsweetened apple juice

1 (3-inch) cinnamon stick

2 tablespoons chopped fresh mint

1 Sprinkle the pork chops with $\frac{1}{4}$ teaspoon of the salt and $\frac{1}{8}$ teaspoon of the pepper. Heat 1 teaspoon of the oil in a large nonstick skillet set over medium-high heat. Add the pork and cook until browned, about 2 minutes on each side. Transfer to a plate.

2 Reduce the heat to medium. Heat the remaining 1 teaspoon of oil in the skillet. Add the onions, thyme, and the remaining $\frac{1}{2}$ teaspoon of salt and $\frac{1}{8}$ teaspoon of pepper; cook, stirring occasionally, until the onions are softened and golden, 10–12 minutes. Remove the skillet from the heat; set aside.

3 Put 12 of the dates in the bottom of a 5- or 6-quart slow cooker, spacing evenly; top with the pork chops. Place the onions on top in an even layer; top with the remaining 12 dates. Pour in the apple juice and nestle the cinnamon stick in the onions. Cook, covered, until the pork is fork-tender, 3–4 hours on high or 6–8 hours on low. Remove the cinnamon stick and sprinkle the pork chops with the mint before serving.

PER SERVING (1 pork chop and $\frac{1}{2}$ cup onion mixture): 374 Cal, 10 g Fat, 3 g Sat Fat, 0 g Trans Fat, 63 mg Chol, 481 mg Sod, 50 g Carb, 5 g Fib, 25 g Prot, 55 mg Calc.
POINTS value: 8.

MAKE IT CORE

To fit this recipe into the **Core Plan,** substitute 1 peeled and diced Golden Delicious apple for the dates and use reduced-sodium chicken broth instead of the apple juice.

Kielbasa and Vegetable Paella

HANDS-ON PREP 15 MIN ■ COOK 1 HR 10 MIN ■ SERVES 6

2 teaspoons olive oil

2 red bell peppers, seeded and chopped

1 large onion, chopped

3 garlic cloves, minced

6 ounces reduced-fat kielbasa, sliced

1 (8-ounce) box yellow rice mix

2 cups water

1 (14-ounce) can quartered artichoke hearts, drained

1 (10-ounce) package frozen mixed vegetables, thawed

1 Heat the oil in a large nonstick skillet set over medium-high heat. Add the bell peppers, onion, and garlic; cook, stirring occasionally, until beginning to soften, 2–3 minutes. With a slotted spoon, transfer the vegetables to a 5- or 6-quart slow cooker.

2 Add the kielbasa to the skillet and cook, stirring occasionally, until browned, 5–6 minutes. Add the kielbasa, rice mix, and water to the slow cooker; mix well. Cook, covered, until the rice is tender and the liquid is absorbed, 1–2 hours on high or 3–4 hours on low.

3 About 25 minutes before the cooking time is up, stir the artichoke hearts and thawed vegetables into the slow cooker. Cook, covered, on high until the vegetables are heated through. Serve at once.

PER SERVING (about 1 cup): **244 Cal, 3 g Fat, 1 g Sat Fat, 0 g Trans Fat, 10 mg Chol, 975 mg Sod, 46 g Carb, 4 g Fib, 10 g Prot, 44 mg Calc.**

POINTS value: 4.

FOOD NOTE

The word *paella* has come to mean a Spanish rice dish that often contains chicken, sausage, and a variety of seafood. But the word originally referred only to the pan in which this dish was cooked, *paellera* from the Latin word for "pan." Paella pans, which are shallow, wide, and often with two brightly colored handles, range in diameter from 10 inches to 3 feet!

Provençal Leg of Lamb ☑

HANDS-ON PREP 10 MIN ■ COOK 3 HR 10 MIN ■ SERVES 8

2 teaspoons olive oil

3 garlic cloves, minced

2 tablespoons chopped fresh rosemary

1 tablespoon chopped fresh oregano

1 tablespoon chopped fresh thyme

$1/2$ teaspoon salt

$1/4$ teaspoon freshly ground pepper

1 (2-pound) piece boneless leg of lamb, butterflied

2 tablespoons horseradish mustard

$1/2$ cup reduced-sodium chicken broth

1 bay leaf

1 Combine 1 teaspoon of the oil, the garlic, rosemary, oregano, thyme, salt, and pepper in a small bowl until mixed well. Brush both sides of the lamb with the mustard, then press the herb mixture evenly over the lamb.

2 Heat the remaining 1 teaspoon of oil in a large nonstick skillet set over medium-high heat. Add the lamb and cook until browned on all sides, about 8 minutes. Transfer the lamb to a 5- or 6-quart slow cooker.

3 Add the broth and bay leaf to the skillet; bring to a boil, stirring constantly to scrape the brown bits from the bottom of the skillet. Pour over the lamb. Cook, covered, until the lamb is fork-tender, 3–4 hours on high or 6–8 hours on low. Transfer the lamb to a cutting board and cut into 16 slices. Remove the bay leaf before serving.

PER SERVING (2 slices): 159 Cal, 7 g Fat, 2 g Sat Fat, 0 g Trans Fat, 65 mg Chol, 329 mg Sod, 1 g Carb, 0 g Fib, 21 g Prot, 20 mg Calc.
POINTS value: 4.

FOOD NOTE

When a piece of meat, chicken, or fish is butterflied, it is split open horizontally almost all the way through, then opened up like a book. It is sometimes flattened to an even thickness. If you don't see butterflied leg of lamb in the meat case of your supermarket, ask the butcher to prepare one for you.

Fresh Lemon and Herb Chicken ☑

HANDS-ON PREP 10 MIN ■ COOK 3 HR 10 MIN ■ SERVES 6

3 garlic cloves, minced

1 tablespoon olive oil

1 1/2 teaspoons fines herbes

1 teaspoon salt

1/4 teaspoon freshly ground pepper

1 (3- to 3 1/2-pound) chicken

1/4 cup reduced-sodium chicken broth

3 tablespoons fresh lemon juice

1 teaspoon grated lemon zest

1 Combine the garlic, oil, fines herbes, salt, and pepper in a small bowl. With your fingers, loosen the skin on the breasts, thighs, and legs of the chicken. Rub half the garlic mixture on the meat under the skin. Rub the remaining garlic mixture in the cavity of the chicken.

2 Spray a large nonstick skillet with nonstick spray and set over medium-high heat. Add the chicken, breast side down, and cook until browned on all sides, 6–8 minutes. Transfer to a 5- or 6-quart slow cooker.

3 Add the broth to the skillet; bring to a boil, stirring constantly to scrape the brown bits from the bottom of the skillet; add 1 tablespoon of the lemon juice. Pour the broth mixture over the chicken. Cook, covered, until the chicken is fork-tender, 3–4 hours on high or 6–8 hours on low.

4 About 20 minutes before the cooking time is up, combine the remaining 2 table-spoons of lemon juice and the lemon zest in a bowl. Add the lemon mixture to the slow cooker. Cook, covered, on high until fragrant.

5 Transfer the chicken to a platter; discard the wings. Remove the skin before eating. Skim off any fat from the broth and discard. Slice the chicken and serve with the broth.

PER SERVING (1/6 of chicken and about 1/4 cup broth): 183 Cal, 8 g Fat, 2 g Sat Fat, 0 g Trans Fat, 73 mg Chol, 476 mg Sod, 2 g Carb, 0 g Fib, 24 g Prot, 23 mg Calc.
POINTS value: 4.

TRY IT

Fines herbes (FEEN-erb) is the French term for a fragrant mix of finely chopped herbs, including chervil, chives, parsley, and tarragon. Once you try it, you will use fines herbes again and again to flavor food.

No-Fuss Chicken Mole

HANDS-ON PREP 15 MIN ■ COOK 3 HR 10 MIN ■ SERVES 6

1 (3- to 3½-pound) chicken, wings discarded, cut into 6 pieces, and skinned

2 teaspoons Mexican or taco seasoning

½ teaspoon salt

3 ears of corn, silk and husks removed, each cut crosswise into 4 pieces

1 onion, sliced

½ cup reduced-sodium chicken broth

3 tablespoons prepared mole sauce

1 serrano pepper, sliced into thin rounds (wear gloves to prevent irritation)

1 Sprinkle the chicken with the Mexican seasoning and salt. Spray a large nonstick skillet with nonstick spray and set over medium-high heat. Add the chicken and cook until browned on all sides, 8–10 minutes. Transfer to a 5- or 6-quart slow cooker; add the corn.

2 Combine the onion, broth, mole sauce, and serrano in a medium bowl; pour over the chicken; mix well. Cook, covered, until the chicken and vegetables are fork-tender, 3–4 hours on high or 6–8 hours on low.

3 Arrange the chicken and corn on a platter; spoon the sauce over the chicken.

PER SERVING (1 piece chicken, 2 pieces corn, and ¼ cup sauce): 238 Cal, 9 g Fat, 2 g Sat Fat, 0 g Trans Fat, 67 mg Chol, 452 mg Sod, 15 g Carb, 2 g Fib, 25 g Prot, 16 mg Calc.
POINTS value: 5.

FOOD NOTE

Mole (MOH-lay) is a dark brown Mexican sauce made from dried chiles, nuts, spices, vegetables, and sometimes chocolate. Traditional mole sauce takes a great deal of time to make. But prepared mole is widely available in Latino markets, making this delicious dish a snap to throw together.

Country Chicken with Mushrooms and Leeks

HANDS-ON PREP 20 MIN ■ COOK 4 HR 15 MIN ■ SERVES 6

1 (3- to 3¹/₂-pound) chicken, cut into 6 pieces, and skinned (wings discarded)

1 teaspoon paprika

³/₄ teaspoon salt

¹/₄ teaspoon freshly ground pepper

2 pounds leeks, cleaned, halved length-wise, and cut into ¹/₂-inch-thick slices (white and light green parts only),

¹/₂ pound fresh white mushrooms, sliced

2 carrots, sliced

¹/₂ cup reduced-sodium chicken broth

4 teaspoons quick-cooking tapioca

1 teaspoon poultry seasoning

2 tablespoons chopped fresh dill

1   Sprinkle the chicken with the paprika, ¹/₄ teaspoon of the salt, and ¹/₈ teaspoon of the pepper. Spray a large nonstick skillet with nonstick spray and set over medium-high heat. Add the chicken and cook until browned on all sides, 8–10 minutes. Transfer to a 5- or 6-quart slow cooker.

2   Add the leeks, mushrooms, and carrots to the skillet; cook, stirring occasionally, until the vegetables begin to soften, 4–5 minutes. Add the broth; cook about 2 minutes longer. Pour the vegetable mixture over the chicken. Add the tapioca, poultry seasoning, and the remaining ¹/₂ teaspoon of salt and ¹/₈ teaspoon of pepper to the slow cooker; mix well. Cook, covered, until the chicken is fork-tender, 4–5 hours on high or 8–10 hours on low. Serve sprinkled with the dill.

PER SERVING (1 piece chicken, ¹/₂ cup vegetables, and ¹/₃ cup broth): 216 Cal, 6 g Fat, 2 g Sat Fat, 0 g Trans Fat, 67 mg Chol, 376 mg Sod, 16 g Carb, 2 g Fib, 25 g Prot, 64 mg Calc. *POINTS* value: 4.

GOOD IDEA

Put a thick slice of toasted country-style bread on each plate for sopping up all of the tasty sauce (1 slice of toasted country-style bread will increase the per-serving *POINTS* value by **2**).

Spicy Apricot Chicken

HANDS-ON PREP 20 MIN ■ COOK 3 HR 10 MIN ■ SERVES 4

3 teaspoons Asian (dark) sesame oil

4 (6-ounce) bone-in chicken breast halves, skinned

$1/2$ cup apricot preserves

2 tablespoons unseasoned rice vinegar

3 garlic cloves, minced

1 tablespoon grated minced fresh ginger

1 tablespoon chili garlic sauce

2 teaspoons reduced-sodium soy sauce

1 Heat 2 teaspoons of the sesame oil in a large nonstick skillet set over medium-high heat. Add the chicken breasts and cook until browned, 2–3 minutes on each side. Transfer the chicken to a 5- or 6-quart slow cooker.

2 Combine the remaining 1 teaspoon of sesame oil, the preserves, vinegar, garlic, ginger, chili garlic sauce, and soy sauce in a small bowl; pour over the chicken. Cook, covered, until the chicken is fork-tender, 3–4 hours on high or 6–8 hours on low.

3 Transfer the chicken to a platter; keep warm. Pour the sauce into a small saucepan; bring to a boil over medium-high heat. Cook, stirring occasionally, until slightly thickened, 3–4 minutes.

PER SERVING (1 chicken breast half and about $1/4$ cup sauce): 283 Cal, 7 g Fat, 1 g Sat Fat, 0 g Trans Fat, 76 mg Chol, 342 mg Sod, 27 g Carb, 1 g Fib, 28 g Prot, 26 mg Calc. *POINTS* value: 6.

PLAN AHEAD

Get a jump start on your prep work by marinating the chicken in advance. Combine the sauce ingredients in a large zip-close plastic bag and add the chicken. Squeeze out the air and seal the bag; turn to coat the chicken. Refrigerate, turning the bag occasionally, up to overnight. When ready to cook, skip step 1 and pour the contents of the bag directly into the slow cooker.

Jamaican Jerk Drumsticks

HANDS-ON PREP 10 MIN ■ COOK 3 HR ■ SERVES 4

6 scallions, chopped

2 serrano peppers, stemmed and halved
(wear gloves to prevent irritation)

2 tablespoons fresh lemon juice

2 tablespoons honey

1 tablespoon canola oil

1 tablespoon Jamaican jerk seasoning

1 teaspoon salt

8 chicken drumsticks (about 1 1/2
pounds), skinned

1 Put the scallions, serranos, lemon juice, honey, oil, jerk seasoning, and salt in a blender; process until a smooth paste forms, 1–2 minutes.

2 Combine the drumsticks and jerk paste in a 5- or 6-quart slow cooker; mix well. Cover and cook until the drumsticks are fork-tender, 3–4 hours on high or 6–8 hours on low.

PER SERVING (2 drumsticks): 244 Cal, 13 g Fat, 3 g Sat Fat, 0 g Trans Fat, 71 mg Chol, 1,024 mg Sod, 11 g Carb, 1 g Fib, 22 g Prot, 25 mg Calc.
POINTS value: **6.**

GOOD IDEA

Jerk is the national dish of Jamaica. It is the food, a cooking method, and for many, a way of life. Authentic jerk is made with searingly-hot Scotch bonnet peppers, but we prefer serranos, which are tamer—but not too tame! Serve this chicken with beer and fluffy white rice to help tone down the heat. (A 12-ounce bottle of non-alcoholic beer and 1/2 cup cooked rice with each serving will increase the **POINTS** value by **3**).

Cornish Hens with Tarragon Butter

HANDS-ON PREP 15 MIN ■ COOK 3 HR ■ SERVES 4

4 tablespoons chopped fresh tarragon

1 tablespoon unsalted butter, softened

3/4 teaspoon salt

1/4 teaspoon freshly ground pepper

2 (1 1/2 - to 1 3/4 -pound) Cornish hens

1/2 cup reduced-sodium chicken broth

1/4 cup dry white wine

2 tablespoons quick-cooking tapioca

1/8 teaspoon ground allspice

1/4 cup fat-free half-and-half

1 With a fork, mash 3 tablespoons of the tarragon, the butter, 1/2 teaspoon of the salt and 1/8 teaspoon of the pepper in a small bowl until combined. With your fingers, loosen the skin on the breasts, thighs, and legs of the hens; pat the meat dry with paper towels. Spread the butter mixture on the meat under the skin, then press the skin back in place. Transfer the hens to a 5- or 6-quart slow cooker.

2 Combine the broth, wine, tapioca, allspice, and the remaining 1/4 teaspoon of salt and 1/8 teaspoon of pepper in a bowl; pour over the hens. Cook, covered, until the hens are fork-tender, 3–4 hours on high or 6–8 hours on low.

3 Transfer the hens to a cutting board; cover loosely with foil. Strain the sauce through a sieve set over a small saucepan, pressing the solids through with a rubber spatula. Bring the sauce to a boil over medium-high heat; stir in the remaining 1 tablespoon of tarragon and the half-and-half. Remove the saucepan from the heat. Remove the skin from the hens; cut each in half. Serve with the sauce.

PER SERVING (1/2 hen and 1/3 cup sauce): 246 Cal, 8 g Fat, 3 g Sat Fat, 0 g Trans Fat, 154 mg Chol, 653 mg Sod, 7 g Carb, 0 g Fib, 33 g Prot, 50 mg Calc.
POINTS value: 6.

FOOD NOTE

Fresh tarragon adds a distinctive anise (licorice-like) flavor to this French-inspired dish. If you're not a fan of tarragon, substitute an equal amount of chopped fresh parsley or dill. Cornish hens are just the right size for neat servings. If your butcher carries *poussins* (poo-SAHN), baby chickens, you can use them instead of the hens.

Turkey Breast with 40 Cloves of Garlic ☑

HANDS-ON PREP 20 MIN ■ COOK 4 HR 10 MIN ■ SERVES 12

2 tablespoons chopped fresh rosemary

1 tablespoon chopped fresh sage

1 tablespoon chopped fresh thyme

1 teaspoon salt

¹/₄ teaspoon freshly ground pepper

1 (6-pound) bone-in turkey breast

1 onion, chopped

1 carrot, chopped

1 celery stalk, chopped

40 garlic cloves, unpeeled

1 Combine the rosemary, sage, thyme, salt, and pepper in a small bowl. With your fingers, loosen the skin on the breast. Rub the herb mixture on the meat under the skin, then press the skin back in place.

2 Spray a large nonstick skillet with nonstick spray and set over medium-high heat. Add the turkey, skin side down, and cook until browned on all sides, 6–8 minutes.

3 Combine the onion, carrot, and celery in a 5- or 6-quart slow cooker. Place the turkey, right side up, on top of the vegetables. Add the garlic cloves. Cook, covered, until the turkey is fork-tender and the garlic is very soft, 4–5 hours on high or 8–10 hours on low.

4 Remove the garlic; set aside. Transfer the turkey to a cutting board; remove the skin and carve the breast. Strain the vegetables and broth through a sieve set over a bowl; discard the vegetables but reserve the garlic. Serve the turkey with the broth and garlic.

PER SERVING (¹/₁₂ of turkey, about 2¹/₂ tablespoons broth, and about 3 garlic cloves): 208 Cal, 1 g Fat, 0 g Sat Fat, 0 g Trans Fat, 118 mg Chol, 270 mg Sod, 4 g Carb, 0 g Fib, 43 g Prot, 40 mg Calc.

POINTS value: 4.

GOOD IDEA

We love the combination of fresh rosemary, sage, and thyme with turkey, but you can use any single herb or combination of herbs you like or happen to have on hand. You can also grate some lemon or orange zest and combine it with the herbs for a bit of a citrusy zing.

Turkey Breast with Spice Butter

HANDS-ON PREP 15 MIN ▪ COOK 4 HR ▪ SERVES 12

2 tablespoons unsalted butter, softened

2 garlic cloves, minced

2 teaspoons fennel seeds, crushed

1 teaspoon salt

1/2 teaspoon ground coriander

1/4 teaspoon freshly ground pepper

1 (6-pound) bone-in turkey breast

2 onions, sliced

1/4 cup dry white wine or dry vermouth

2 tablespoons cornstarch

1 With a fork, mash the butter, garlic, fennel seeds, salt, coriander, and pepper in a small bowl until well combined. With your fingers, loosen the skin on the breast. Pat the meat dry with paper towels. Rub the butter mixture on the meat under the skin, then press the skin back in place.

2 Combine the onions, wine, and cornstarch in a 5- or 6-quart slow cooker. Place the turkey on top of the onion mixture. Cook, covered, until the turkey is fork-tender, 4–5 hours on high or 8–10 hours on low.

3 Transfer the turkey to a serving platter; remove the skin and carve the breast. Strain the onions from the broth and discard. Serve the turkey with the broth.

PER SERVING (1/12 **of turkey and about 2**1/2 **tablespoons broth): 215 Cal, 3 g Fat, 2 g Sat Fat, 0 g Trans Fat, 123 mg Chol, 268 mg Sod, 2 g Carb, 0 g Fib, 43 g Prot, 23 mg Calc.** *POINTS* **value: 5.**

HOW WE DID IT

Crushing fennel seeds just before using them brings out all their flavor and fragrance, which greatly adds to the finished dish. To crush the seeds, put them in a small zip-close plastic bag and pound with a mallet or the bottom of a small saucepan until crushed.

Two-Bean Burritos

HANDS-ON PREP 5 MIN ■ COOK 3 HR ■ SERVES 8

1 (14½-ounce) can diced tomatoes with green chiles

1 (15½-ounce) can pinto beans, rinsed and drained

1 (15½-ounce) can black beans, rinsed and drained

1 (8¾-ounce) can corn kernels (no salt added), drained

3 tablespoons Mexican or taco seasoning

8 (8-inch) fat-free flour tortillas, warmed

16 tablespoons light sour cream

1 Pour off ½ cup of the liquid from the diced tomatoes; discard. Combine the tomatoes and the remaining liquid, the pinto beans, black beans, corn, and Mexican seasoning in a 5- or 6-quart slow cooker. Cook, covered, until the flavors are blended, 3–4 hours on high or 6–8 hours on low.

2 With a potato masher or wooden spoon, coarsely mash the bean mixture. Spoon about ½ cup of the bean mixture over each warm tortilla. Top each burrito with 2 tablespoons of the sour cream. Fold two opposite sides of each burrito over the filling, then roll up jelly-roll style to enclose the filling.

PER SERVING (1 burrito): 207 Cal, 4 g Fat, 2 g Sat Fat, 0 g Trans Fat, 12 mg Chol, 804 mg Sod, 35 g Carb, 6 g Fib, 7 g Prot, 66 mg Calc.
POINTS value: 4.

GOOD IDEA

For burritos deluxe, in addition to the sour cream, top the filling in step 2 with salsa and cheddar cheese (2 tablespoons fat-free salsa and 2 tablespoons reduced-fat cheddar cheese with each burrito will increase the **POINTS** value by **2**).

New Orleans Shrimp Gumbo

HANDS-ON PREP 10 MIN ■ COOK 3 HR 25 MIN ■ SERVES 4

2 1/2 tablespoons unsalted butter

3 tablespoons all-purpose flour

1 (14 1/2-ounce) can stewed tomatoes

1 cup reduced-sodium chicken broth

1 (10-ounce) box frozen cut okra

1/2 teaspoon dried thyme

1/4 teaspoon dried oregano

1 1/2 pounds large shrimp, peeled and deveined

2 cups hot cooked white rice (optional)

1 Melt the butter in a small nonstick skillet set over medium-high heat. Add the flour and cook, stirring constantly, until the mixture turns reddish brown, 4–5 minutes.

2 Combine the butter mixture, tomatoes, broth, okra, thyme, and oregano in a 5- or 6-quart slow cooker; mix well. Cook, covered, until the sauce thickens and the okra is tender, 3–4 hours on high or 6–8 hours on low.

3 About 20 minutes before the cooking time is up, stir in the shrimp. Cook, covered, on high until the shrimp are just opaque in the center, about 20 minutes. Spoon the rice if using in each of 4 large mugs or soup bowls and ladle the gumbo on top.

PER SERVING (about 1 1/2 cups without rice): 269 Cal, 9 g Fat, 5 g Sat Fat, 0 g Trans Fat, 271 mg Chol, 839 mg Sod, 16 g Carb, 4 g Fib, 31 g Prot, 143 mg Calc.
POINTS value: 5.

EXPRESS LANE

To save prep time, look for bags of frozen uncooked peeled shrimp in your grocer's freezer. Thaw the shrimp according to the package directions before adding them to the slow cooker in step 3. Also, if you're serving the gumbo with the rice, increase the *POINTS* value by 2 for 1/2 cup.

Stuffed Peppers with Rice and Beans

HANDS-ON PREP 15 MIN ■ COOK 2 HR ■ SERVES 4

1½ cups cooked basmati or brown rice

1 (15½-ounce) can black beans, rinsed and drained

1 small onion, finely chopped

¾ cup grated Parmesan cheese

1 (14½-ounce) can diced tomatoes with mushrooms and garlic

1 teaspoon Italian seasoning

4 assorted color bell peppers, tops cut off and seeded

1 Combine the rice, beans, onion, Parmesan, ¼ cup of the tomatoes, and the Italian seasoning in a large bowl. Spoon ¾ cup of the rice mixture into each of the bell peppers.

2 Stand the bell peppers in a 5- or 6-quart slow cooker. Pour the remaining tomatoes over them. Cook, covered, until the bell peppers are very tender but still hold their shape, 2–3 hours on high or 4–6 hours on low.

PER SERVING (1 stuffed pepper and ¼ cup sauce): 280 Cal, 5 g Fat, 3 g Sat Fat, 0 g Trans Fat, 12 mg Chol, 831 mg Sod, 45 g Carb, 8 g Fib, 14 g Prot, 305 mg Calc.
POINTS value: 5.

FOOD NOTE

Although green bell peppers would be tasty in this easy vegetable entrée, we prefer the sweeter varieties, such as the red, yellow, or orange bell peppers.

CHAPTER ELEVEN

15-Minute Dishes

Tapenade and Roast Beef Crostini

HANDS-ON PREP 10 MIN ■ COOK 2 MIN ■ SERVES 8 (AS AN APPETIZER)

½ baguette, cut on the diagonal into 24 (¼-inch-thick) slices

2 tablespoons prepared tapenade

12 arugula leaves, torn in half

6 thin slices lean deli roast beef (¼ pound), quartered

2 tablespoons crumbled blue, Gorgonzola, or feta cheese

1 Preheat the broiler. Arrange the baguette slices on the broiler rack and broil 3 inches from the heat until lightly browned, about 45 seconds on each side.

2 Spread each baguette slice with ¼ teaspoon of the tapenade; top each with half an arugula leaf and 1 piece of roast beef. Lightly scatter a little of the crumbled cheese over each crostini.

PER SERVING (3 crostini): 101 Cal, 3 g Fat, 1 g Sat Fat, 0 g Trans Fat, 8 mg Chol, 421 mg Sod, 13 g Carb, 1 g Fib, 5 g Prot, 32 mg Calc.
POINTS value: 2.

GOOD IDEA

Look for crumbled blue, Gorgonzola, or feta cheese in plastic pouches or in containers at the supermarket alongside the other cheeses. Just use the amount you need, and save yourself the mess and time of crumbling the cheese yourself.

Spiced Shrimp Salsa ☑

HANDS-ON PREP 15 MIN ■ COOK NONE ■ SERVES 12 (AS AN APPETIZER)

1/2 pound cooked peeled, and deveined shrimp, coarsely chopped

1/2 medium jicama, peeled and diced

2 tablespoons fresh lime juice

2 tablespoons chopped fresh cilantro

1 tablespoon finely chopped red onion

1 teaspoon olive oil

1/4 teaspoon ground cumin

1/8 teaspoon salt

1/8 teaspoon hot pepper sauce

Combine all of the ingredients in a serving bowl. Serve at once or cover and refrigerate up to 8 hours.

PER SERVING (1/4 cup): 33 Cal, 1 g Fat, 0 g Sat Fat, 0 g Trans Fat, 37 mg Chol, 68 mg Sod, 3 g Carb, 1 g Fib, 4 g Prot, 11 mg Calc.
POINTS value: 1.

GOOD IDEA

For added color and crunch, serve vegetables as nature's own salsa scoops: seeded red and yellow bell peppers cut into wedges, radicchio leaves, or large mushrooms cut crosswise in half.

Sesame Beef Satay

HANDS-ON PREP 8 MIN ■ COOK 6 MIN ■ SERVES 4

1/4 cup packed fresh cilantro leaves

1 tablespoon minced peeled fresh ginger

2 garlic cloves, quartered

2 teaspoons Asian (dark) sesame oil

1/2 teaspoon teriyaki sauce

1 pound boneless sirloin steak, trimmed and cut into 1/4-inch-thick slices

2 teaspoons toasted sesame seeds

1 Spray the broiler rack with nonstick spray and preheat the broiler.

2 Put the cilantro, ginger, garlic, sesame oil, and teriyaki sauce in a mini food processor or a blender; process until it forms a paste. Transfer to a medium bowl; add the beef and toss to coat evenly.

3 Thread the beef slices onto 4 (12-inch) metal skewers, piercing each strip in at least two places so it lies flat. Place on the broiler rack and broil 5 inches from the heat, turning once, until cooked through, about 6 minutes. Sprinkle the satay with the toasted sesame seeds just before serving. Serve warm or at room temperature.

PER SERVING (1 skewer): 174 Cal, 8 g Fat, 2 g Sat Fat, 0 g Trans Fat, 64 mg Chol, 77 mg Sod, 1 g Carb, 0 g Fib, 22 g Prot, 12 mg Calc.
POINTS value: 4.

TRY IT

Substitute a tablespoon of chopped pickled ginger slices or 1 teaspoon ground ginger if you're out of fresh ginger.

Beef-Vegetable Fried Rice

HANDS-ON PREP 5 MIN ■ COOK 10 MIN ■ SERVES 4

3 scallions, thinly sliced

2 garlic cloves, minced

½ pound ground lean beef (7% fat or less)

1 teaspoon five-spice powder

½ teaspoon ground ginger

¼ teaspoon crushed red pepper

1 (10-ounce) box frozen mixed vegetables, thawed

2 cups cooked brown rice

1 tablespoon reduced-sodium soy sauce

2 teaspoons hoisin sauce or oyster sauce

1 Spray a large nonstick wok or deep nonstick skillet with nonstick spray and set over high heat until a drop of water sizzles in it. Add the scallions and garlic; stir-fry until fragrant, about 1 minute. Add the ground beef and cook, breaking it apart with a wooden spoon, until browned, about 3 minutes.

2 Add the five-spice powder, ginger, and crushed red pepper; stir-fry until fragrant, about 20 seconds. Add the mixed vegetables and stir-fry 2 minutes. Add the brown rice and stir-fry 2 minutes. Add the soy sauce and hoisin sauce; stir-fry until heated through, about 1 minute.

PER SERVING (1¼ cups): 245 Cal, 4 g Fat, 2 g Sat Fat, 0 g Trans Fat, 31 mg Chol, 259 mg Sod, 35 g Carb, 5 g Fib, 17 g Prot, 47 mg Calc.
POINTS value: 4.

MAKE IT CORE

To fit this recipe into the **Core Plan,** omit the hoisin sauce and add an extra tablespoon of soy sauce.

Stir-Fried Beef and Snow Peas

HANDS-ON PREP 8 MIN ■ COOK 7 MIN ■ SERVES 4

3 scallions, thinly sliced

2 garlic cloves, minced

1 tablespoon minced peeled fresh ginger

³/₄ pound boneless sirloin steak, trimmed and cut into thin 2-inch-long slices

¹/₂ pound fresh snow peas, trimmed, or thawed frozen snow peas

1 cup canned sliced water chestnuts, drained

2 tablespoons reduced-sodium soy sauce

2 tablespoons orange juice

1 teaspoon cornstarch

1 tablespoon water

1 Spray a large nonstick wok or deep skillet with nonstick spray and set over high heat until a drop of water sizzles in it. Add the scallions, garlic, and ginger; stir-fry until fragrant, about 1 minute. Add the beef and stir-fry until browned, about 3 minutes. Add the snow peas and stir-fry about 1 minute. Add the water chestnuts and stir-fry 30 seconds. Stir in the soy sauce and orange juice; bring to a simmer and cook 20 seconds.

2 Stir together the cornstarch and water in a small bowl until smooth. Add to the wok and cook, stirring constantly, until the sauce bubbles and thickens, about 30 seconds.

PER SERVING (1 cup): 132 Cal, 3 g Fat, 1 g Sat Fat, 0 g Trans Fat, 45 mg Chol, 316 mg Sod, 7 g Carb, 2 g Fib, 19 g Prot, 45 mg Calc.
POINTS value: 2.

GOOD IDEA

Turn this tasty dish into a noodle bowl by serving with cooked spaghetti or linguine (¹/₂ cup cooked spaghetti will increase the per-serving POINTS value by 2).

Hungarian-Style Pork Chops with Baby Spinach ☑

HANDS-ON PREP 7 MIN ■ COOK 8 MIN ■ SERVES 4

4 (¹/₄-pound) boneless pork loin chops, trimmed

¹/₂ teaspoon salt

¹/₄ teaspoon freshly ground pepper

³/₄ cup reduced-sodium chicken broth

1 teaspoon onion powder

1 (5- to 6-ounce) bag baby spinach

2 tablespoons fat-free sour cream

2 tablespoons paprika

1 Place the pork chops between 2 sheets of wax paper. Pound to ¹/₄-inch thickness using the smooth side of a meat mallet or the bottom of a heavy saucepan. Season the chops with the salt and pepper.

2 Spray a large nonstick skillet with nonstick spray and set over medium-high heat. Add the pork chops and cook until browned and cooked through, about 2 minutes on each side. Transfer to a plate; keep warm.

3 Add the broth to the skillet, scraping up any browned bits from the bottom of the pan. Stir in the onion powder and spinach. Reduce the heat and simmer, covered, about 1 minute.

4 Stir in the sour cream and paprika; cook until heated through, about 30 seconds (do not let boil). Slip the pork chops and any accumulated juices into the sauce, stirring well until blended.

PER SERVING (1 chop and ¹/₃ cup sauce with spinach): **224 Cal, 9 g Fat, 3 g Sat Fat, 0 g Trans Fat, 70 mg Chol, 664 mg Sod, 9 g Carb, 4 g Fib, 28 g Prot, 95 mg Calc.**
POINTS value: 4.

FOOD NOTE

Paprika can taste mildly sweet or devilishly hot. The powder is made from a wide variety of peppers from Spain, Morocco, California, or Hungary. Paprika is an absolute must-have ingredient for paprikash and other goulash-type dishes.

Pan-Fried Chicken Cutlets with Chunky Nectarine Salsa ☑

HANDS-ON PREP 8 MIN ■ COOK 6 MIN ■ SERVES 4

2 large nectarines, halved, pitted, and chopped

1/4 cup chopped onion

1/4 cup chopped fresh basil

2 teaspoons balsamic vinegar

3/4 teaspoon salt

1/2 teaspoon freshly ground pepper

2 tablespoons yellow cornmeal

2 egg whites

4 (1/4-pound) thin-sliced chicken breast cutlets

2 teaspoons canola oil

1 To make the salsa, combine the nectarines, onion, basil, vinegar, 1/4 teaspoon of the salt, and 1/4 teaspoon of pepper in a small bowl; set aside.

2 Combine the cornmeal, the remaining 1/2 teaspoon salt and 1/4 teaspoon pepper on a sheet of wax paper. Lightly beat the egg whites in a shallow bowl. Dip the chicken cutlets, one at a time, in the egg whites, then coat with the cornmeal mixture, pressing firmly so it adheres.

3 Heat the oil in a large nonstick skillet set over medium-high heat. Add the chicken and cook, turning once, until lightly browned and cooked through, about 3 minutes on each side. Serve with the salsa.

PER SERVING (1 piece chicken and generous 1/3 cup salsa): 207 Cal, 5 g Fat, 1 g Sat Fat, 0 g Trans Fat, 63 mg Chol, 519 mg Sod, 14 g Carb, 2 g Fib, 26 g Prot, 25 mg Calc.
POINTS value: 4.

TRY IT

Look for blue cornmeal in specialty food stores and Latino groceries and use it instead of the more typical yellow variety. It has the same crunchy texture as regular cornmeal, but its unusual color is guaranteed to be a conversation starter. It's also great in corn muffins.

Spicy Moroccan Chicken Soup ☑

HANDS-ON PREP 5 MIN ■ COOK 10 MIN ■ SERVES 6

1 (32-ounce) carton reduced-sodium chicken broth

1 (15 1/2-ounce) can chickpeas, rinsed and drained

1 (14 1/2-ounce) can diced tomatoes with roasted garlic

1 (6-ounce) bag shredded carrots

1 teaspoon curry powder

1/8 teaspoon cinnamon

1/8 teaspoon cayenne

2 cups cubed cooked chicken breast

1 (6-ounce) bag baby arugula

1/2 cup couscous

1 Combine the broth, chickpeas, tomatoes, carrots, curry powder, cinnamon, and cayenne in a large saucepan; bring to a boil over medium-high heat. Reduce the heat and simmer, covered, until the carrots are tender, about 2 minutes. Add the chicken and cook until heated through, about 1 minute.

2 Stir in the arugula and couscous. Remove the saucepan from the heat. Let stand, covered, until the couscous is tender and the arugula is wilted, about 5 minutes.

PER SERVING (generous 1 cup): 205 Cal, 4 g Fat, 1 g Sat Fat, 0 g Trans Fat, 26 mg Chol, 637 mg Sod, 26 g Carb, 5 g Fib, 17 g Prot, 78 mg Calc.
POINTS value: 4.

FOOD NOTE

If you enjoy cooking Moroccan-style food, consider purchasing *ras-al-hanout*, a tasty blend of 15 or more toasted ground spices. It can be found at many Middle Eastern grocery stores or ordered from online sources. You can easily replace the spices in this recipe with *ras-al-hanout*, but add a little at a time to ensure that you get the flavor you like.

Chicken Sausage and Bean Stew

HANDS-ON PREP 5 MIN ■ COOK 10 MIN ■ SERVES 4

6 ounces fully cooked Italian-style
  chicken sausages, diced

2 zucchini, diced

1 small onion, chopped

1 (15½-ounce) can red kidney beans,
  rinsed and drained

1 (14½-ounce) can diced tomatoes

1 (8-ounce) can tomato sauce

¼ cup water

1 tablespoon chopped fresh oregano
  or 1 teaspoon dried

2 cups packed baby spinach

1 Spray a large nonstick skillet with nonstick spray and set over high heat. Add the sausages, zucchini, and onion; cook, stirring frequently until the vegetables soften, about 6 minutes.

2 Stir in the beans, tomatoes, tomato sauce, water, and oregano; bring to a boil. Reduce the heat and simmer until the vegetables are tender, about 2 minutes. Remove the skillet from the heat and stir in the spinach until it wilts, about 1 minute.

PER SERVING (1½ cups): 249 Cal, 6 g Fat, 2 g Sat Fat, 0 g Trans Fat, 24 mg Chol, 1,079 mg Sod, 34 g Carb, 8 g Fib, 18 g Prot, 89 mg Calc.
POINTS value: 5.

GOOD IDEA

To make this a hearty meal in a bowl, stir in 1 cup of cooked orzo or other small pasta just before serving (it will increase the per-serving **POINTS** value by 1).

Curried Chicken Patties on Lemony Rice

HANDS-ON PREP 5 MIN ■ COOK 10 MIN ■ SERVES 4

1 pound ground skinless chicken breast

1/2 cup plain low-fat yogurt

1/2 small onion, grated

1 tablespoon plain dried bread crumbs

1 tablespoon curry powder

1/2 teaspoon salt

1/4 teaspoon freshly ground pepper

2 cups quick-cooking brown rice

2 teaspoons grated lemon zest

1/2 cup prepared mango chutney

1 Spray the broiler rack with nonstick spray and preheat the broiler.

2 Combine the chicken, 1/4 cup of the yogurt, the onion, bread crumbs, curry powder, salt, and pepper in a medium bowl. Form into 4 patties.

3 Place the patties on the broiler rack; broil 4 inches from the heat until an instant-read thermometer inserted into the side of a patty registers 165°F, 5–6 minutes on each side.

4 Meanwhile, cook the rice according to the package directions, omitting the salt if desired. Add the lemon zest and fluff the rice with a fork. Divide the rice among 4 plates and top with the chicken patties. Serve with the remaining 1/4 cup yogurt and the chutney.

PER SERVING (1 patty, 2/3 cup rice, 1 tablespoon yogurt, and 2 tablespoons chutney): 380 Cal, 3 g Fat, 1 g Sat Fat, 0 g Trans Fat, 77 mg Chol, 409 mg Sod, 53 g Carb, 7 g Fib, 33 g Prot, 101 mg Calc.

POINTS value: 7.

PLAY IT SAFE

To help keep harmful bacteria from spreading, wear disposable plastic gloves when forming the patties, then discard the gloves. Look for them at kitchen-supply stores and in some supermarkets.

Spiced Shrimp with Mango Puree

HANDS-ON PREP 5 MIN ■ COOK 10 MIN ■ SERVES 4

I pound jumbo shrimp, unpeeled

I tablespoon curry powder

1/2 teaspoon ground allspice

1/2 teaspoon salt

2 cups frozen mango cubes, thawed

1/4 cup water

2 teaspoons canola oil

I small red onion, finely chopped

I tablespoon minced peeled fresh ginger

1 1/2 teaspoons sugar

2 tablespoons finely chopped fresh cilantro

1 Toss together the shrimp, curry powder, allspice, and ¼ teaspoon of the salt in a medium bowl until the shrimp are evenly coated. Let stand about 5 minutes.

2 Meanwhile, put the mango and water in a blender or food processor and puree; set aside.

3 Heat the oil in a medium nonstick saucepan set over medium-high heat. Add the red onion, ginger, sugar, and remaining ¼ teaspoon of salt; cook, stirring frequently, until lightly browned, about 3 minutes. Add the mango puree; bring to a boil, stirring occasionally. Reduce the heat and simmer 1 minute. Remove the saucepan from the heat.

4 Spray a large nonstick skillet with nonstick spray and set over medium-high heat. Add the shrimp and cook until lightly browned and just opaque in the center, about 2 minutes on each side. Sprinkle with the cilantro and serve with the sauce and plenty of napkins.

PER SERVING (about 7 shrimp and ⅓ cup sauce): 171 Cal, 4 g Fat, 1 g Sat Fat, 0 g Trans Fat, 161 mg Chol, 484 mg Sod, 17 g Carb, 2 g Fib, 18 g Prot, 53 mg Calc.
POINTS value: 3.

HOW WE DID IT

Here's how to devein unpeeled shrimp: With kitchen scissors, snip down along the curved side of the shrimp, cutting through the shell and flesh. Then with your fingers or a toothpick remove the black vein.

Microwave Cod with Parsley

HANDS-ON PREP 5 MIN ■ COOK 10 MIN ■ SERVES 4

1 (1 1/4-pound) skinless cod fillet, cut into 4 pieces

2 tablespoons fresh lemon juice

3/4 teaspoon salt

1/8 teaspoon ground white pepper

2 tablespoons all-purpose flour

1 cup low-fat (1%) milk

1/4 cup finely chopped fresh parsley

1 teaspoon grated lemon zest

1 Spray a 2-quart microwavable covered dish with nonstick spray. Add the cod and sprinkle with the lemon juice, salt, and pepper. Cover the dish and microwave on High until the fish is just opaque in the center, 5–6 minutes; let stand, covered, 1 minute. Drain the fish juices into a cup; reserve. Re-cover the dish.

2 Meanwhile, stir together the flour and 1/4 cup of the milk in a medium saucepan until a smooth paste forms. Stir in the remaining 3/4 cup of milk, the parsley, and lemon zest. Cook, stirring constantly, until the mixture bubbles and thickens, about 3 minutes. Stir in the reserved fish juices and heat through. Serve the cod with the sauce.

PER SERVING (1 piece cod and generous 1/4 cup sauce): 171 Cal, 2 g Fat, 1 g Sat Fat, 0 g Trans Fat, 60 mg Chol, 569 mg Sod, 7 g Carb, 0 g Fib, 31 g Prot, 93 mg Calc.
POINTS value: 4.

ZAP IT

Fish is one of the most microwave-friendly foods because of its high moisture content. Always test fish carefully for doneness: It should be almost opaque throughout and just flake easily with a fork. The fish will continue to cook for a minute or two from the residual heat, so remove it from the microwave just before it looks done.

Crab Lovers' Sandwiches

HANDS-ON PREP 15 MIN ■ COOK NONE ■ SERVES 4

3 tablespoons low-fat mayonnaise

2 scallions, finely chopped (white and light green parts only)

1 tablespoon fresh lime juice

2 teaspoons Dijon mustard

$1/8$ teaspoon cayenne

$1/2$ pound fresh or canned lump or jumbo crabmeat, drained if canned, picked over

1 celery stalk, finely chopped

8 slices crusty whole-wheat bread, toasted

1 Combine the mayonnaise, scallions, lime juice, mustard, and cayenne in a medium bowl. Add the crabmeat and celery; mix well, lightly flaking the crabmeat with a fork but leaving some of the pieces whole.

2 Spread a scant $1/2$ cup of the crabmeat mixture on each of 4 slices of the bread. Top with the remaining 4 slices of bread.

PER SERVING (1 sandwich): 207 Cal, 4 g Fat, 1 g Sat Fat, 0 g Trans Fat, 38 mg Chol, 619 mg Sod, 30 g Carb, 4 g Fib, 15 g Prot, 95 mg Calc.
POINTS value: 4.

MAKE IT CORE

To fit this recipe into the **Core Plan,** use fat-free mayonnaise and substitute a bed of green leaf lettuce for the bread.

Soy-Pasta Bolognese

HANDS-ON PREP 7 MIN ■ COOK 8 MIN ■ SERVES 4

1 (8-ounce) package fresh ziti or linguine

1 tablespoon extra-virgin olive oil

1 fennel bulb, cored and finely chopped

1 onion, chopped

3 garlic cloves, minced

2 cups frozen soy protein crumbles

2 cups prepared marinara sauce

2 teaspoons dried basil

$1/4$ teaspoon freshly ground pepper

$1/3$ cup grated Parmesan cheese

1 Cook the pasta according to the package directions, omitting the salt if desired. Drain and keep warm.

2 Meanwhile, heat the oil in a large nonstick skillet set over medium-high heat. Add the fennel, onion, and garlic; cook, stirring, until slightly softened, about 4 minutes. Stir in the soy crumbles and heat through, about 1 minute. Reduce the heat and add the pasta sauce, basil, and pepper; cook until hot and bubbling, about 3 minutes.

3 Divide the pasta evenly among 4 shallow bowls; top with the sauce and sprinkle with the Parmesan.

PER SERVING (I cup pasta, $3/4$ cup sauce, and generous 1 tablespoon Parmesan): 355 Cal, 7 g Fat, 2 g Sat Fat, 0 g Trans Fat, 5 mg Chol, 901 mg Sod, 51 g Carb, 7 g Fib, 22 g Prot, 174 mg Calc.
POINTS value: 7.

FOOD NOTE

There is a noticeable difference in the textures of cooked dry and fresh pasta. When cooked perfectly, dried pasta should be al dente, or have a bit of tooth to the bite, while fresh pasta should be cooked until soft. Using fresh pasta in this dish best complements the silky texture of the fennel and onion in the sauce.

Double-Cheese Mini Pizzas

HANDS-ON PREP 5 MIN ■ COOK 8 MIN ■ SERVES 4

1 (15 1/2-ounce) can pinto beans, rinsed and drained

2 tablespoons fresh lemon juice

1 tablespoon extra-virgin olive oil

1 tablespoon chopped fresh oregano or 1 teaspoon dried

1/4 teaspoon freshly ground pepper

4 (6-inch) pitas

1 cup fat-free ricotta cheese

1 tomato, chopped

4 tablespoons grated Parmesan cheese

1 Preheat the oven to 425°F. Spray a baking sheet with nonstick spray.

2 Combine the beans, lemon juice, oil, oregano, and pepper in a medium bowl. Mix well with a wooden spoon, coarsely mashing the beans.

3 Spread one-fourth of the bean mixture over each pita; top each with 1/4 cup of the ricotta, one-fourth of the chopped tomato, and 1 tablespoon of the Parmesan cheese. Place on the baking sheet and bake until the topping is hot and the pitas are crisp, about 8 minutes.

PER SERVING (1 mini pizza): 366 Cal, 6 g Fat, 2 g Sat Fat, 0 g Trans Fat, 11 mg Chol, 443 mg Sod, 55 g Carb, 7 g Fib, 23 g Prot, 301 mg Calc.
POINTS value: 7.

GOOD IDEA

You (and the kids too) can get creative with these fun-to-eat pizzas by layering on no-**POINTS**-added yet big-on-flavor extras, such as capers, crushed red pepper, parsley, and garlic powder.

Cheesy Herbed Omelette ☑

4 large eggs

4 egg whites

³/₄ teaspoon salt

¹/₄ teaspoon freshly ground pepper

4 teaspoons extra-virgin olive oil

1 onion, chopped

1 plum tomato, chopped

1 teaspoon dried basil

¹/₄ cup fat-free ricotta cheese

¹/₄ cup shredded fat-free cheddar cheese

2 tablespoons chopped fresh chives

1 Lightly beat the eggs, egg whites, ¹/₂ teaspoon of the salt, and ¹/₈ teaspoon of the pepper in a medium bowl; set aside.

2 Heat 2 teaspoons of the oil in a large nonstick skillet set over medium-high heat. Add the onion, tomato, basil, and the remaining ¹/₄ teaspoon salt and ¹/₈ teaspoon pepper; cook, stirring occasionally, until the onion is softened, about 2 minutes. Transfer to a bowl and stir in the ricotta, cheddar, and 1 tablespoon of the chives.

3 Wipe out the skillet with a paper towel. Add the remaining 2 teaspoons of oil to the skillet and set over medium-low heat. Pour in the egg mixture and cook, lifting the edges frequently with a spatula to allow the uncooked egg to run underneath, until the eggs are just set, about 3 minutes. Spoon the cheese mixture over half of the egg mixture, then fold the unfilled portion of eggs over to enclose the filling. Cook, turning once, until the filling is heated through, about 2 minutes. Cut the omelette in to 4 portions. Sprinkle with the remaining 1 tablespoon of chives.

PER SERVING (¹/₄ of omelette): 177 Cal, 10 g Fat, 2 g Sat Fat, 0 g Trans Fat, 215 mg Chol, 658 mg Sod, 7 g Carb, 1 g Fib, 14 g Prot, 128 mg Calc.

POINTS value: 4.

TRY IT

To make the omelette extra-fluffy, add 1 or 2 tablespoons of water to the eggs as you beat them. The age-old advice of adding milk actually results in a *tougher* omelette.

Classic Rice and Beans
Cuban-Style ☑

HANDS-ON PREP 5 MIN ■ COOK 10 MIN ■ SERVES 4

3/4 cup quick-cooking brown rice

1 tablespoon extra-virgin olive oil

1 onion, chopped

2 assorted-color bell peppers, seeded and chopped

4 garlic cloves, minced

1 teaspoon dried oregano

1/2 teaspoon ground cumin

1 (15 1/2-ounce) can black beans, undrained

1/4 teaspoon hot pepper sauce

4 lime wedges

1 Prepare the rice according to the package directions, omitting the salt if desired; keep warm.

2 Meanwhile, heat the oil in a large saucepan set over high heat. Add the onion, bell peppers, garlic, oregano, and cumin; cook, stirring, until softened, about 5 minutes. Stir in the beans with their liquid and the pepper sauce. Reduce the heat and simmer, covered, until the sauce thickens slightly, about 5 minutes. Serve over the rice with the lime wedges.

PER SERVING (scant 1/2 cup rice and 3/4 cup beans): 301 Cal, 5 g Fat, 1 g Sat Fat, 0 g Trans Fat, 0 mg Chol, 337 mg Sod, 48 g Carb, 10 g Fib, 11 g Prot, 90 mg Calc.
POINTS value: 6.

FOOD NOTE

Canned beans are a great convenience food, but use dried beans if you prefer. When purchasing dried beans, look for whole, perfect-looking beans, and buy them in a store where there is a fast turnover. The older the beans, the longer they take to cook and the less nutritious they become. Have any old dried beans at the back of your pantry? Toss them!

CHAPTER TWELVE

Sweet Desserts

Boston Cream Pie

HANDS-ON PREP 25 MIN ■ COOK 35 MIN ■ SERVES 12

CAKE

1 cup cake flour

1 1/2 teaspoons baking powder

1/4 teaspoon salt

3 large eggs, at room temperature

3/4 cup granulated sugar

1/4 cup warm water

2 tablespoons unsalted butter, melted

1 1/2 teaspoons vanilla extract

CUSTARD

1/3 cup granulated sugar

3 tablespoons cornstarch

1/4 teaspoon salt

1 1/2 cups low-fat (1%) milk

1 large egg

1 tablespoon unsalted butter

2 teaspoons vanilla extract

GLAZE

1/3 cup confectioners' sugar

3 tablespoons Dutch-process cocoa powder

1/2 cup fat-free sweetened condensed milk

1/2 teaspoon vanilla extract

1/4 teaspoon chocolate extract (optional)

1 To make the cake, preheat the oven to 350°F. Spray two 9-inch round cake pans with nonstick spray. Line with wax paper rounds and spray with nonstick spray.

2 Whisk together the flour, baking powder, and salt in a medium bowl; set aside. With an electric mixer on high speed, beat the eggs until thickened, about 3 minutes. Gradually add the granulated sugar, beating until light and fluffy, about 3 minutes. Reduce the speed to low. Add the water, butter, and vanilla; beat until blended. Add the flour mixture; beat just until blended. Pour the batter into the pans, dividing it evenly. Bake until a toothpick inserted into the center comes out clean, 25–30 minutes. Let cool completely in the pans on racks. Run a knife around the edges of the cakes to loosen them from the pans; invert onto the racks. Remove the wax paper.

3 To make the custard, whisk together the granulated sugar, cornstarch, and salt in a medium saucepan. Whisk in the milk and egg until blended. Cook over medium heat, stirring constantly, until the mixture simmers, about 3 minutes. Cook, stirring constantly, until thickened, about 1 minute longer. Remove the saucepan from the heat; stir in the butter and vanilla. Press a piece of plastic wrap directly onto the surface; let cool.

4 To make the glaze, sift together the confectioners' sugar and cocoa into a small saucepan; stir in the condensed milk and set over low heat. Cook, stirring, until the mixture bubbles and thickens, about 2 minutes; cook 1 minute. Remove the pan from the heat; stir in the vanilla extract and chocolate extract if using. Let cool until thickened, about 10 minutes.

5 To assemble the cake, place 1 cake layer, bottom side up, on a serving plate. Whisk the custard until smooth; spread evenly over the layer, leaving a ½-inch border. Top with the remaining layer, top side up. Using a narrow metal spatula, spread the chocolate glaze evenly over the cake layer.

PER SERVING (¹/₁₂ of cake): 224 Cal, 5 g Fat, 3 g Sat Fat, 0 g Trans Fat, 80 mg Chol, 212 mg Sod, 40 g Carb, 1 g Fib, 5 g Prot, 120 mg Calc.
POINTS value: 5.

FOOD NOTE

As the story goes, in 1855 in Boston, the Parker House's pastry chef decided to dress up the hotel's Boston Pie, a two-layer sponge filled with custard and dusted with confectioners' sugar, by topping it with a rich chocolate glaze. He renamed it Parker House Chocolate Pie, but over the years its name became Boston Cream Pie. It remains the signature dessert at the Parker House and is the official State dessert of Massachusetts.

Nectarine-Strawberry Cobbler

HANDS-ON PREP 20 MIN ■ COOK 35 MIN ■ SERVES 6

½ cup strawberry jam

⅓ cup apricot nectar

1 tablespoon cornstarch

¾ teaspoon cinnamon

1½ pounds firm-ripe nectarines (about 5 medium), halved, pitted, and thinly sliced

1 cup all-purpose flour

3 tablespoons sugar

1 teaspoon baking powder

¼ teaspoon baking soda

½ cup low-fat buttermilk

2 tablespoons unsalted butter, melted

1 Preheat the oven to 375°F. Whisk together the jam, apricot nectar, cornstarch, and cinnamon in a microwavable 9-inch deep-dish pie plate or casserole dish until blended. Add the nectarines and stir to coat well. Microwave on High, stirring occasionally, until the mixture begins to bubble, 6–7 minutes. Transfer the mixture to a 1½- to 2-quart baking pan.

2 Meanwhile, to make the topping, whisk together the flour, 2 tablespoons of the sugar, the baking powder, and baking soda in a medium bowl. Make a well in the center and pour in the buttermilk and melted butter. Using a wooden spoon, stir just until a moist dough forms.

3 Drop the dough by tablespoonfuls onto the hot fruit, forming 6 mounds. Sprinkle the remaining 1 tablespoon of sugar over the biscuits. Bake until the biscuits are golden and the fruit mixture is bubbly, about 25 minutes. Serve warm.

PER SERVING (⅙ of cobbler): 247 Cal, 4 g Fat, 3 g Sat Fat, 0 g Trans Fat, 11 mg Chol, 167 mg Sod, 51 g Carb, 3 g Fib, 4 g Prot, 85 mg Calc.

POINTS value: 5.

HOW WE DID IT

If you prefer to use peaches instead of nectarines, here's how to peel them: Plunge the peaches into boiling water just long enough to loosen their skins, which will take from 1 to 3 minutes. Immediately transfer the peaches to a bowl of ice water to cool them; when cool enough to handle, slip off the skins.

Pineapple Bread Pudding with Chocolate Sauce

HANDS-ON PREP 15 MIN ■ COOK 45 MIN ■ SERVES 10

$1/3$ cup sweetened flaked coconut

1 (20-ounce) can pineapple chunks in juice, drained

3 large eggs

2 egg whites

$1/2$ cup sugar

1 teaspoon salt

$2 1/4$ cups fat-free milk

1 cup light (reduced-fat) coconut milk

1 tablespoon vanilla extract

5 cups ($3/4$-inch) cubes French bread

2 ounces bittersweet or semisweet chocolate, chopped

2 teaspoons Dutch-process cocoa powder

1 Preheat the broiler.

2 Spread the coconut in a broiler pan and broil 5 inches from the heat until lightly browned, about 1 minute. Transfer the coconut to a plate and let cool. Put the pineapple chunks in the broiler pan in a single layer and broil, turning once, until lightly browned, about 3 minutes. Transfer to the same plate and let cool.

3 Place an oven rack in the center of the oven and preheat the oven to 350°F. Spray a 7 x 11-inch baking dish with nonstick spray.

4 Whisk together the eggs, egg whites, sugar, and salt in a large bowl until blended. Whisk in 2 cups of the milk, the coconut milk, and vanilla. Add the bread cubes, pressing down on the bread so it soaks up the liquid. Allow to sit about 10 minutes.

5 Stir the coconut and pineapple into the bread mixture until evenly combined. Bake until puffed and browned, 40–50 minutes. Place on a rack and let cool slightly.

6 Meanwhile, combine the remaining $1/4$ cup of milk, the chocolate, and cocoa powder in a 1-cup glass measuring cup. Microwave on High until melted, about 45 seconds; stir until blended and smooth. Serve the bread pudding with the chocolate sauce.

PER SERVING ($1/10$ **of pudding and about 1 tablespoon sauce): 200 Cal, 7 g Fat, 3 g Sat Fat, 0 g Trans Fat, 65 mg Chol, 398 mg Sod, 30 g Carb, 1 g Fib, 7 g Prot, 102 mg Calc.** *POINTS* value: 4.

PLAN AHEAD

If you want to get a jump start on the prep, follow steps 1 through 4, then stir in the coconut and pineapple and refrigerate the mixture overnight. The next day, bake the pudding as directed.

Date-Raisin Baklava

HANDS-ON PREP 35 MIN ■ COOK 30 MIN ■ SERVES 16

BAKLAVA

2 cups pitted dates, chopped

1 cup dried sour cherries

2 tablespoons + 1/2 cup sugar

1 tablespoon grated lemon zest

1/2 teaspoon cinnamon

3 tablespoons orange juice

2 tablespoons fresh lemon juice

1/2 cup finely chopped walnuts

12 (12 x 17-inch) sheets frozen phyllo
dough, thawed

GLAZE

1/3 cup sugar

2 tablespoons water

3 tablespoons honey

2 tablespoons fresh lemon juice

1 Preheat the oven to 350°F. Spray an 8-inch square baking dish with nonstick spray.

2 To make the baklava, put the dates, cherries, 2 tablespoons of the sugar, the lemon zest, and cinnamon in a food processor; pulse until the dates and cherries are finely chopped. Add the orange juice and lemon juice; pulse until the mixture forms a thick paste. Transfer to a medium bowl and stir in the walnuts; set aside.

3 Stack the phyllo sheets on a cutting board. Using the bottom of the baking dish as a guide, cut out 2 (8-inch square) stacks of phyllo; discard the trimmings. Cover the phyllo with a damp paper towel and plastic wrap to keep it from drying out. Place 1 phyllo sheet in the bottom of the baking dish. Lightly spray with nonstick spray and sprinkle with 1 teaspoon of the remaining sugar. Repeat the layering with 9 more phyllo sheets and the sugar, spraying each phyllo sheet with nonstick spray. Spread with half of the date mixture, then top with 4 more layers of phyllo and sugar. Spread with the remaining date mixture, then top with 10 more layers of phyllo and sugar.

4 With a sharp knife, cut through the baklava to mark 16 squares, being careful not to cut all the way through to the bottom. Bake until crisp and lightly golden, about 30 minutes.

5 Meanwhile, to make the glaze, combine the sugar and water in a small saucepan; bring to a boil over medium heat. Cook, without stirring, until the sugar is dissolved, about 1 minute. Remove the saucepan from the heat. Stir in the honey and lemon juice; let cool.

6 Cut the baklava into squares along the scored lines. Drizzle the glaze over the top; let cool completely.

PER SERVING (1 square): 219 Cal, 4 g Fat, 1 g Sat Fat, 0 g Trans Fat, 0 mg Chol, 70 mg Sod, 47 g Carb, 3 g Fib, 2 g Prot, 18 mg Calc.
POINTS value: 4.

Crêpes Suzette

HANDS-ON PREP 20 MIN ■ COOK 15 MIN ■ SERVES 6

3/4 cup low-fat (1%) milk

2 large eggs, lightly beaten

1/2 teaspoon vanilla extract

1/2 cup all-purpose flour

4 tablespoons sugar

1/8 teaspoon salt

2 oranges, peeled and cut into segments

1 tablespoon grated orange zest

1/3 cup fresh orange juice

2 tablespoons orange-flavored liqueur (optional)

3 tablespoons light unsalted butter

1 To make the crêpe batter, combine the milk, eggs, and vanilla in a small bowl. Combine the flour, 1 tablespoon of the sugar, and the salt in a medium bowl; set aside. Gradually whisk the milk mixture into the flour mixture until blended; let stand 15 minutes.

2 Spray a small nonstick skillet or crêpe pan with nonstick spray and set over medium heat. When a drop of water sizzles in the skillet, stir the batter. Pour a scant 1/4 cupful of the batter into the skillet, quickly tilting the pan to evenly coat the bottom with the batter. Cook the crêpe until golden brown, 1–2 minutes. Turn the crêpe; cook until golden brown on the second side, about 15 seconds longer. Flip the crêpe onto a plate and cover with a sheet of wax paper. Repeat with the remaining batter to make 6 crêpes in all, stacking them between wax paper. Cover loosely with plastic wrap and set aside.

3 Combine the orange segments and their juice, the orange zest and juice, and the remaining 3 tablespoons of sugar in a large skillet and set over medium heat. Cook, stirring occasionally, until the sugar is dissolved, about 2 minutes. Dip the crêpes, one at a time, into the hot juice mixture. Fold each crêpe into quarters and transfer to a warm platter. Add the liqueur if using to the skillet and bring to a boil; boil 30 seconds. Remove the skillet from the heat and add the butter, swirling the skillet until the butter is melted. Spoon the orange mixture over the crêpes and serve at once.

PER SERVING (1 crêpe and about 1/3 cup orange mixture without liqueur): 161 Cal, 5 g Fat, 3 g Sat Fat, 0 g Trans Fat, 82 mg Chol, 86 mg Sod, 25 g Carb, 2 g Fib, 5 g Prot, 68 mg Calc.
POINTS value: 3.

HOW WE DID IT

When making crêpe batter, it is always recommended to allow the batter to sit for anywhere from 15 to 30 minutes before cooking it. This gives the gluten in the flour time to relax, yielding tender crêpes.

Lemon-Glazed Orange Loaf

HANDS-ON PREP 15 MIN ■ COOK 40 MIN ■ SERVES 16

2 cups all-purpose flour

2 teaspoons grated orange zest

1 teaspoon baking powder

1/2 teaspoon baking soda

1/4 teaspoon salt

1 cup granulated sugar

1/2 cup fresh orange juice

1/3 cup canola oil

2 large eggs

2 teaspoons vanilla extract

3/4 cup confectioners' sugar

1 teaspoon grated lemon zest

2 tablespoons lemon juice

1 Preheat the oven to 350°F. Spray a 5 x 9-inch loaf pan with nonstick spray. Dust with flour and tap out the excess.

2 To make the batter, whisk together the flour, orange zest, baking powder, baking soda, and salt in a large bowl; set aside. Whisk together the granulated sugar, orange juice, oil, eggs, and vanilla in a medium bowl. Add the orange juice mixture to the flour mixture, stirring until well combined. Pour into the pan. Bake until a toothpick inserted into the center of the loaf comes out clean, 40–45 minutes. Let cool in the pan on a rack 10 minutes. Remove the loaf from the pan and let cool completely on the rack.

3 To make the glaze, whisk together the confectioners' sugar and lemon zest and juice in a medium bowl until smooth. With a narrow metal spatula, spread the glaze evenly over the top of the loaf. Let stand until the glaze sets, about 10 minutes. Cut into 16 slices.

PER SERVING (1 slice): 183 Cal, 5 g Fat, 1 g Sat Fat, 0 g Trans Fat, 27 mg Chol, 108 mg Sod, 31 g Carb, 1 g Fib, 3 g Prot, 12 mg Calc.
POINTS value: 4.

GOOD IDEA

Come the holidays, consider using this delectable loaf cake for a festive fruit trifle. It is lighter than a traditional pound cake but just as delicious. If you like, leave off the glaze.

Tiramisù

HANDS-ON PREP 25 MIN ■ COOK NONE ■ SERVES 6

1/4 cup boiling water

2 1/2 teaspoons instant espresso powder

1 1/2 teaspoons + 1/2 cup sugar

6 ounces fat-free pound cake, cut into 1/2-inch-thick slices

1 (8-ounce) package tub-style fat-free cream cheese

1/2 teaspoon vanilla extract

1/2 (8-ounce) container thawed frozen fat-free whipped topping

2 ounces semisweet chocolate, grated

Dutch-process cocoa powder (optional)

1 Combine the boiling water, espresso powder, and 1 1/2 teaspoons of the sugar in a small bowl, stirring until the espresso and sugar are dissolved; let cool slightly.

2 Spray an 8-inch square baking dish or casserole with nonstick spray. Line the bottom of the disk with the cake slices, cutting them to fit as needed. Brush with the espresso mixture; set aside.

3 Put the cream cheese, the remaining 1/2 cup of sugar, and the vanilla in a food processor; process just until smooth. Transfer to a medium bowl. Gently fold in the whipped topping and spoon over the cake, spreading it evenly; sprinkle with the chocolate and dust with cocoa powder if using. Cover the dish with plastic wrap, being careful not to let the wrap touch the tiramisù. Refrigerate until chilled, at least 4 hours or up to 2 days.

PER SERVING (1/6 of tiramisù without cocoa powder): **268 Cal, 4 g Fat, 2 g Sat Fat, 0 g Trans Fat, 6 mg Chol, 345 mg Sod, 50 g Carb, 1 g Fib, 8 g Prot, 191 mg Calc.**
POINTS value: **5.**

ZAP IT

Save time by bringing the water to a boil in a glass measuring cup in the microwave. It will take about 20 seconds on High, depending on the wattage of the microwave oven.

Dried Blueberry Scones

HANDS-ON PREP 15 MIN ■ COOK 20 MIN ■ SERVES 12

1 1/2 cups all-purpose flour

1/2 cup whole-wheat flour

1/2 cup sugar

1 1/2 teaspoons baking powder

1/2 teaspoon baking soda

1/4 teaspoon salt

4 tablespoons cold unsalted butter, cut into pieces

3/4 cup dried blueberries

3/4 cup low-fat buttermilk

1 large egg, lightly beaten

2 teaspoons grated lemon zest

1 Preheat the oven to 350°F. Spray a large baking sheet with nonstick spray.

2 Whisk together the all-purpose flour, whole-wheat flour, sugar, baking powder, baking soda, and salt in a large bowl. With a pastry blender, cut in the butter until the mixture resembles coarse crumbs. Stir in the dried blueberries; set aside.

3 Put 2 tablespoons of the buttermilk in a cup; set aside. Combine the remaining buttermilk, the egg, and lemon zest in a small bowl. Add the buttermilk mixture to the flour mixture, stirring with a wooden spoon just until the flour mixture is moistened. Knead the dough in the bowl once or twice. On a lightly floured surface, pat the dough into a 6 x 10-inch rectangle. Cut lengthwise in thirds, then crosswise in fourths to make 12 scones.

4 Place the scones on the baking sheet about 1 inch apart. Brush with the reserved buttermilk. Bake until golden and a toothpick inserted into a scone comes out clean, 20–22 minutes. Transfer to a rack and let cool 5 minutes to serve warm or let cool completely.

PER SERVING (1 scone): 175 Cal, 5 g Fat, 3 g Sat Fat, 0 g Trans Fat, 29 mg Chol, 171 mg Sod, 31 g Carb, 1 g Fib, 3 g Prot, 35 mg Calc.
POINTS value: 4.

EXPRESS LANE

Here's how to get freshly-baked scones on the table without a lot of morning fuss. The night before, combine the dry ingredients as directed in step 2, and cover and refrigerate. Combine the buttermilk, egg, and lemon zest in a small bowl; cover and refrigerate. The next day, while the oven is preheating, combine the wet and dry ingredients as directed, and fabulous scones will be on the table in about 30 minutes.

Raspberry-Corn Muffins

HANDS-ON PREP 15 MIN ■ COOK 15 MIN ■ SERVES 12

1 cup all-purpose flour

3/4 cup yellow cornmeal

1/2 cup sugar

2 teaspoons baking powder

1/4 teaspoon salt

1/2 cup fat-free milk

1/4 cup canola oil

1 large egg, lightly beaten

1 cup fresh or frozen raspberries

1 Preheat the oven to 425°F. Spray a 12-cup muffin pan with nonstick spray.

2 Whisk together the flour, cornmeal, sugar, baking powder, and salt in a large bowl; set aside. Beat the milk, oil, and egg in a small bowl. Add the milk mixture to the flour mixture, stirring just until cornmeal mixture is moistened. Gently fold in the raspberries.

3 Fill each muffin cup two-thirds full with batter. Bake until a toothpick inserted into a muffin comes out clean, 12–15 minutes. Remove the muffins from the pan and let cool completely on a rack.

PER SERVING (1 muffin): 176 Cal, 5 g Fat, 1 g Sat Fat, 0 g Trans Fat, 18 mg Chol, 124 mg Sod, 30 g Carb, 1 g Fib, 3 g Prot, 35 mg Calc.
POINTS value: 4.

PLAN AHEAD

These muffins freeze beautifully, so bake up an extra batch. Cool the extra muffins as directed; then wrap each one in plastic wrap. Transfer the wrapped muffins to a large zip-close plastic freezer bag and freeze up to 1 month. The individual wrapping makes it easy to grab a muffin or two at a time. Set out on the counter to thaw overnight.

Dried Cranberry–Stuffed Baked Apples

HANDS-ON PREP 10 MIN ■ COOK 30 MIN ■ SERVES 4

4 medium apples, peeled and cored

1/4 cup dried cranberries

1 tablespoon pure maple syrup

1 tablespoon unsalted butter, softened

1/4 teaspoon pumpkin pie spice

1/2 cup apple juice

1 Preheat the oven to 350°F.

2 Cut a thin slice off the bottoms of the apples if necessary so they stand upright. Stand the apples in a small shallow baking dish or pie plate.

3 Combine the cranberries, maple syrup, butter, and pumpkin pie spice in a small bowl. Spoon about 1 tablespoon of the mixture into the cavity of each apple. Pour the apple juice over the apples and cover with foil. Bake until the apples are soft but still hold their shape, about 30 minutes. Spoon the cooking juices over the apples and serve at once.

PER SERVING (1 apple): 150 Cal, 3 g Fat, 2 g Sat Fat, 0 g Trans Fat, 8 mg Chol, 11 mg Sod, 32 g Carb, 3 g Fib, 1 g Prot, 15 mg Calc.
POINTS value: 3.

FOOD NOTE

To make the best baked apples, it is crucial to use fruit that not only tastes delicious but is sure to hold its shape during baking; we recommend both McIntosh and Granny Smith apples. Choose Macs if you prefer a sweeter baked apple and Granny Smiths if a bit more tang suits your taste. If you happen to have dark or golden raisins on hand, you can use them instead of the cranberries.

Pomegranate and Star Anise–Poached Grapefruit

HANDS-ON PREP 15 MIN ■ COOK 15 MIN ■ SERVES 4

1 1/4 cups water

1/2 cup sugar

2 (3-inch-long) strips orange zest, removed with a vegetable peeler

2 (3-inch-long) strips lemon zest, removed with a vegetable peeler

1 (3-inch) cinnamon stick

1 star anise

3 pink grapefruit

1/4 cup pomegranate juice

1 Combine the water, sugar, orange zest, lemon zest, cinnamon stick, and star anise in a large skillet and set over medium heat. Cover and bring to a simmer; cook 10 minutes.

2 Meanwhile, cut off the rind and white pith from the grapefruit, then cut each grapefruit into 8 wedges. Add the grapefruit to the simmering liquid; remove the skillet from the heat. Stir in the pomegranate juice and transfer to a serving bowl; let cool to room temperature. Refrigerate, covered, up to 4 days. Serve chilled or at room temperature.

PER SERVING (about 3/4 cup): 189 Cal, 0 g Fat, 0 g Sat Fat, 0 g Trans Fat, 0 mg Chol, 1 mg Sod, 44 g Carb, 2 g Fib, 1 g Prot, 25 mg Calc.
POINTS value: 3.

FOOD NOTE

Once difficult to find, pure pomegranate juice is now available in large supermarkets and specialty food stores. If you like, however, you can make your own. Here's how: Wearing rubber gloves and an apron to prevent staining, cut the crown end off a pomegranate, then lightly score the rind in several places. Immerse the fruit in a bowl of water; soak for 5 minutes. Hold the fruit underwater and break the sections apart, separating the seeds from the membrane. The seeds will sink, while the rind and membrane float. With a slotted spoon, skim off and discard the membranes and rind. Pour the seeds into a colander; drain and pat dry, then wrap the seeds in a damp cloth and squeeze over a bowl, pressing out the juice. You should have about 1/2 cup of juice.

Lime-Grilled Pineapple, Mango, and Plums

HANDS-ON PREP 20 MIN ■ COOK 10 MIN ■ SERVES 8

1/4 cup sugar

3 tablespoons water

1 teaspoon grated lime zest

3 tablespoons fresh lime juice

1 teaspoon vanilla extract

1 pineapple, trimmed, rind removed, halved, and cored

1 mango, halved, pitted, and peeled

4 red plums, halved and pitted

1 Combine the sugar and water in a small saucepan and set over medium heat. Bring to a simmer; cook until syrupy, about 2 minutes. Stir in the lime zest and juice and vanilla; set aside.

2 Preheat the grill to medium, prepare a medium fire, or preheat the broiler.

3 Meanwhile, cut each pineapple half crosswise into 1/2-inch-thick slices. Cut each mango half lengthwise into 1/2-inch-thick slices. Spray the pineapple, mango, and plums on both sides with nonstick spray. Place the fruit on the grill rack. Grill, turning once, until softened, about 4 minutes. Brush the fruit with the lime syrup and turn the fruit; grill 1 minute. Brush again with the syrup; turn and grill until the syrup is slightly caramelized, about 1 minute longer. Transfer the fruit to a platter and brush with the remaining syrup. Serve warm, at room temperature, or chilled.

PER SERVING (about 4 pineapple slices, about 1 mango slice, and 1 plum half): 88 Cal, 0 g Fat, 0 g Sat Fat, 0 g Trans Fat, 0 mg Chol, 3 mg Sod, 24 g Carb, 2 g Fib, 1 g Prot, 10 mg Calc. POINTS value: 1.

PLAN AHEAD

The sugar syrup can be prepared up to 5 days ahead and stored in the refrigerator in a covered glass jar. The syrup is an easy and tasty way to sweeten iced tea and fruit drinks or to moisten a simple one-layer cake. The recipe can also be doubled or tripled. If you like, add additional flavor by simmering the syrup with a whole star anise or cinnamon stick. Or you can add orange or lemon zest as well as the lime zest.

Broiled Pineapple with Passion Fruit Sorbet and Toasted Coconut

HANDS-ON PREP 10 MIN ■ COOK 5 MIN ■ SERVES 4

1 peeled pineapple (about 1 pound), cut into 12 rounds

3 tablespoons packed light brown sugar

1 1/3 cups passion fruit sorbet, softened slightly

4 teaspoons toasted sweetened flaked coconut

1 Preheat the broiler. Spray a baking sheet with nonstick spray.

2 Arrange the pineapple slices on the baking sheet in a single layer. Sprinkle evenly with the brown sugar and broil 5 inches from the heat until lightly browned, about 5 minutes.

3 Place 3 pineapple slices on each of 4 dessert plates. Top each plate with a 1/3-cup scoop of the sorbet and 1 teaspoon of the toasted coconut. Serve at once.

PER SERVING (1 plate): 168 Cal, 1 g Fat, 1 g Sat Fat, 0 g Trans Fat, 0 mg Chol, 16 mg Sod, 40 g Carb, 2 g Fib, 2 g Prot, 21 mg Calc.

POINTS value: 3.

EXPRESS LANE

To toast your own coconut, preheat an oven or toaster oven to 350°F. Spread the untoasted coconut in an even layer on a baking sheet and bake until lightly browned, 4–6 minutes., Or you can toast the coconut in a dry nonstick skillet set over medium-low heat, stirring often, until golden, 4–6 minutes.

Mixed Fruit Fool

HANDS-ON PREP 10 MIN ■ COOK NONE ■ SERVES 4

1 (8-ounce) container thawed frozen fat-free whipped topping

3 tablespoons raspberry preserves

3 tablespoons peach preserves

1 cup fresh or thawed frozen raspberries

12 fresh mint leaves

1 Divide the whipped topping evenly between 2 small bowls. With a rubber spatula, gently fold the raspberry preserves into 1 bowl of topping and the peach preserves into the other.

2 Gently spoon the raspberry mixture into 4 dessert dishes, dividing it evenly; spoon the peach mixture on top. Spoon ¼ cup of raspberries over the peach mixture and garnish each serving with 3 mint leaves. Serve at once or refrigerate up to 1 hour.

PER SERVING (1 dish): 185 Cal, 0 g Fat, 0 g Sat Fat, 0 g Trans Fat, 0 mg Chol, 32 mg Sod, 42 g Carb, 2 g Fib, 0 g Prot, 7 mg Calc.
POINTS value: 3.

FOOD NOTE

A fool is part of a very British family of desserts that includes trifles, syllabubs, crumbles, and other sweets that date back as far as the sixteenth century. Why did the British come up with so many berry desserts? Some believe it is because the lush countryside yielded a bountiful variety of berries, including raspberries, gooseberries, blackberries, and mulberries.

Fruit Mélange with Minty Lemon Syrup

HANDS-ON PREP 10 MIN ■ COOK 10 MIN ■ SERVES 4

1/2 cup sugar

1/2 cup water

3 tablespoons fresh lemon juice

2 tablespoons chopped fresh mint

2 teaspoons grated lemon zest

2 cups cubed honeydew melon (about 3/4 pound)

2 cups cubed cantaloupe (about 3/4 pound)

2 cups fresh or thawed frozen blueberries

1 Combine the sugar, water, and lemon juice in a small saucepan and bring to a boil. Boil until the mixture is syrupy and the sugar is dissolved, about 5 minutes. Remove the saucepan from the heat and stir in the mint and lemon zest; let stand 2 minutes.

2 Combine the honeydew, cantaloupe, and blueberries in a large bowl. Pour the syrup mixture over the fruit and gently toss. Serve at once or cover and refrigerate up to overnight and serve chilled.

PER SERVING (1 1/2 cups): 200 Cal, 1 g Fat, 0 g Sat Fat, 0 g Trans Fat, 0 mg Chol, 21 mg Sod, 51 g Carb, 4 g Fib, 2 g Prot, 26 mg Calc.
POINTS value: 3.

GOOD IDEA

Most berries, including blueberries, strawberries, blackberries, and raspberries freeze well. The trick is to spread them on a baking sheet in one layer and place in the freezer until individually frozen so they don't clump into a solid mass. Transfer the frozen berries to zip-close plastic freezer bags; date and label. In a 0°F freezer, berries will keep up to 1 year; otherwise, store up to 6 months.

Ruby Port–Poached Plums

HANDS-ON PREP 15 MIN ■ COOK 25 MIN ■ SERVES 6

1/2 cup honey

1/2 cup ruby port

1/2 cup pomegranate juice

2 (3-inch) cinnamon sticks

4 slices peeled fresh ginger

4 whole cloves

1 1/2 pounds red plums (about 9 medium), halved and pitted

1 tablespoon fresh lemon juice

1 Put the honey, port, and pomegranate juice in a medium saucepan. Put the cinnamon sticks, ginger, and cloves in the center of a 5-inch square of cheesecloth. Gather up the ends of the cheesecloth and tie into a bundle with kitchen string; add to the saucepan. Cover and bring to a simmer over medium heat; cook about 10 minutes.

2 Cut each plum half into 3 wedges. Add to the port mixture in the saucepan and return to a simmer. Cook, covered, until the plums soften, 10–12 minutes. Remove the saucepan from the heat and stir in the lemon juice; let cool. Transfer to a serving bowl and refrigerate, covered, until chilled, at least 2 hours or up to 4 days. Remove the spice bag before serving. Serve chilled or at room temperature.

PER SERVING (scant 1/2 cup): 171 Cal, 1 g Fat, 0 g Sat Fat, 0 g Trans Fat, 0 mg Chol, 10 mg Sod, 37 g Carb, 2 g Fib, 1 g Prot, 22 mg Calc.
POINTS value: 3.

GOOD IDEA

To dress up the plums a bit, spoon them into glass dessert dishes and top each portion with a generous dollop of brown sugar–sweetened fat-free sour cream (For 6 servings, 3/4 cup of sour cream sweetened with 2 tablespoons of brown sugar will increase the per-serving *POINTS* value by 1). If you prefer an alcohol-free version of this homey dessert, substitute orange juice or additional pomegranate juice for the port.

Mocha Granita with Hazelnut Liqueur

HANDS-ON PREP 10 MIN ■ COOK 6 MIN ■ SERVES 4

$^1/_2$ cup sugar

$^1/_3$ cup Dutch-process cocoa powder

2 cups strong brewed coffee

5 tablespoons hazelnut or walnut liqueur

1 Combine the sugar and cocoa in a medium saucepan. Stir in the coffee. Bring to a boil over medium-high heat. Reduce the heat and simmer 3 minutes. Remove the saucepan from the heat and let cool to room temperature.

2 Stir 3 tablespoons of the liqueur into the cooled coffee mixture. Pour into a 9-inch square baking pan. Freeze until the mixture is frozen along the edges but still slushy in the center, about 1$^1/_2$ hours. Using a fork, break up the ice crystals. Return the granita to the freezer; freeze just until solid in the center and firm around the edges, about 1$^1/_2$ hours. Tightly wrap the pan in heavy-duty foil and freeze until solid, at least 4 hours or up to 1 month.

3 Use a fork to scrape across the surface of the granita, transferring the ice shards to each of 4 wineglasses, dividing them evenly. Drizzle with the remaining 2 tablespoons of liqueur and serve at once.

PER SERVING ($^2/_3$ cup granita and 1$^1/_2$ teaspoons liqueur): 178 Cal, 1 g Fat, 1 g Sat Fat, 0 g Trans Fat, 0 mg Chol, 5 mg Sod, 37 g Carb, 2 g Fib, 1 g Prot, 11 mg Calc. *POINTS* value: 3.

PLAN AHEAD

Granita is part of the "family" of frozen ice desserts that includes sorbet and sherbet. Granitas are special in that once frozen, their icy shards are scraped into dessert dishes. A sorbet is a sweetened mixture, often a fruit puree, that is scooped for serving, while sherbet is made from a sweetened fruit puree that also contains either milk or beaten egg white.

Chocolate-Banana Smoothie

HANDS-ON PREP 5 MIN ■ COOK NONE ■ SERVES 4

1 medium banana, cut into chunks

1 cup ice cubes

1 cup fat-free chocolate milk

1 cup vanilla fat-free yogurt

Put all of the ingredients in a blender and puree. Pour into 4 chilled glasses and serve at once.

PER SERVING (1 cup): 119 Cal, 0 g Fat, 0 g Sat Fat, 0 g Trans Fat, 2 mg Chol, 72 mg Sod, 25 g Carb, 1 g Fib, 6 g Prot, 182 mg Calc.
POINTS value: 2.

GOOD IDEA

Almost any favorite flavor combination works well in a smoothie. Just use this basic formula: 1 cup fruit, 1 cup ice cubes, 1 cup milk (or juice), and 1 cup yogurt. Possible combinations include: strawberries, orange juice, and vanilla yogurt; mixed berries, blueberry yogurt, and milk; banana, chocolate milk, coffee yogurt, and cinnamon; and peaches, milk, raspberry yogurt, and vanilla extract.

Dry and Liquid Measurement

If you are converting the recipes in this book to metric measurements, use the following chart as a guide.

TEASPOONS	TABLESPOONS	CUPS	FLUID OUNCES
3 teaspoons	1 tablespoon		1/2 fluid ounce
6 teaspoons	2 tablespoons	1/8 cup	1 fluid ounce
8 teaspoons	2 tablespoons plus 2 teaspoons	1/6 cup	
12 teaspoons	4 tablespoons	1/4 cup	2 fluid ounces
15 teaspoons	5 tablespoons	1/3 cup minus 1 teaspoon	
16 teaspoons	5 tablespoons plus 1 teaspoon	1/3 cup	
18 teaspoons	6 tablespoons	1/4 cup plus 2 tablespoons	3 fluid ounces
24 teaspoons	8 tablespoons	1/2 cup	4 fluid ounces
30 teaspoons	10 tablespoons	1/2 cup plus 2 tablespoons	5 fluid ounces
32 teaspoons	10 tablespoons plus 2 teaspoons	2/3 cup	
36 teaspoons	12 tablespoons	3/4 cup	6 fluid ounces
42 teaspoons	14 tablespoons	1 cup minus 2 tablespoons	7 fluid ounces
45 teaspoons	15 tablespoons	1 cup minus 1 tablespoon	
48 teaspoons	16 tablespoons	1 cup	8 fluid ounces

LENGTH	
1 inch	25 millimeters
1 inch	2.5 centimeters

WEIGHT	
1 ounce	30 grams
1/4 pound	120 grams
1/2 pound	240 grams
1 pound	480 grams

VOLUME	
1/4 teaspoon	1 milliliter
1/2 teaspoon	2 milliliters
1 teaspoon	5 milliliters
1 tablespoon	15 milliliters
2 tablespoons	30 milliliters
3 tablespoons	45 milliliters
1/4 cup	60 milliliters
1/3 cup	80 milliliters
1/2 cup	120 milliliters
2/3 cup	160 milliliters
3/4 cup	175 milliliters
1 cup	240 milliliters
1 quart	950 milliliters

OVEN TEMPERATURE			
250°F	120°C	400°F	200°C
275°F	140°C	425°F	220°C
300°F	150°C	450°F	230°C
325°F	160°C	475°F	250°C
350°F	180°C	500°F	260°C
375°F	190°C	525°F	270°C

NOTE: Measurement of less than 1/8 teaspoon is considered a dash or a pinch. Metric volume measurements are approximate.

Index

Recipes by *POINTS* Value

Grilled Chicken with Fresh Corn
  Salsa, 89
Grilled Lamb Chops with Herb Pesto,
  140
Grilled Portobello Mushroom and
  Onion "Burgers," 181
Grilled Swiss with Avocado and
  Tomato, 73
Ham, Mushroom, and Ginger Fried
  Rice, 137
Hungarian-Style Pork Chops with
  Baby Spinach, 252
Kielbasa and Vegetable Paella, 230
Lamb and Vegetable Skewers, 138
Lemon-Glazed Orange Loaf, 277
Microwave Cod with Parsley, 260
Mussels in Spicy Tomato Broth, 157
Pan-Fried Chicken Cutlets with
  Chunky Nectarine Salsa, 253
Pasta with Oven-Roasted Tomatoes
  and Pesto, 15
Pineapple and Honey–Glazed
  Chicken, 86
Pineapple Bread Pudding with
  Chocolate Sauce, 272
Pork and Rice–Stuffed Cabbage, 135
Potato, Gruyère, and Tofu Casserole,
  189
Provençal Leg of Lamb, 231
Quinoa, Fennel, and Sun-Dried
  Tomato Pilaf, 186
Raspberry-Corn Muffins, 280
Red Snapper with Jalapeño Tartar
  Sauce, 156
Rice Salad with Bell Peppers and
  Edamame, 210
Sesame Beef Satay, 248
Skillet Chicken with Lemon and
  Capers, 93
Spicy Black Bean Cakes with Tomato
  Salsa, 187
Spicy Moroccan Chicken Soup, 254
Spring Lamb with Artichoke Hearts,
  141
Sweet Apple and Cheese Pancakes, 11
Teriyaki Pork, 225
Texas-Style Meatloaf, 129
Tex-Mex–Spiced Turkey Breast, 109
Thai Chicken Satay, 94
Turkey Breast with 40 Cloves of
  Garlic, 239
Tuscan Beef with Tomatoes, 218
Two-Bean Burritos, 241
Veal Scaloppine Marsala, 143

5 POINTS value
Almond Butter and Jam–Stuffed
  French Toast, 74
Asparagus and Pea Risotto, 179
Bacon, Egg, and Cheese Casserole, 63
Barbecue-Sauced Sloppy Joes, 113
Beef Tenderloin with Red Wine and
  Mushrooms, 121
Boston Cream Pie, 272
Broccoli-Tomato Quiche, 70
Cheddar, Corn, and Tortilla Casserole,
  182
Chicken Sausage and Bean Stew, 256
Chicken with Green Sauce, 97
Classic New England Dinner, 221
Cuban-Style Picadillo, 128
Golden Cornmeal Pancakes, 68
Grilled Margarita Chicken, 103
Grilled Whole Chicken with Garlic
  and Herbs, 82
Ham and Cheese Soufflé, 10
Harvest Shepherd's Pie, 142
Herb-Grilled Pork Chops with
  Vegetables, 133
Hoisin Duck and Vegetable Stir-Fry,
  117
Hunan Chicken Stir-Fry, 98
Japanese Beef Hot Pot, 123
Meatloaf with Bell Pepper and Onion,
  126
Mini Beef Wellingtons, 122
Nectarine-Strawberry Cobbler, 271
New Orleans Shrimp Gumbo, 243
No-Fuss Chicken Mole, 233
Pasta with Mixed Vegetable Ragu, 169
Penne-Chicken Salad with Creamy
  Ranch Dressing, 30
Pork Chop Salad with Pear-Roquefort
  Dressing, 25
Pork Chops with Cremini
  Mushrooms, 228
Pork Chops with Rosemary-Wine
  Sauce, 134
Saucy Turkey Meatballs, 112
Sesame-Lime Grilled Tuna, 149
Shrimp and Sausage Paella, 163
Smoky Black Bean Soup, 44
Smoky Buffalo Chicken Fingers, 99
Smoky Roast Pork with Peaches and
  Plums, 131
Soy-Ginger Chicken Breasts, 90
Stuffed Peppers with Rice and Beans,
  244
Swiss Steak, 220
Tex-Mex Chicken Wraps, 96

Thai Pork and Rice Bowl, 136
Tiramisù, 278
Turkey and Sweet Potato Soup, 47
Turkey Breast with Spice Butter, 240
Zesty Steak Fajitas, 124

6 POINTS value
Chicken Salad with Grapes and
  Walnuts, 31
Classic Rice and Beans Cuban-Style,
  266
Cornish Hens with Tarragon Butter,
  238
Creole-Seasoned Tilapia, 153
Double Cheese Polenta with
  Mushroom Sauce, 180
Fruited Pork Tenderloin, 224
Italian-Style Beef Rolls, 219
Jamaican Jerk Drumsticks, 237
Mustardy Pot Roast with Vegetables,
  216
Pork Barbecue Sandwiches, 227
Pork with Cherry-Mustard Glaze, 223
Ricotta Cheese Ravioli with
  Butternut Squash Sauce, 170
Santa Fe–Style Baked Eggs, 67
Spaghetti with Spring Vegetables, 167
Tuna and Vegetable Bake, 150
Turkey Sausage with Peppers and
  Polenta, 115

7 POINTS value
Curried Chicken Patties on Lemony
  Rice, 257
Double Cheese Mini Pizzas, 264
Eggplant-Mushroom Lasagna, 166
Ham and Cheese–Stuffed Turkey
  Cutlets, 111
Lemon Chicken with Artichokes, 102
Salmon and Vegetable Packets, 147
Salmon with Tabbouleh Salad, 146
Soy-Pasta Bolognese, 262
Tuna and Bell Pepper Soft Tacos, 151
Turkey Parmesan, 110
Vegetable–Jack Cheese Quesadillas,
  176

8 POINTS value
Braised Pork Chops with Dates and
  Thyme, 229

9 POINTS value
Halibut with Moroccan Tomato Sauce
  and Couscous, 155
Spanish Chicken and Rice, 101

Core Plan Recipes